I08103 95

IMAGES
of America

TRYON PALACE

On the Cover: The entrance to Tryon Palace from Pollock Street originally featured an allée (tree-lined drive) that led from the main gates to the palace gates. The Darlington oaks, though historically accurate, are not well suited to the highly alkaline soil found in New Bern. In October 2003, the trees were removed as they reached the end of their life spans. (Courtesy of Tryon Palace.)

IMAGES
of America

TRYON PALACE

Tryon Palace Commission

ARCADIA
PUBLISHING

ISBN 978-1-4671-2324-2

Published by Arcadia Publishing
Charleston, South Carolina

Printed in the United States of America

Library of Congress Control Number: 2014950961

For all general information, please contact Arcadia Publishing:
Telephone 843-853-2070
Fax 843-853-0044
E-mail sales@arcadiapublishing.com
For customer service and orders:
Toll-Free 1-888-313-2665

Visit us on the Internet at www.arcadiapublishing.com

This book is dedicated to the Dreamers:
Gertrude Sprague Carraway, Minette Chapman Duffy, May Gordon Latham Kellenberger, Maude Moore Latham, and Kate B. Reynolds

Contents

Acknowledgments

The Tryon Palace Commission, created in 1945 by the North Carolina General Assembly to oversee the restoration of Tryon Palace, will celebrate its 70th anniversary in 2015. All of the commission members are proud to see Tryon Palace's continued success and contributions toward educating the public about North Carolina's colonial history. This book would not have been possible without the dedicated support of the many hardworking staff members who have contributed to and continue to contribute to the site's success. We would like to thank Siobhan Fitzpatrick and Penne Sandbeck for researching the institutional history of the site and writing captions for the photographs. We would also like to thank Richard A. Baker for locating many of these images in the site's archives and Craig Ramey for assisting with the layout and editing. Several other individuals assisted with the project, including Philippe Lafargue, Alma Gibbons, Matt Arthur, Sarah Risty-Davis, Cole Dittmer, and John Green. All images appear courtesy of Tryon Palace.

INTRODUCTION

Tryon Palace was not originally built to be a palace at all but instead a permanent seat of government for colonial North Carolina. Royal Governor William Tryon (1729–1788) came from England in 1764 with a mandate to establish more effective and efficient governing within the colony. Tryon was aided by the capable assistance of surveyor and builder John Hawks (c. 1731–1790), who, between 1766 and 1767, drafted a series of plans for a "Government House" in the up-and-coming town of New Bern. Hawks was born in Shipston-on-Stour in Warwickshire. His father, a joiner, taught Hawks the trade, and he was apprenticed to English architect Stiff Leadbeater, who taught him architectural theory and drawing. Hawks created two plans for the palacc; one set remained in the United States, and the other was sent to London for approval. Hawks remained in New Bern, marrying Sarah Rice in 1769. He continued to work on architectural projects in his new home until his death in 1790.

Located near the center of North Carolina's coast and at the confluence of the Neuse and Trent Rivers, New Bern promised to be more easily accessible than previous colony capitals. Tryon gained the British Crown's support for the Government House, obtained several town lots for the site, and sent Hawks north to Philadelphia to find skilled masons and other artisans. As the building and its flanking stable and kitchen took shape, dazzled locals referred to the edifice as a "palace"—a moniker that quickly caught on throughout the colony. When the palace officially opened in December 1770, the colony's legislators convened in the council chamber. It was reported in the *Virginia Gazette* that after much ceremony "a very grand and surprising Exhibition of Fireworks" was set off on the south lawn as crowds warmed by a bonfire and enjoyed a "great plenty of Liquor."

The palace's elegant Palladian details—from regularly-spaced sash windows delineated by a handsome brick stringcourse to a prominent entrance echoing the handsome pediment crowning the building's center section—were framed by a classically-inspired, curving colonnade on each side. The colonnades, which provided shelter, also linked the palace to its ancillary working spaces, the kitchen and stable offices. Some were inspired and proud to have such a state-of-the-art governing center in North Carolina, but other colonists, who seethed at paying taxes for a building that would cost nearly £15,000 to construct, rebelled.

Animosity towards the coastal planter class, which controlled the colonial government, had been growing for years. In 1768, a group known as the "Regulators" refused to pay the taxes imposed on them and eventually resorted to violent retaliation. The Regulators did not have a strong leader, and they were underfunded, but their large numbers were indicative of the growing unrest in the colonies prior to the American Revolution. In 1771, Tryon called up the colonial militia to disperse the Regulators and the well-supplied and -armed militia crushed the Regulators with few casualties at the Battle of Alamance on May 16. Tryon was sent to New York to take over as royal governor in 1772, and he held that position until the outbreak of the American Revolution, when he joined the British army with the rank of major general.

After Tryon left for New York, Josiah Martin (1737–1786) succeeded him as royal governor of North Carolina. Martin was born in Dublin and raised throughout the British Empire at his family's homes is Ireland, Antigua, and England. He briefly studied law and the military before taking his first political appointment. Martin received word that he was to become royal governor of North Carolina in 1770 while he was living in New York with his wife, Elizabeth, and their children. However, he was undergoing medical treatment at the time and did not leave for North Carolina until the following year. Martin worked to reduce tensions still present after the Regulators' rebellion by passing legislation to relieve the war debt. Unfortunately, his early success did not last, and in 1774, the people of North Carolina convened the First Provincial Congress in New Bern. Fearing for their safety, Martin sent his family to New York and later followed them in 1776, making him the first royal governor to desert his post. By 1779, all of his property had been sold by the new State of North Carolina, and his wife had died. Martin spent the remainder of the war fighting with Lord Charles Cornwallis before leaving for England in 1781.

By 1776, New Bern was no longer subject to the Crown, and Tryon Palace became the state's first house of government. Richard Caswell, North Carolina's first governor, was inaugurated there on January 16, 1777, as were subsequent governors Abner Nash, Alexander Martin, and Samuel Johnston. However, only Caswell and Nash lived in the palace. The North Carolina General Assembly did not use New Bern or Tryon Palace as a regular meeting location during the American Revolution. With its prominent location on the Neuse and Trent Rivers and easy access from the Atlantic Ocean, it was deemed too vulnerable. It was not until after the war that the general assembly began regularly meeting in New Bern again; however, by the time the general assembly last convened at the palace in 1792, the push for a more central seat of government led officials to the new town of Raleigh. Only one year before, Pres. George Washington had attended a ball at the palace, pronouncing it "a good brick building but now hastening to Ruins." In 1798, the slowly deteriorating building was destroyed by fire.

This book explores the story of Tryon Palace after the fire of 1798 and its rise from the ashes, beginning with the immediate aftermath of the destruction and the many incarnations of the salvaged stable office, through the battle to restore the palace, and beyond to the present day. Tryon Palace is no longer just a grand government building; it is a thriving cultural heritage site that explores the history of New Bern and Eastern North Carolina from the 18th century through the 20th century. The Tryon Palace Commission invites everyone to discover the history of the modern Tryon Palace.

One

The Palace Fire of 1798

The North Carolina General Assembly convened for the last time at Tryon Palace in 1792, leaving the first permanent capitol building in North Carolina unused and with no full-time residents for the next several years. Once considered to be the grandest building in the colony, Tryon Palace slid into disrepair; it first served as a dancing school and private academy, then as a Masonic lodge, while other sections were used as warehouse space. A fire on February 27, 1798, began in the palace cellar, which was being used for storage, and swept through the building and offices. There is no evidence to suggest that the fire was set intentionally; the likely culprit was improperly stored grain. The main building and east wing—or kitchen office—were beyond repair, but the stables were partially salvaged. The fire of 1798 ended the short 28-year existence of Tryon Palace, and the area was eventually sold off as lots on which new homes were built. Highway 70 was even built directly over the archeological remains of the palace. The only reminder of New Bern's past as the first state capital was the west wing—the remains of the stables. It would be over 100 years before Tryon Palace had the chance to shine again.

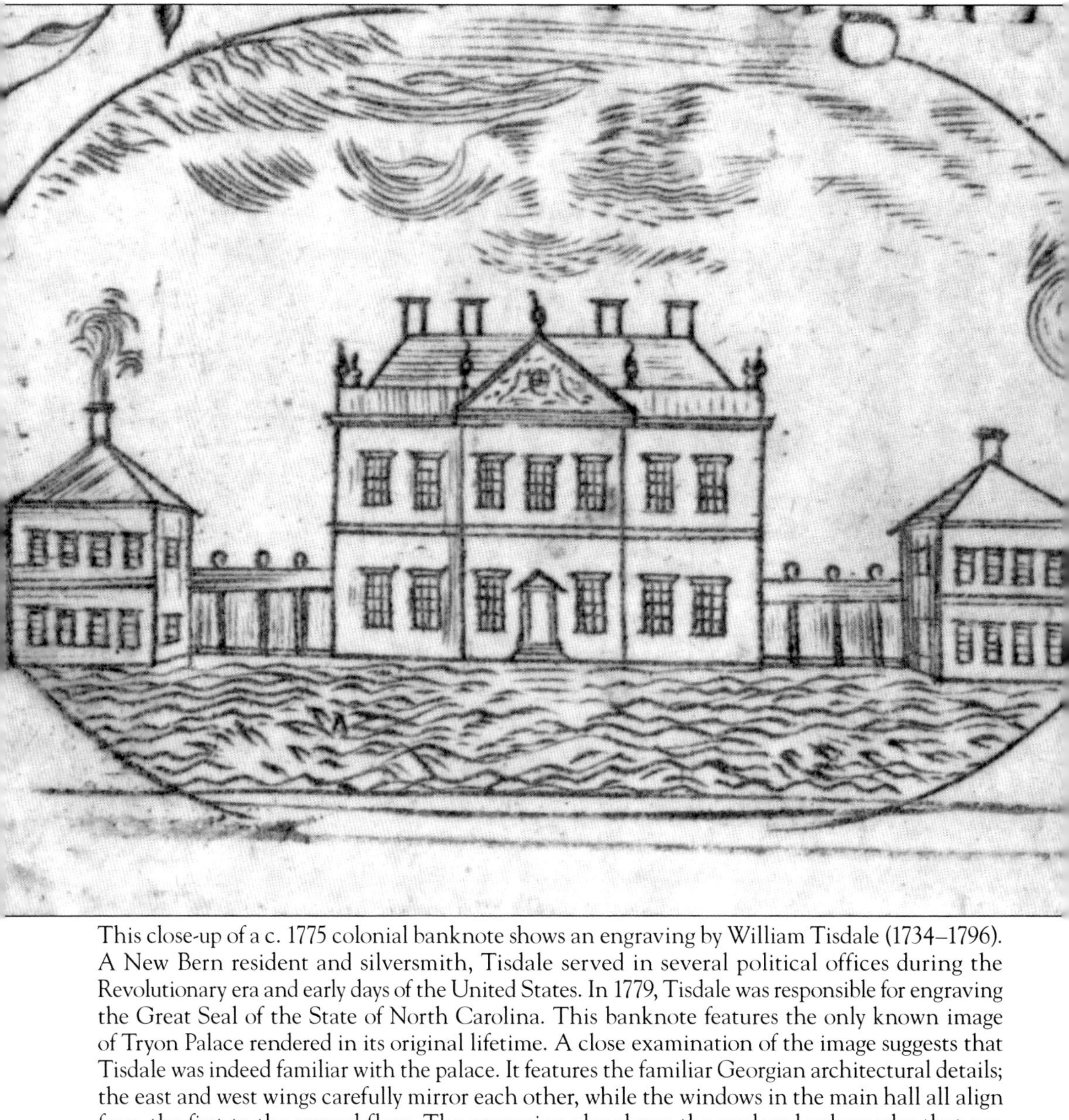

This close-up of a c. 1775 colonial banknote shows an engraving by William Tisdale (1734–1796). A New Bern resident and silversmith, Tisdale served in several political offices during the Revolutionary era and early days of the United States. In 1779, Tisdale was responsible for engraving the Great Seal of the State of North Carolina. This banknote features the only known image of Tryon Palace rendered in its original lifetime. A close examination of the image suggests that Tisdale was indeed familiar with the palace. It features the familiar Georgian architectural details; the east and west wings carefully mirror each other, while the windows in the main hall all align from the first to the second floor. The engraving also shows the enclosed colonnades that run between the east and west wings (kitchen and stable offices). The smoke emanating from the east wing chimney also indicates that Tisdale was familiar with the layout of the palace and the busy schedule of the kitchen.

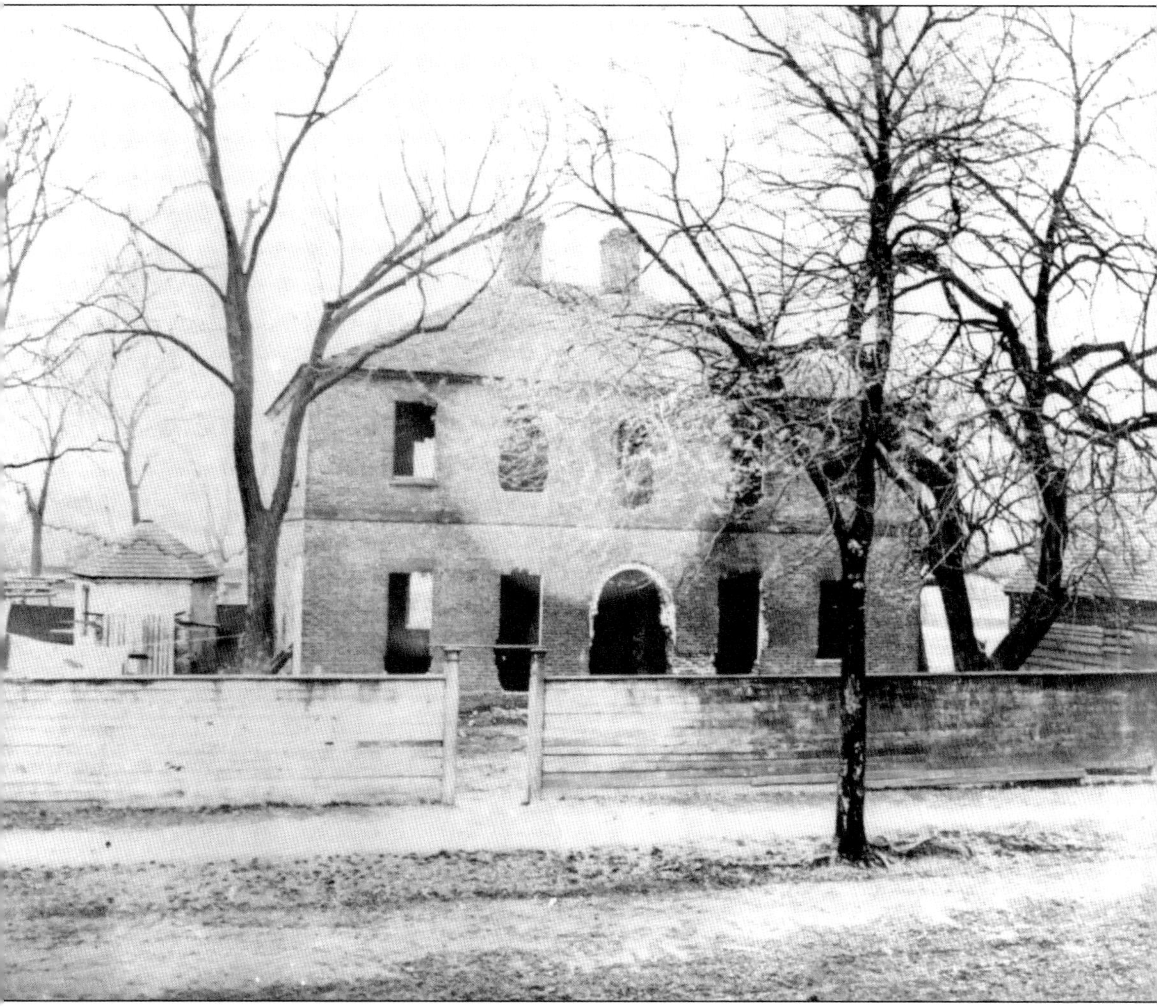

There are no known images of Tryon Palace created in the immediate aftermath of the fire of 1798, making it difficult for historians to get an impression of the severity of the damage. Some sections of the palace may have survived the initial fire; however, it was common practice in the late 17th and early 18th centuries to repurpose brick from older buildings for new buildings. As a result, sections of the palace walls may have become part of neighboring structures as the area around the palace was sold off as lots by the State of North Carolina. The earliest known photograph of the surviving palace wing is this tintype taken by a Union soldier in 1862. The tintype shows the former stable office surrounded by a wooden fence, laundry drying on a line at left, and a log cabin at right. At this point, the building appears to still be in use as a stable or possibly a shop.

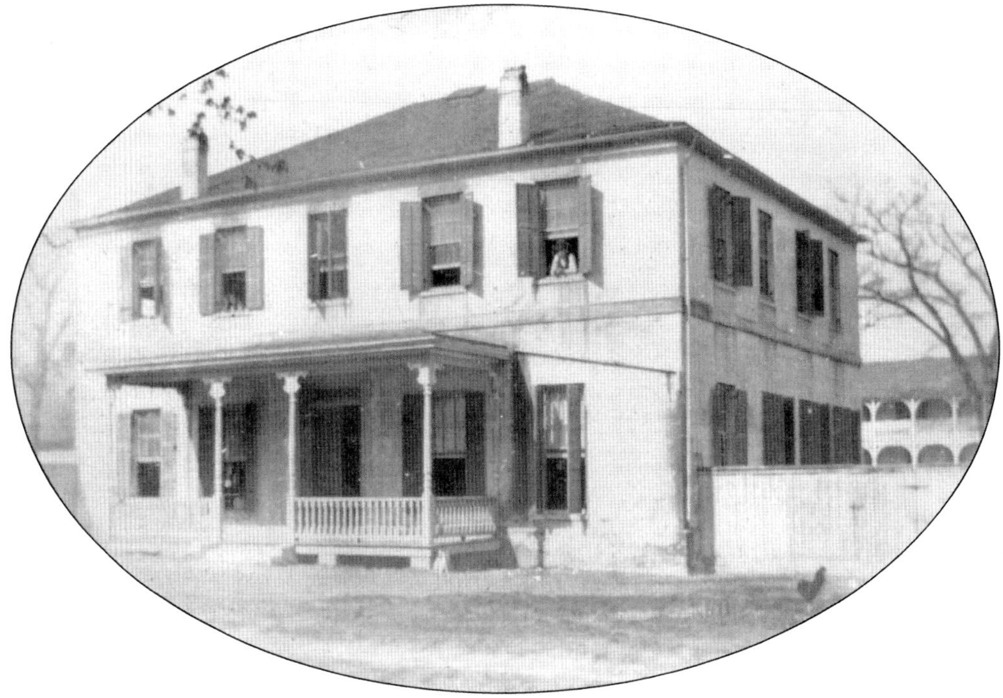

The former stable office took on a variety of uses between 1798 and its restoration in the 1950s, including a machine shop, a Sunday school for Christ Episcopal Church, and an apartment dwelling. The c. 1900 photograph above shows an early view of the stable office (or west wing) when it was converted to a dwelling but still had its original hip roof. The c. 1940 photograph below shows a later view of the stable building shortly before it was restored. At this point, it was being used as apartments, and the roof had been converted to a cross-gabled roof.

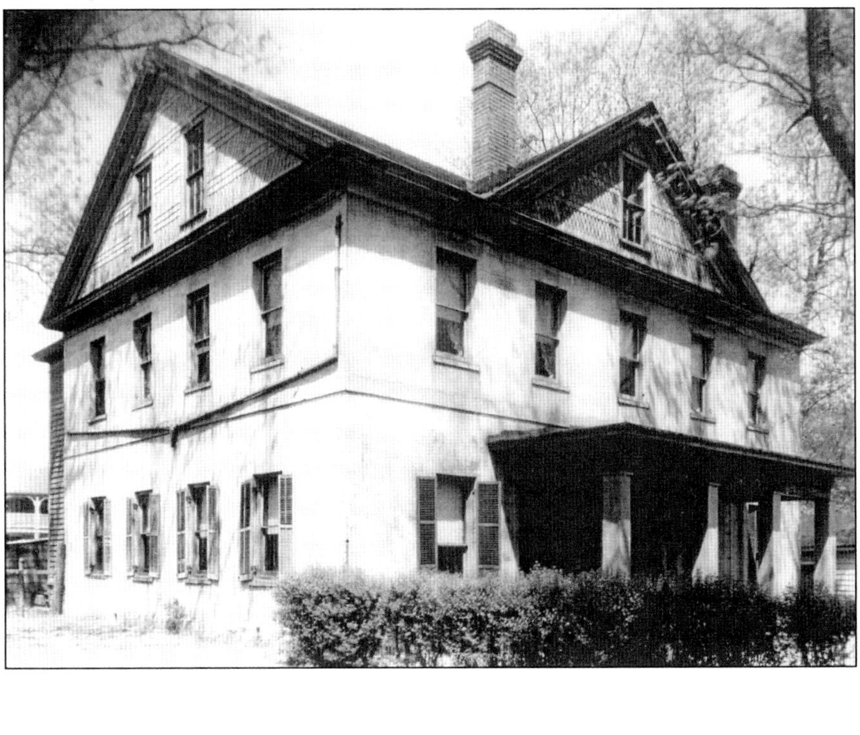

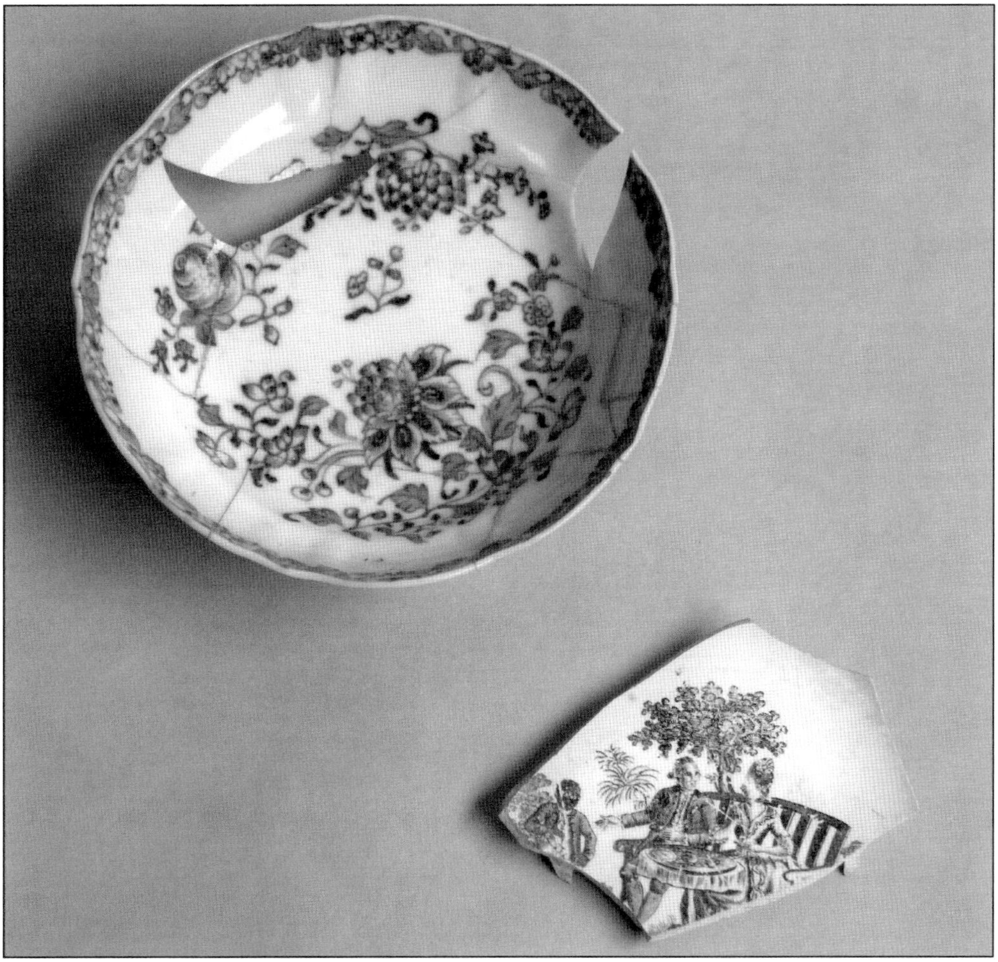

In 1952, before reconstruction began on the palace, an archeological excavation of the grounds was performed. The excavation uncovered the original foundation of the palace, remnants of the building materials, and fragments from different decorative elements that had once filled the palace. Pictured above are a few of the ceramic fragments found during the excavation; the small fragment shows a pattern known as the "Tea Party." When furnishing Tryon Palace during its reconstruction, the curator and commission members sought period pieces with the same patterns as these fragments and others that were found on-site. Pictured below are a few of the building materials that were uncovered, including fragments of window glass, keys, keyhole plates, and hand-wrought nails.

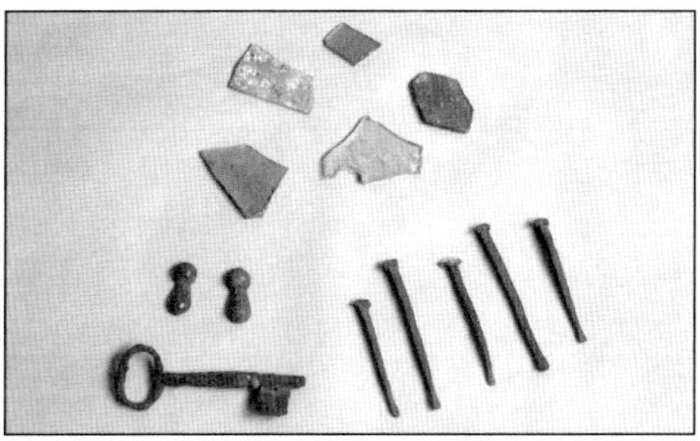

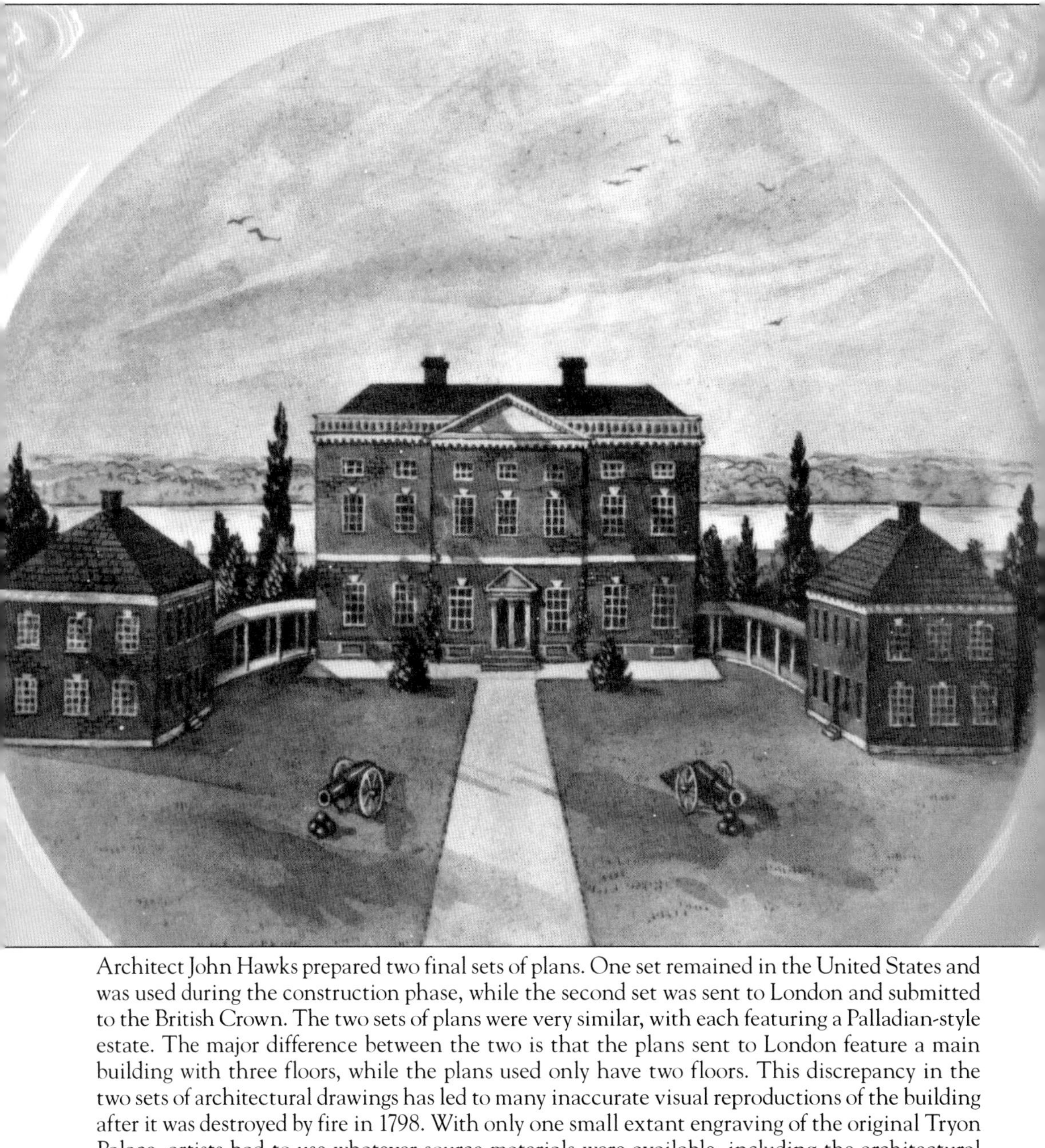

Architect John Hawks prepared two final sets of plans. One set remained in the United States and was used during the construction phase, while the second set was sent to London and submitted to the British Crown. The two sets of plans were very similar, with each featuring a Palladian-style estate. The major difference between the two is that the plans sent to London feature a main building with three floors, while the plans used only have two floors. This discrepancy in the two sets of architectural drawings has led to many inaccurate visual reproductions of the building after it was destroyed by fire in 1798. With only one small extant engraving of the original Tryon Palace, artists had to use whatever source materials were available, including the architectural plans in London; the "palace" with the three-story edifice continued to appear on promotional material well into the 1900s.

Two

Rebirth of Tryon Palace

By the 1920s, there seemed little hope that the palace would be restored to its former glory; a highway ran over Tryon Palace's deeply buried footprint, and the last remaining visage of the original structure—the stable—had been converted into apartments. However, a group of dedicated preservationists and historians believed in restoring the palace, and these individuals began raising funds and building awareness of New Bern's historical importance. By the end of the 1930s, their efforts had been recognized by the North Carolina State Historical Commission. The Dreamers, a dedicated group of women who had grown up in New Bern and wished to preserve the history of Tryon Palace, spearheaded the preservation efforts beginning in the 1940s. While World War II temporarily halted their plans, these women worked to convince the state legislature to redirect Highway 70 in order to have the palace rebuilt. By the late 1940s, the Tryon Palace Commission was buying properties that needed to be demolished before Tryon Palace and its grounds could be fully restored. In 1952, construction began based on John Hawks's original plans and incorporating the archeological evidence uncovered during excavations. The construction of the new palace and restoration of the stables were nearly complete in 1957, when work began in earnest on the gardens, and by 1959, the palace and gardens were complete.

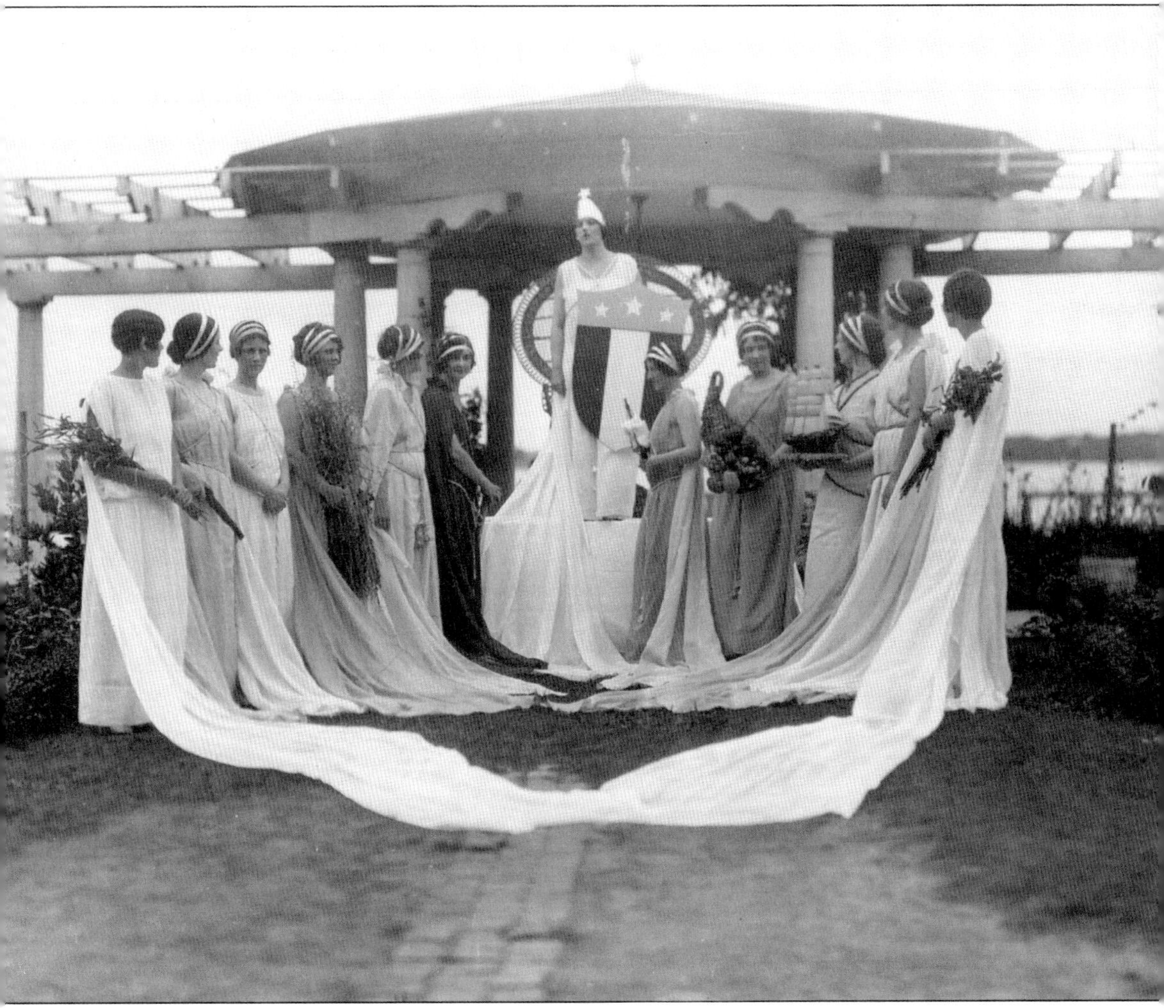

The New Bern Historic Celebration and Pageant, held on June 11, 1929, featured a tableau entitled "America, attended by spirits of North Carolina's New Bern." The central figure in the tableau (holding the shield) is America, accompanied by figures of New Bern, North Carolina, Agriculture, Commerce, Art, Labor, Industry, Religion, Thanksgiving, Peace, and Remembrance. Agriculture is represented by the sheath of wheat she carries, Commerce by the three-masted ship before her, Thanksgiving carries a cornucopia, and Industry holds a cotton-covered spindle. The tableau was part of the "History of New Bern" pageant held later that night and attended by 8,000 people. Other events of the day included a parade, an open house, and a Swiss Ball. The event was attended by dignitaries from all over the country honoring the founding of the state of North Carolina and New Bern's role in the history of the state.

This garden party was held on June 11, 1929, in Mrs. Sam Smallwood's yard. Guests ate under a 700-year-old cypress tree while enjoying the band and party games. The party was part of a larger series of celebrations held in New Bern during the Historic Celebration and Pageant.

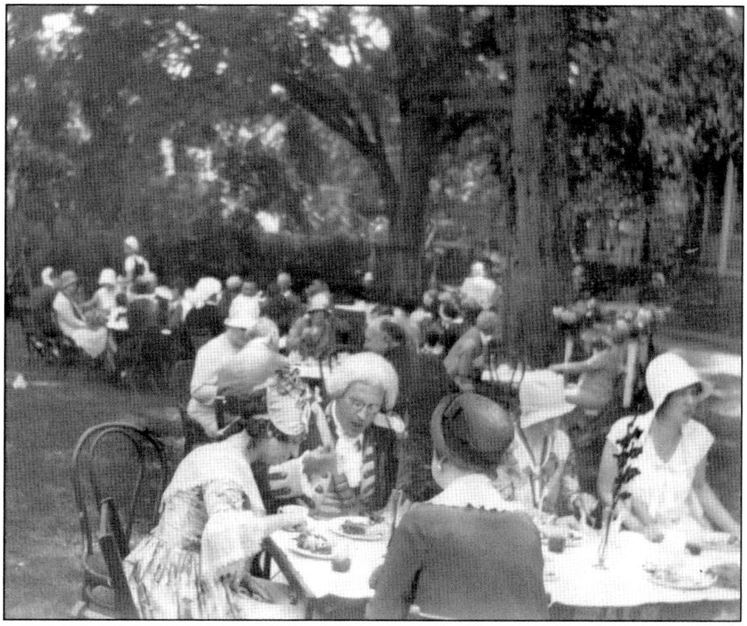

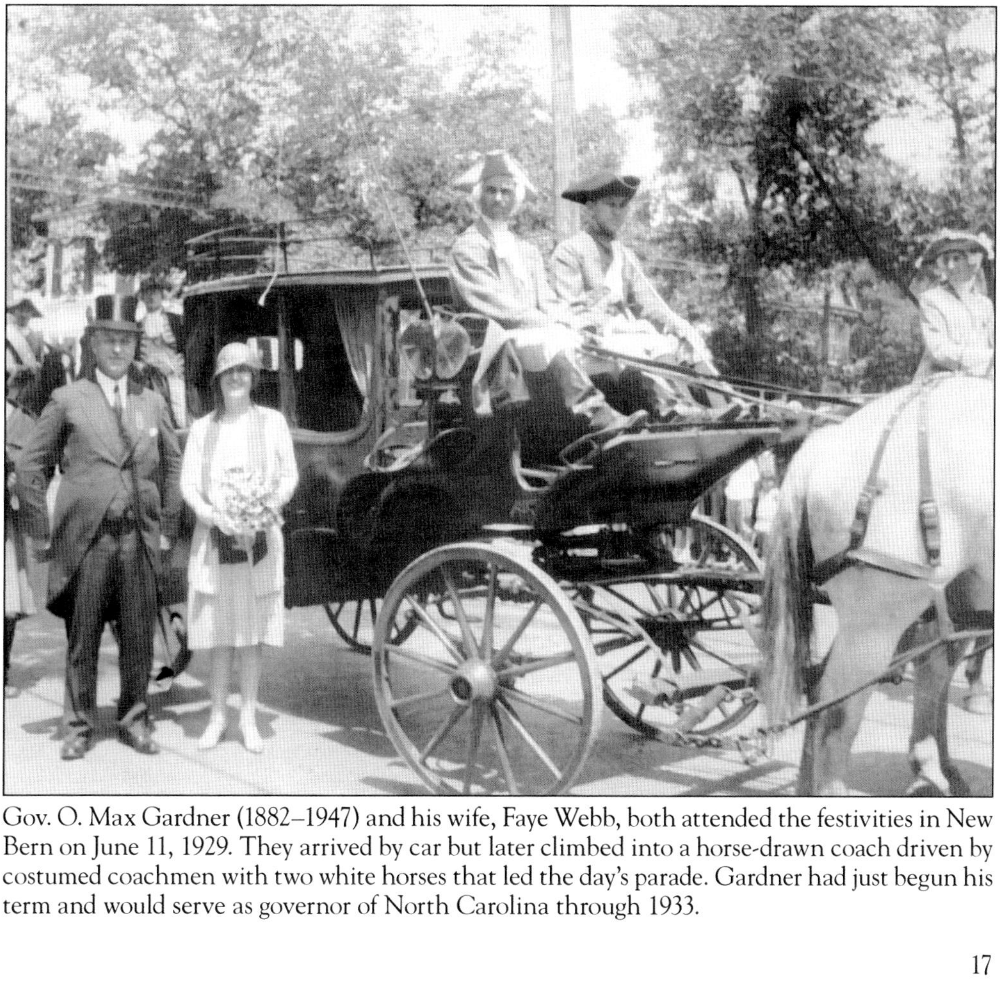

Gov. O. Max Gardner (1882–1947) and his wife, Faye Webb, both attended the festivities in New Bern on June 11, 1929. They arrived by car but later climbed into a horse-drawn coach driven by costumed coachmen with two white horses that led the day's parade. Gardner had just begun his term and would serve as governor of North Carolina through 1933.

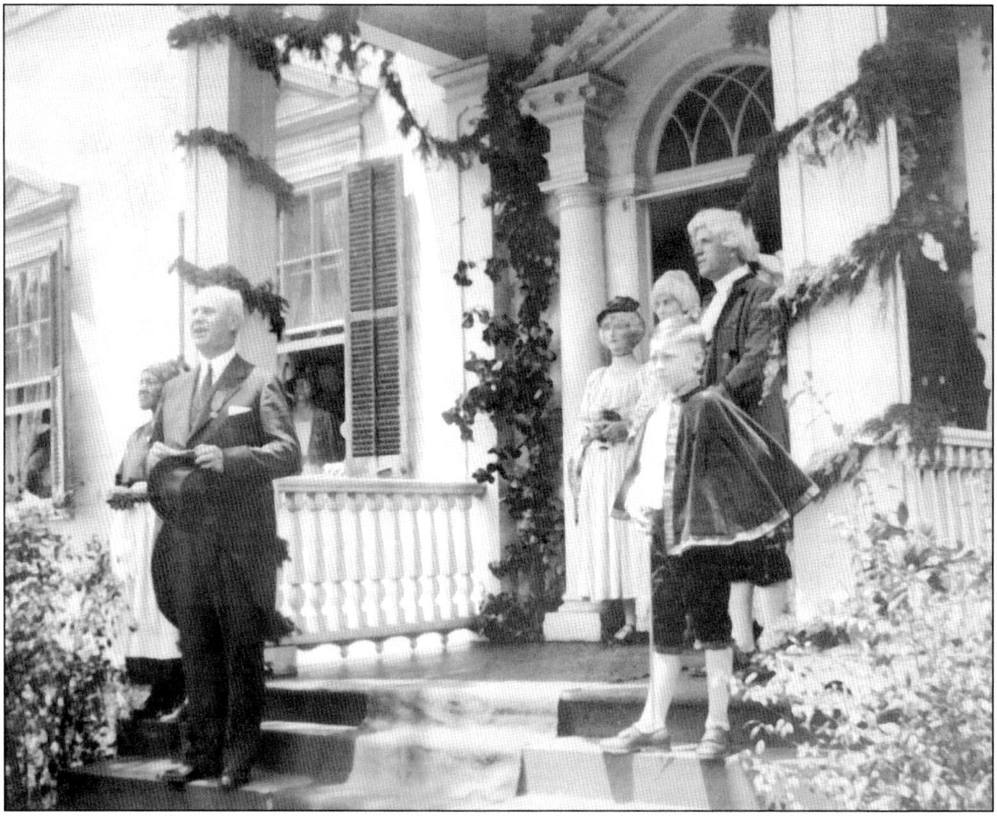

On June 11, 1929, Gov. O. Max Gardner addressed the crowd in front of the John Wright Stanly House. After his speech, everyone retired to the house for a party hosted by Mrs. James A. Bryan, who owned the structure in 1929. The house was one of 14 colonial homes that were part of an open house for the celebratory events.

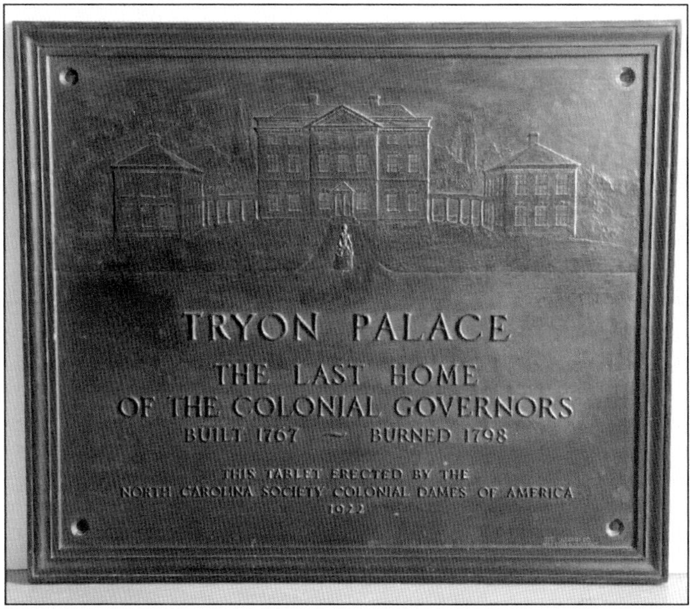

This plaque—erected in 1922 by the North Carolina Society Colonial Dames of America—was the first to recognize the historic significance of Tryon Palace. It reads: "Tryon Palace / The Last Home of the Colonial Governors / Built 1767 ~ Burned 1798." Installing the plaque was an important first step in gaining recognition for the site and ensuring its eventual restoration.

In 1935, the North Carolina State Historical Commission chose to erect a marker for Tryon Palace. This marker recognizes Tryon Palace as the first permanent capitol, provides the 1770 completion date of the palace, and lists the date it was destroyed. It also indicates that there is a surviving wing still standing. The installation of the marker indicated another step toward recognition of the historical importance of the palace.

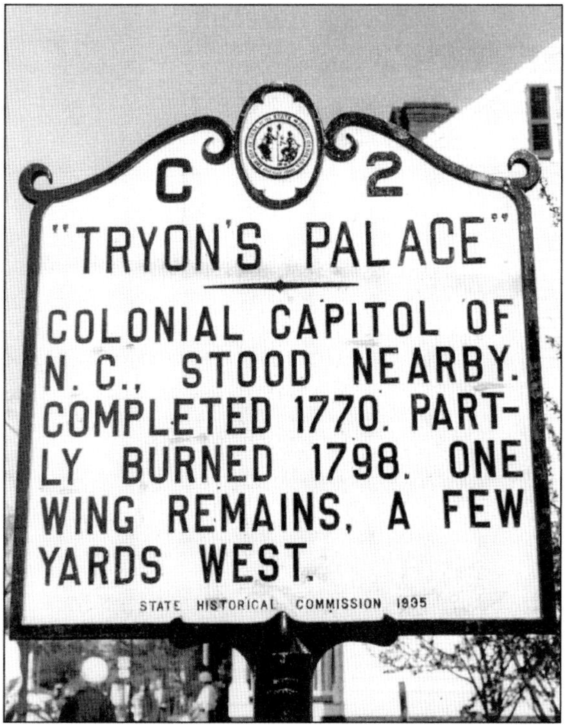

Before the restoration of the stable wing and reconstruction of the palace, additional informational signs were erected in front of the stables to inform passersby of the building's long history. These new signs were hung using newel posts to distinguish them from the nearby signs erected by the state historical commission.

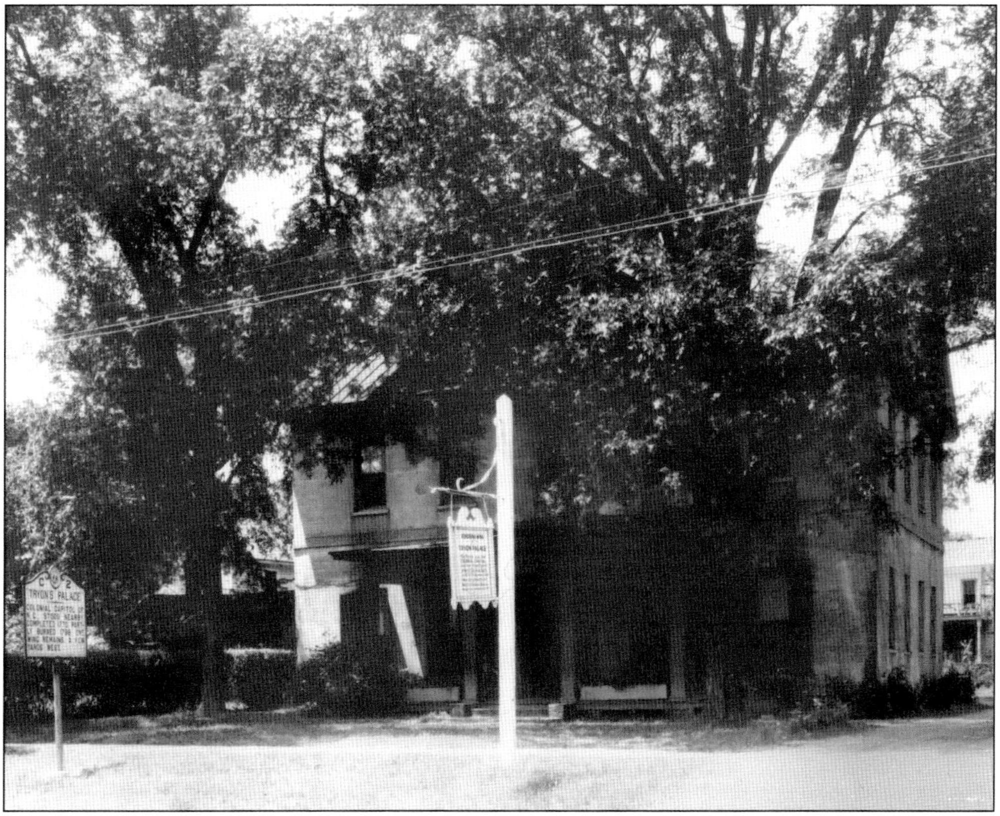

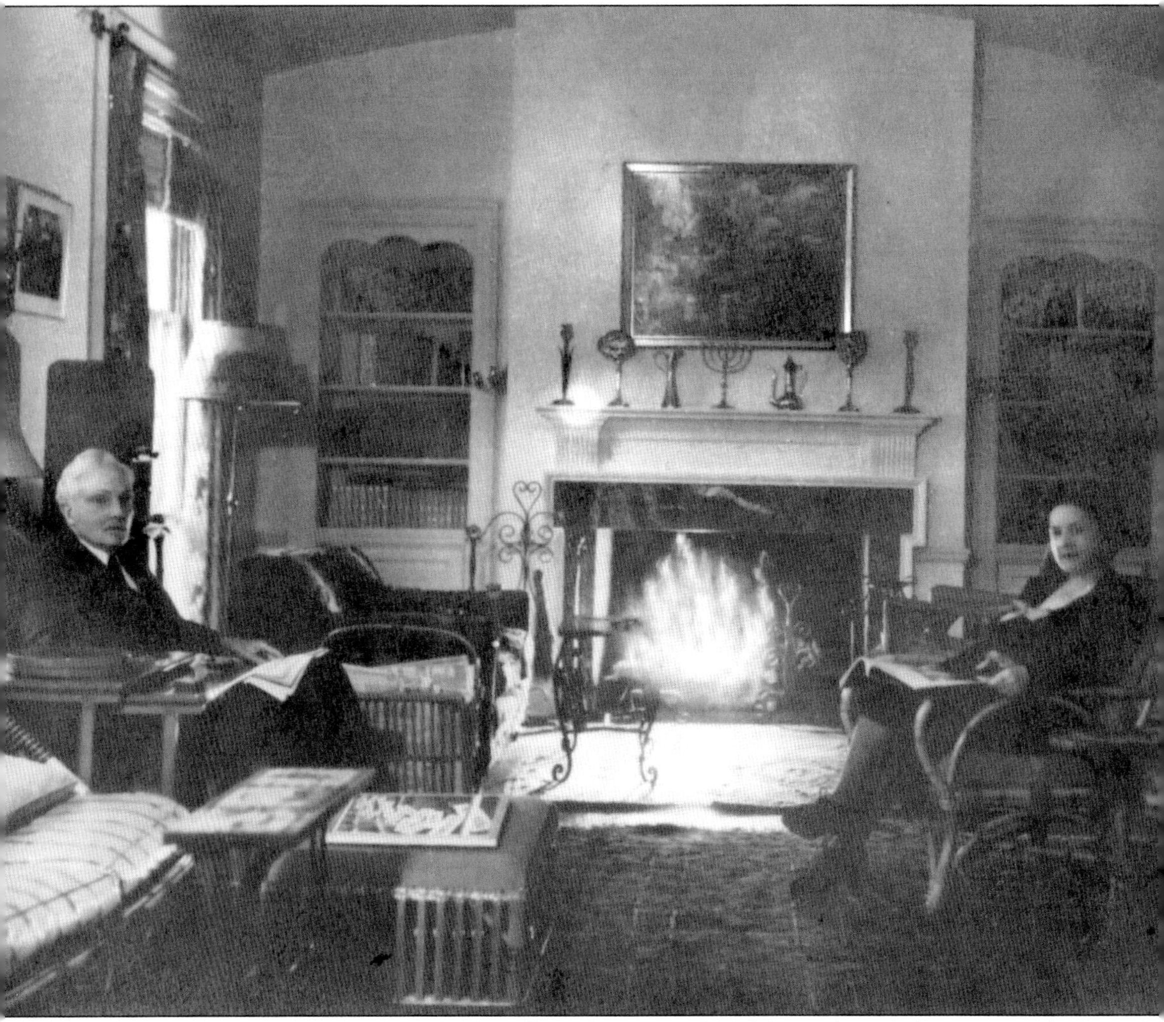

This photograph shows James Edwin Latham (1866–1946) and his wife, Maude Moore Latham (1871–1951), at their Greensboro home around 1937; they used this picture for their Christmas card that year. Born in New Bern, Maude was a strong supporter of the arts and historic preservation as a member of the North Carolina Art Society, North Carolina Folklore Society, State Literary and Historical Association, Historical Book Club of North Carolina, and Woman's Club of Greensboro. The complete restoration and reconstruction of Tryon Palace became her lifelong dream. With the assistance of James, she financed several state historic preservation projects, including the 1939 publication of *Old Homes and Gardens of North Carolina*, before turning her sole attention and resources toward providing an endowment for the future palace. Maude's tireless support and devotion to Tryon Palace made the project possible.

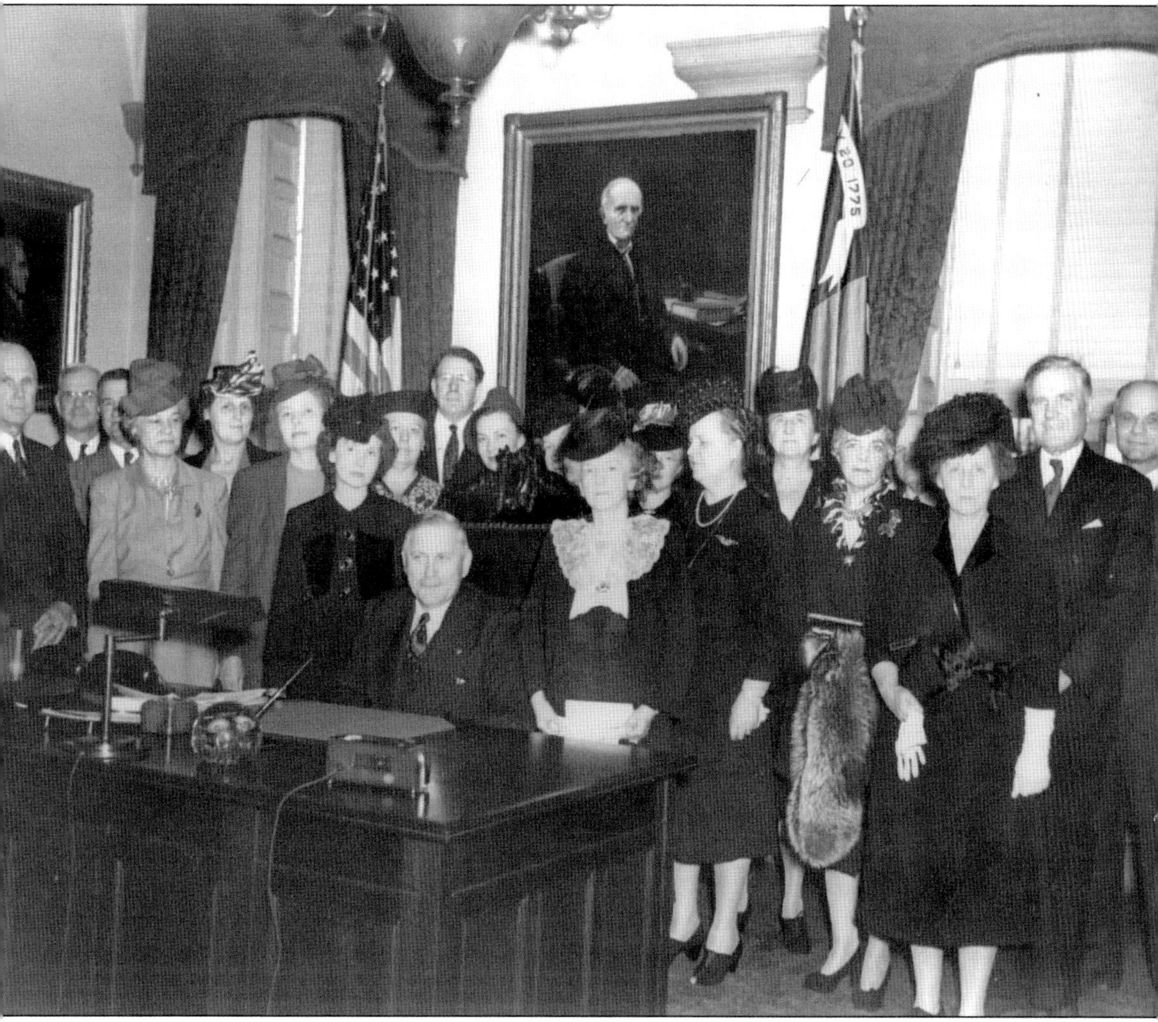

This photograph, taken in November 1945 at the state capitol in Raleigh, shows all of the original members of the Tryon Palace Commission. Maude Moore Latham established a trust for funding the reconstruction of the palace; in return, the State of North Carolina put forward the funds to purchase the needed property and created the Tryon Palace Commission to oversee the reconstruction. Latham was named chairman of the commission. Pictured members of the Tryon Palace Commission and influential political parties include D.L. Ward, R. Bruce Etheridge (State Department of Conservation and Development, the forerunner of the Department of Cultural Resources), attorney general Harry McMullan, Carroll P. Rogers, Martha Gold Winstead Borden, Mrs. J. Wilber Bunn, Mrs. James Samuel Mitchener, May Gordon Latham Kellenberger, Mrs. P.P. McCain, former governor J. Melville Broughton, Elizabeth Dillard Reynolds, Gertrude S. Carraway, Maude Moore Latham, Virginia Horne, Ruth Cannon, Minnette Chapman Duffy, Katherine Clark Pendleton Arrington, Judge R.A. Nunn, Elizabeth Henderson Cotton, Judge Richard D. Dixon, and Rev. Robert L. Pugh. Gov. R. Gregg Cherry is seated.

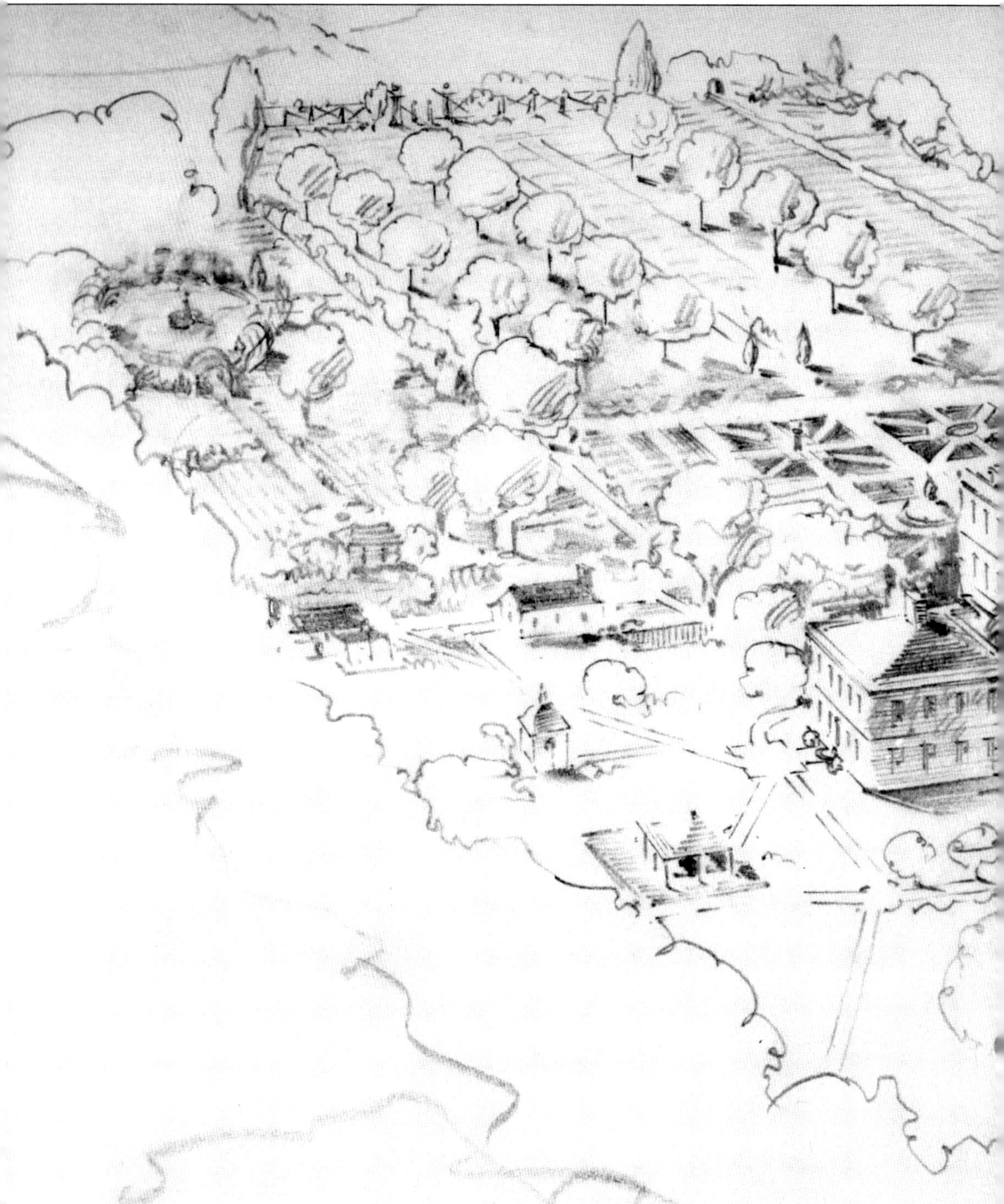

By 1954, the Tryon Palace Commission had drawn plans for both the reconstructed palace and gardens. The palace design was set to follow the original plans created by John Hawks in 1767, while the gardens incorporated design elements common to state gardens during the 18th century. At the front of the palace grounds is a small paddock for horses, an allée (tree-lined drive) leading to

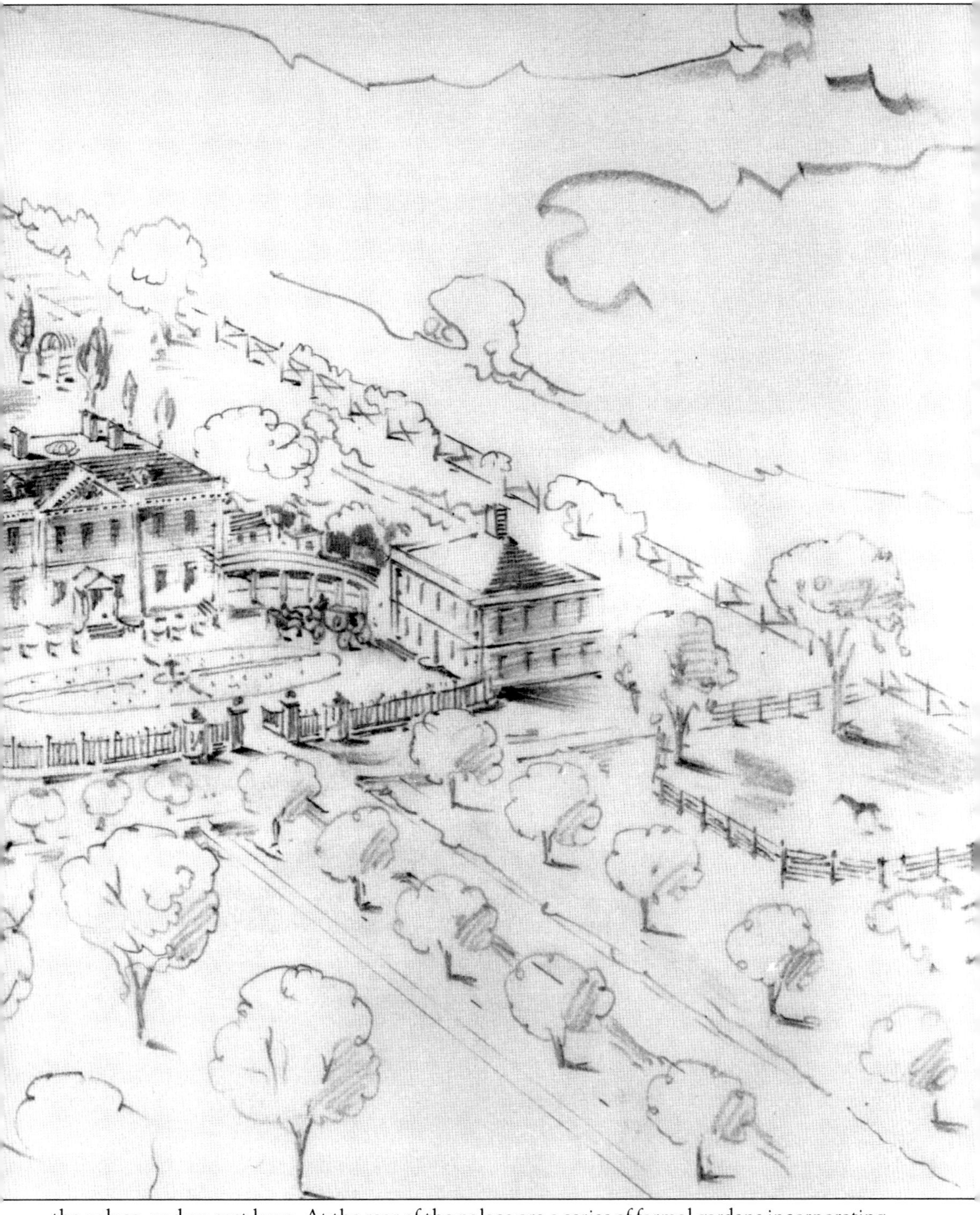

the palace, and an east lawn. At the rear of the palace are a series of formal gardens incorporating shaped planting beds and fountains. In this original design, the rear of the palace would not have had a large lawn space but instead a mall focusing attention on the rear entrance.

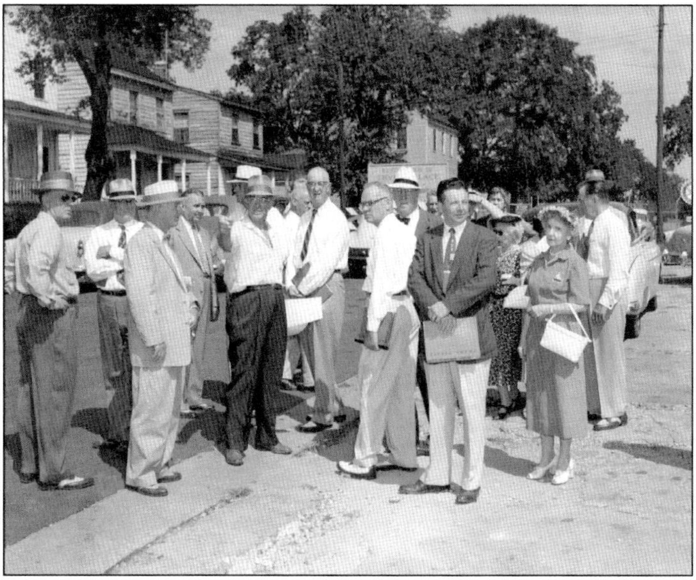

This early-1950s photograph shows Tryon Palace Commission members standing on New Bern's George Street, located in front of the future site of Tryon Palace. The street that they are standing on eventually became the south lawn, and the houses at left were demolished to make way for part of the formal gardens.

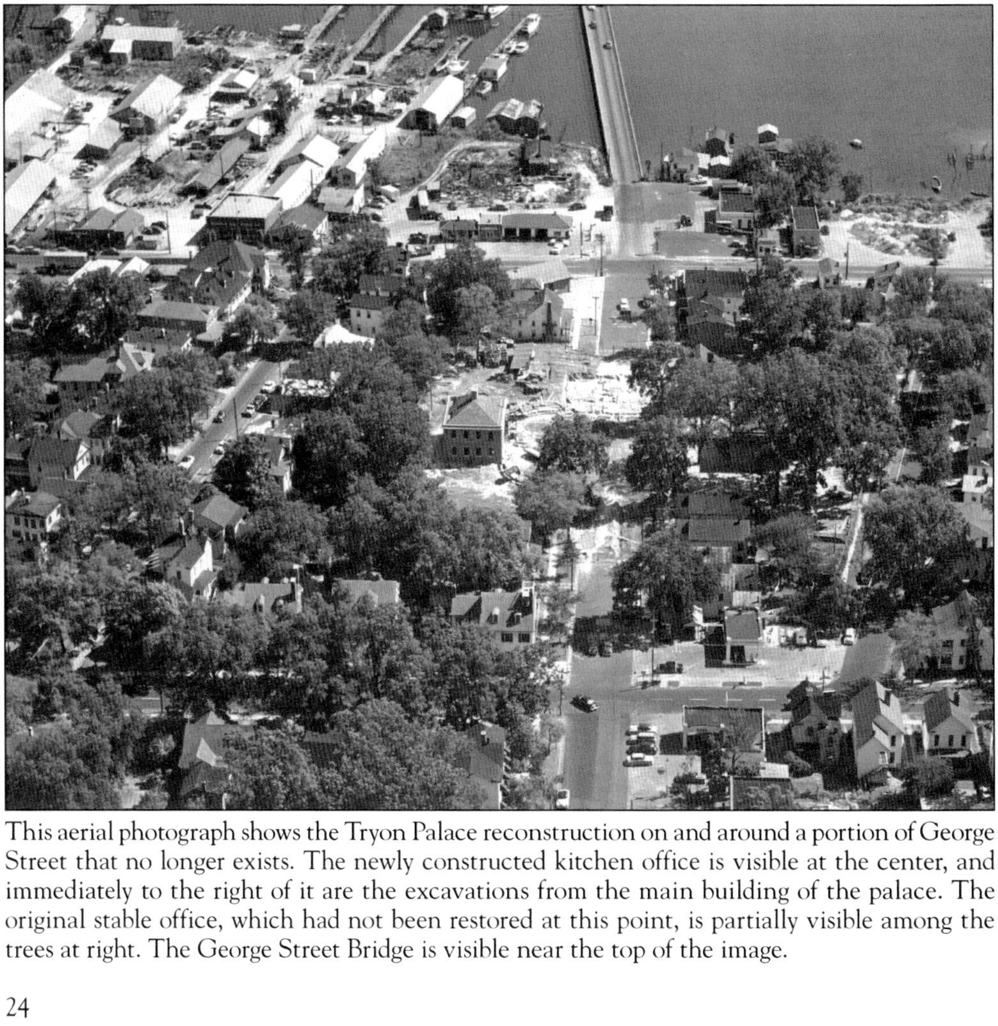

This aerial photograph shows the Tryon Palace reconstruction on and around a portion of George Street that no longer exists. The newly constructed kitchen office is visible at the center, and immediately to the right of it are the excavations from the main building of the palace. The original stable office, which had not been restored at this point, is partially visible among the trees at right. The George Street Bridge is visible near the top of the image.

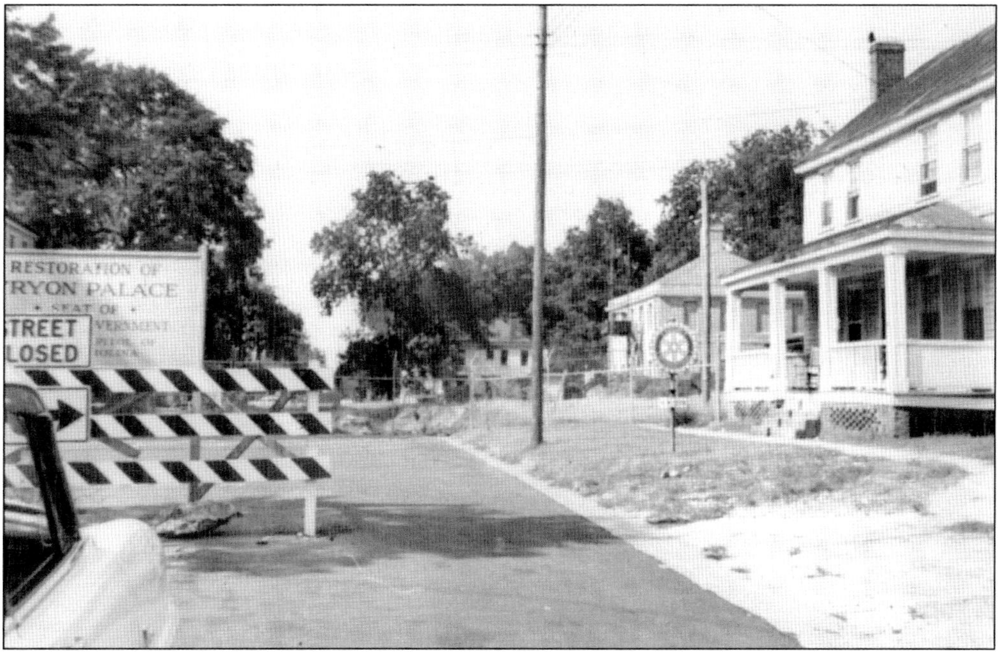

More than 100 New Bern citizens were unhappy with the decision to close George Street and demolish the houses along the road. This photograph shows George Street blocked off during the reconstruction. The house at right was one of several demolished to make way for the reconstructed palace and gardens, and the kitchen office is just behind it.

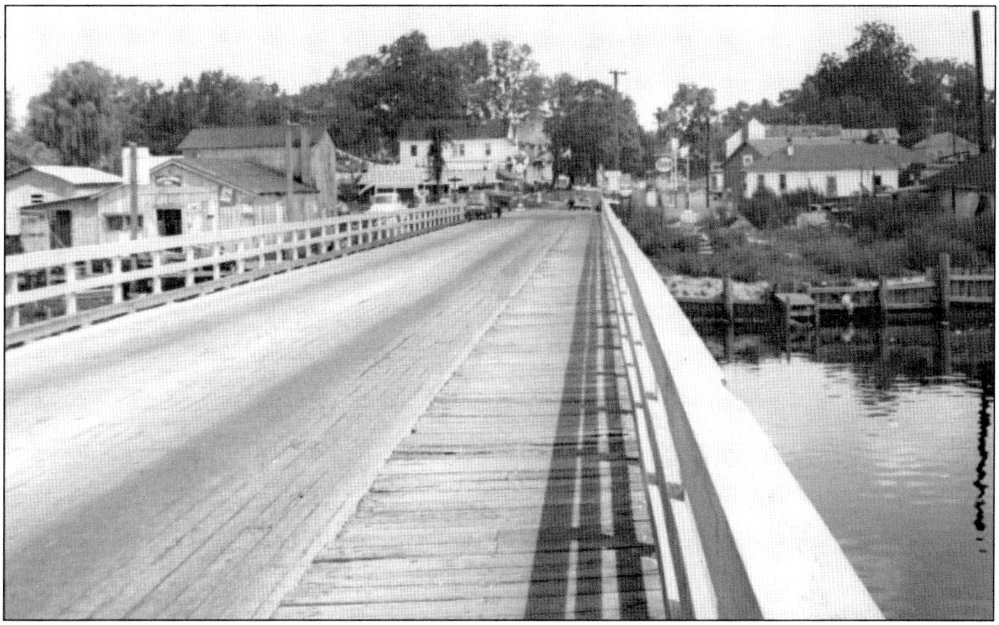

The George Street Bridge was a wooden bridge connecting the two sides of the Trent River. During World War II, Gov. J. Melville Broughton considered it a military necessity to build a new bridge; he was supported by the commanding officers at Camp Lejeune, Camp Davis, and Cherry Point. In September 1944, it was announced by Governor Broughton that the US Army Corps of Engineers would oversee the building of a new concrete bridge.

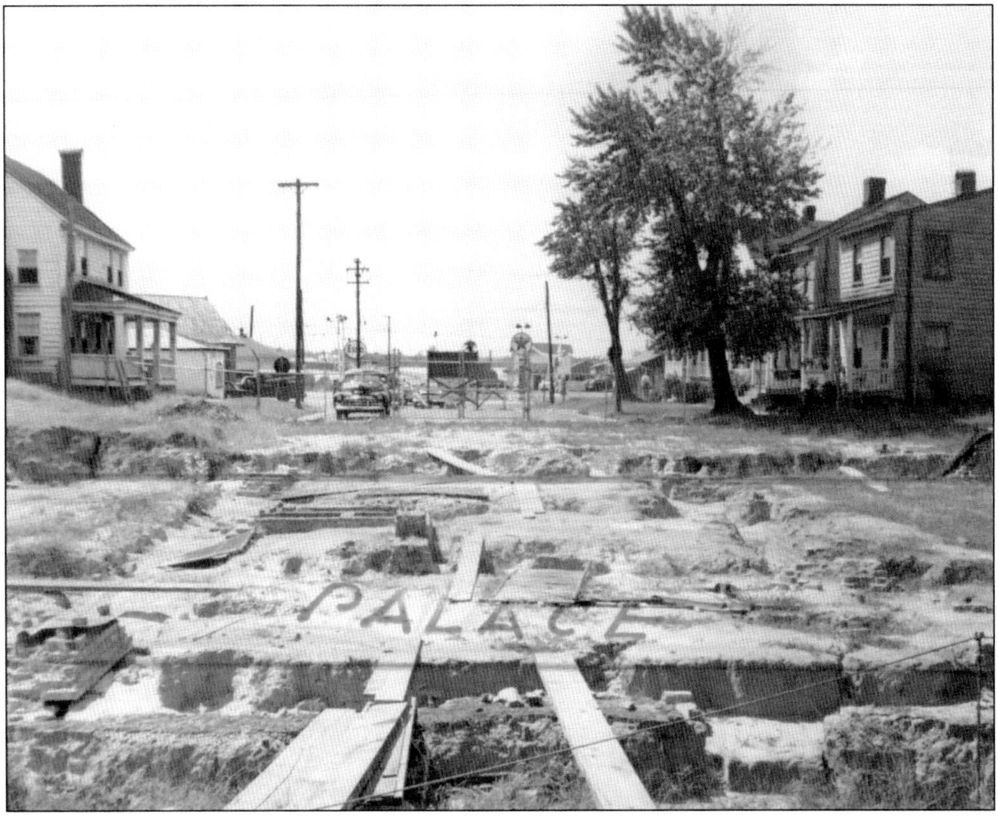

By the 1940s, no physical evidence of Tryon Palace's main building survived on the surface. But based on the location of the stable office, the one surviving palace wing, and the drawings by John Hawks, the Tryon Palace Commission knew the general area where the main building of the palace should be located. When excavations began for the main building, workers discovered the original foundation of the palace, which provided new insight into the original palace and ensured that the reconstruction would be able to follow the footprint of the original structure.

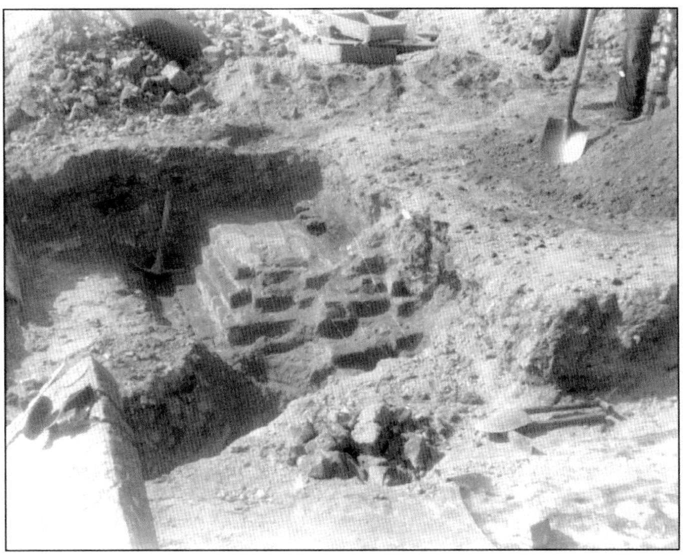

The Tryon Palace reconstruction project began in the 1950s and employed several bricklayers, all African American. M.L. Skinner, a general contractor, was one of many New Bern–based businesses that supplied additional assistance to palace contractors. In this 1953 photograph, a Skinner's pickup truck has brought bricks to the construction site, where workers are unloading them by hand.

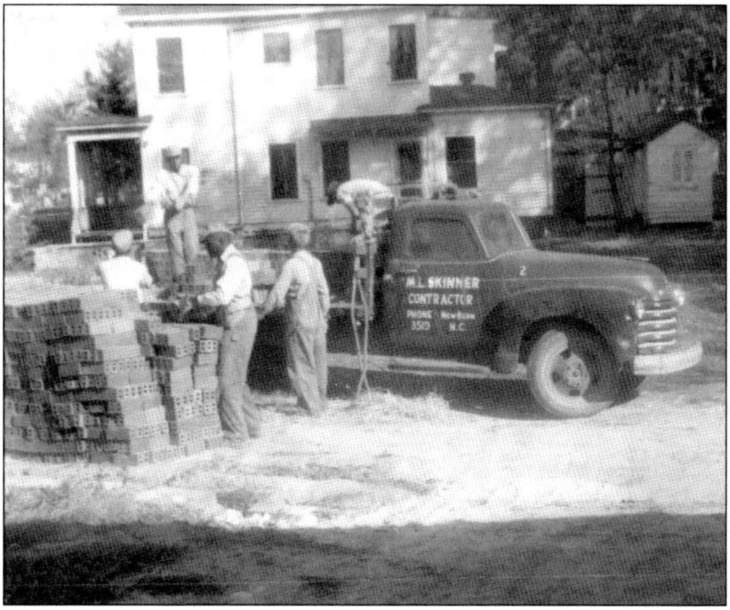

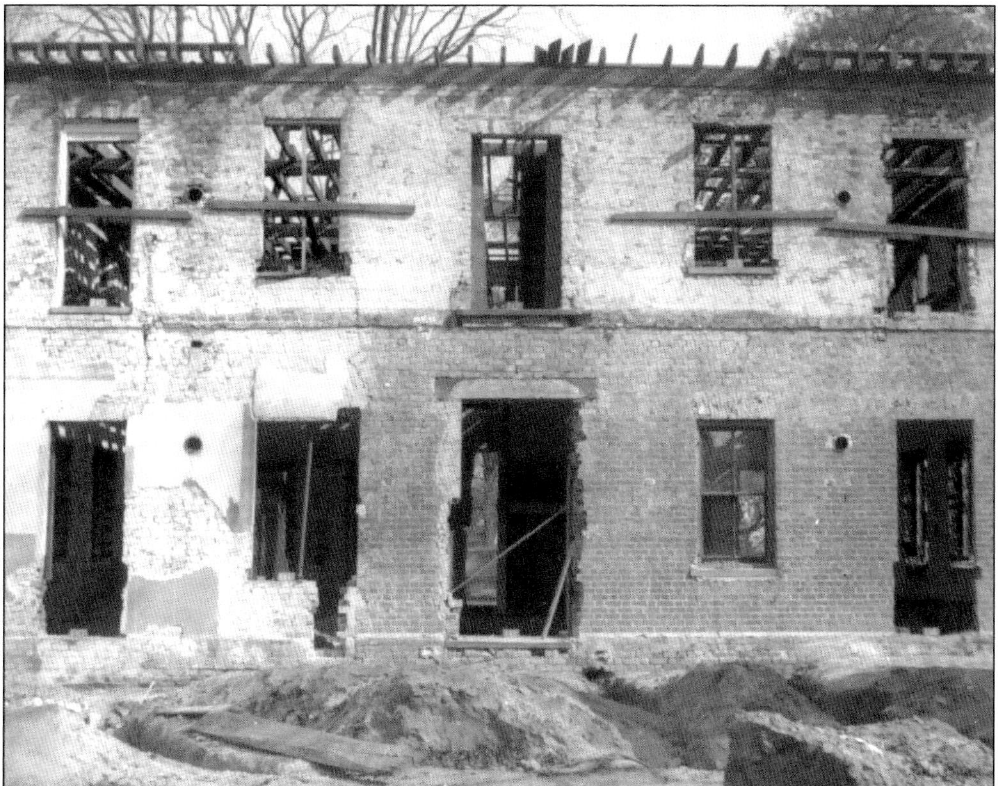

This photograph shows the stable office freshly stripped of the paint and plaster that had covered its surface since the 19th century. This made the stable office's brick walls, stringcourse, and flat arches visible to the public once again. Although it would take more work to restore the stables to their original appearance, approximately 70 percent of the original bricks remained.

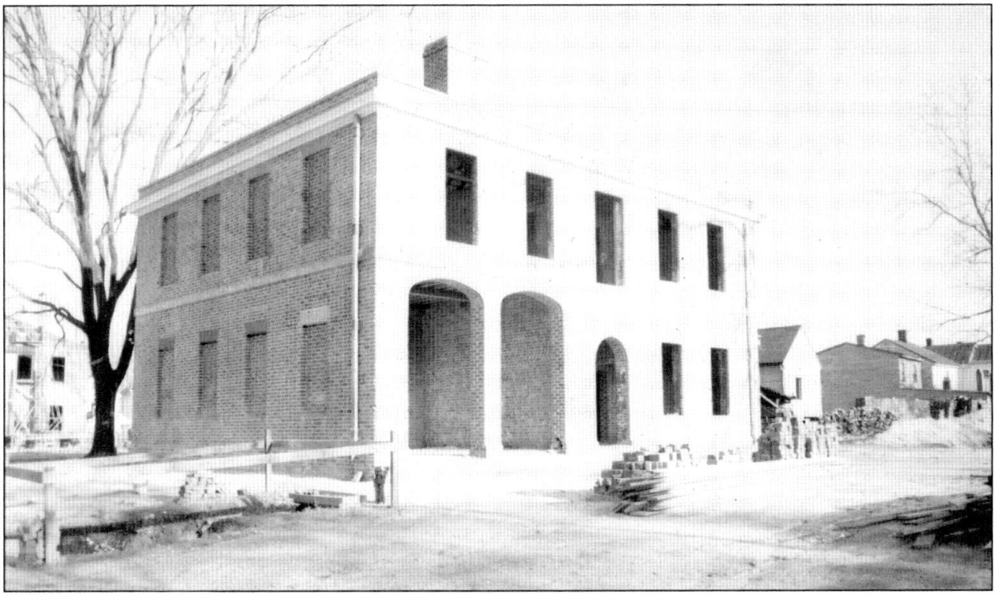

This photograph shows the 1954 rear elevation of the stable office after the brickwork had been restored. The two large archways on the left rear side of the building lead into the coach house that housed the governor's carriage. In 2013, the coach house served as quarters to the *Miss Kay*, a sailboat built in honor of former Tryon Palace director Kay Williams.

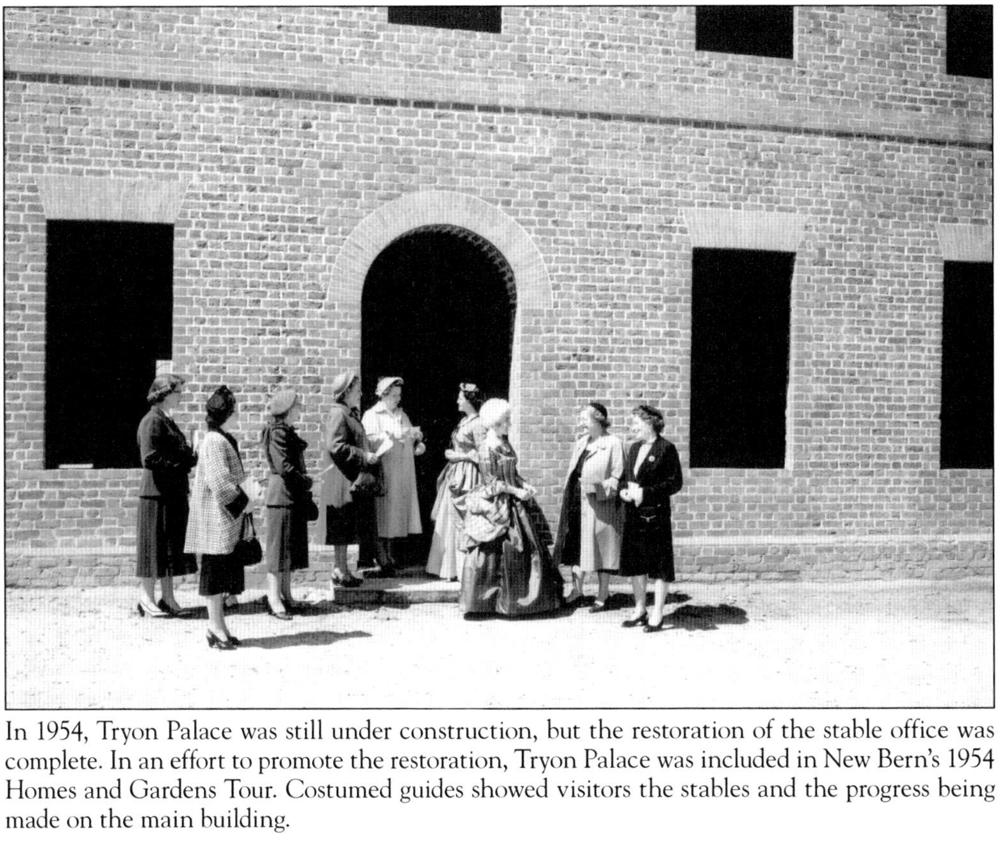

In 1954, Tryon Palace was still under construction, but the restoration of the stable office was complete. In an effort to promote the restoration, Tryon Palace was included in New Bern's 1954 Homes and Gardens Tour. Costumed guides showed visitors the stables and the progress being made on the main building.

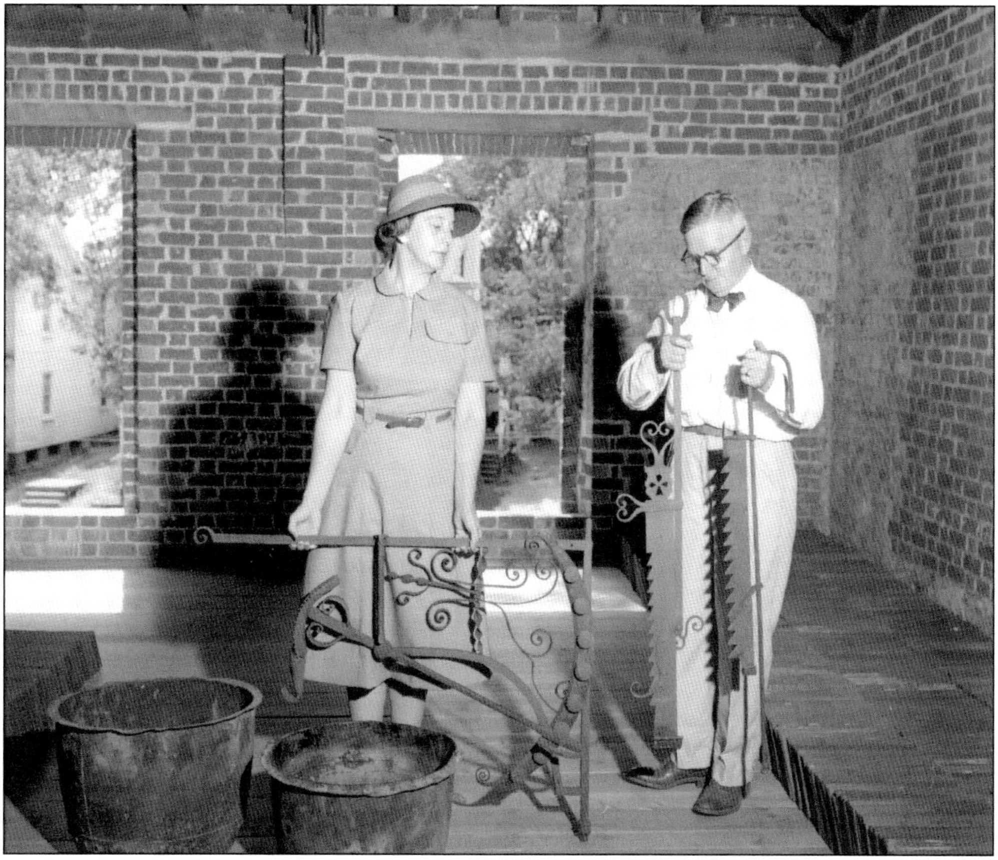

Morley Jeffers Williams—a former professor of landscape architecture from Harvard who had worked on projects at Stratford Hall, Monticello, and Mount Vernon—oversaw the restoration of Tryon Palace's gardens. He incorporated extensive archeological investigations and worked with his wife, Nathalia Uhlman, an MIT-trained architect, on many of his projects. This photograph shows Williams and Uhlman holding some of the new ironwork for Tryon Palace.

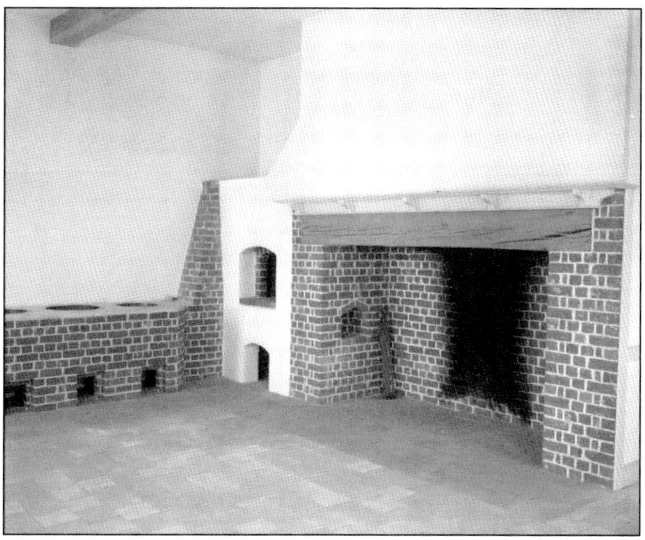

Like many new kitchens, the kitchen office's fireplace hearth, bake oven, and deep-well cookers were yet to receive the patina created by years of roasting, baking, and boiling various delicacies. However, it is probably much as it initially appeared to the first cook who arrived to take the place of Pierre LeBlanc, colonial governor William Tryon's cook, who died before the palace was completed.

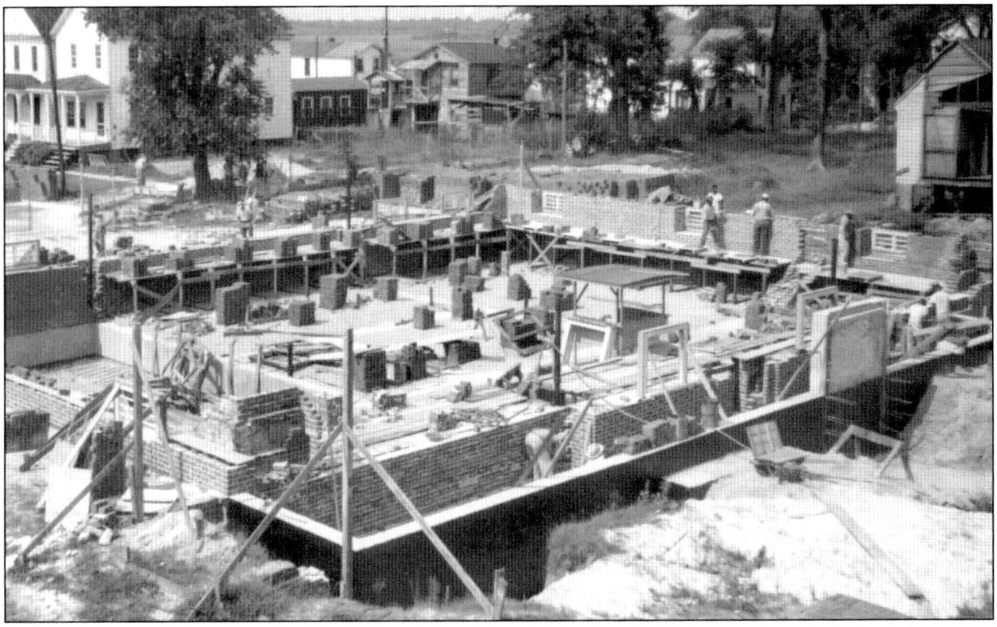

Local New Bern contractor K.R. Wade was the on-site project supervisor and was in charge of making sure the brickmasons, all locals, kept to the construction schedule. This photograph shows the construction of the main building's basement, which incorporates sections of the original walls.

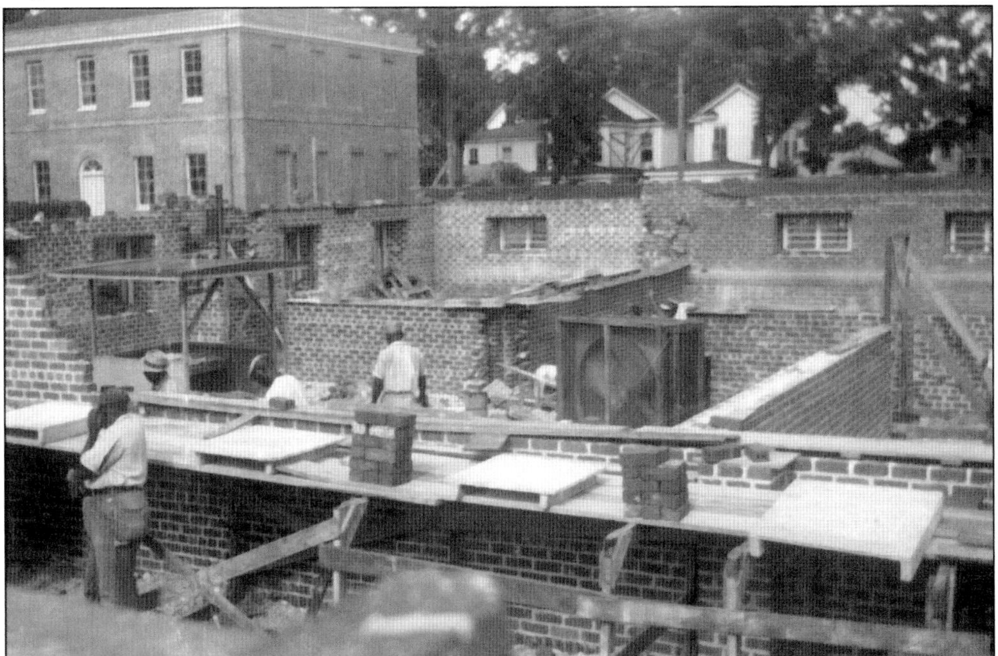

The main building was the last to be completed. In this photograph, the finished kitchen office is visible in the background at left, while the brickmasons continue to work on the main building's basement. The basement level is nearly complete; window casements are visible, and the interior walls are taking shape.

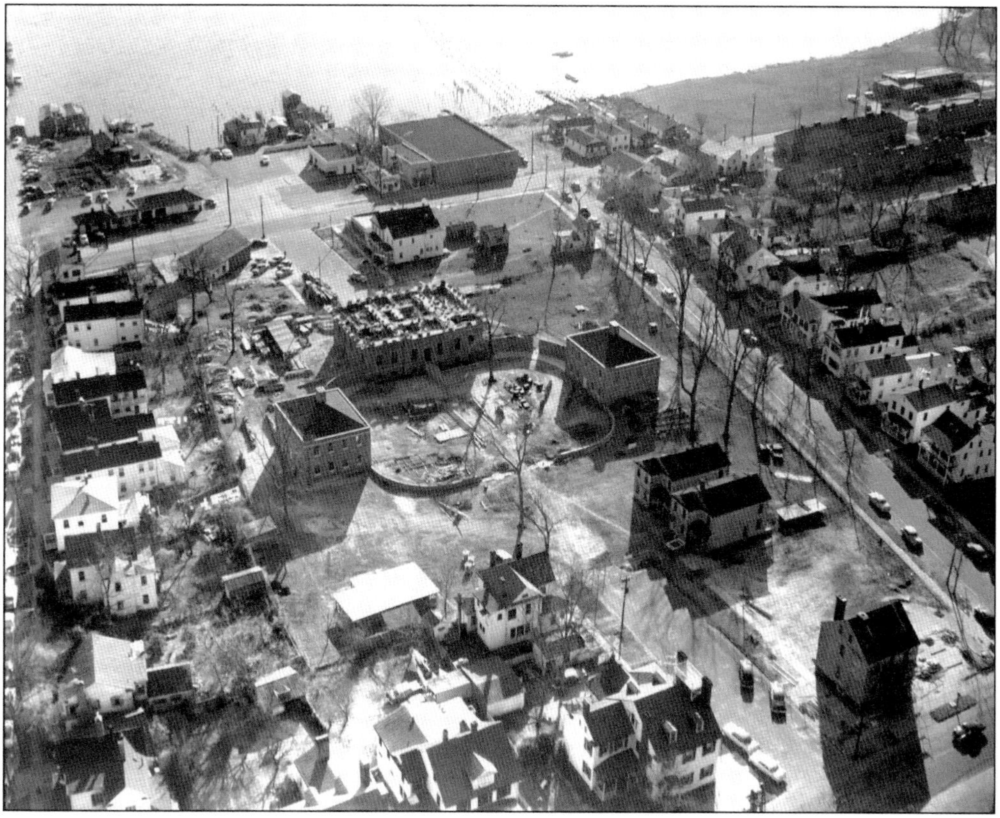

By January 3, 1956, the first floor of the palace was nearly complete, and the John P. Daves House was anchored at its new location flanking the Dixon House. The main gate to the palace grounds now stands between the two houses. More than 15 of the buildings visible in this photograph were demolished over the course of the restoration.

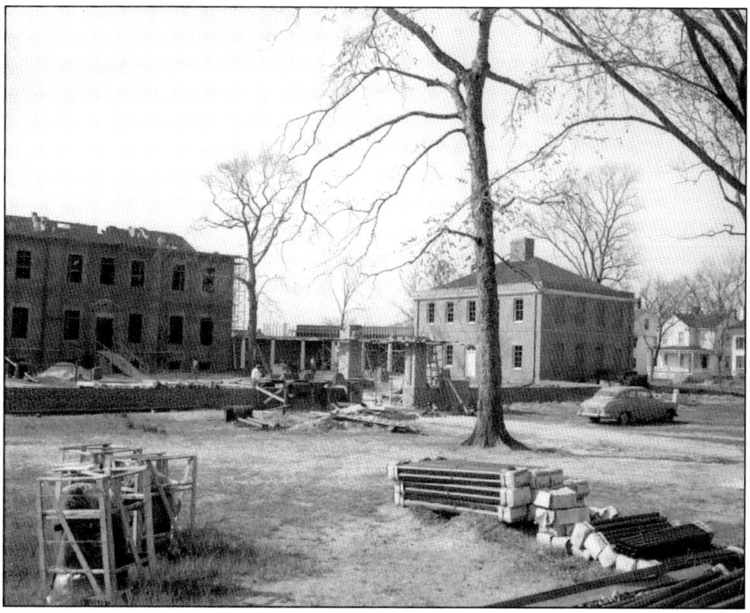

With the second floor of the palace nearly complete, work began on two additional areas: the covered colonnades (which connect the kitchen and stable offices to the main building) and the front gate. While the covered colonnades appear in the original plans, there is no evidence to suggest that the gates were originally part of John Hawks's design.

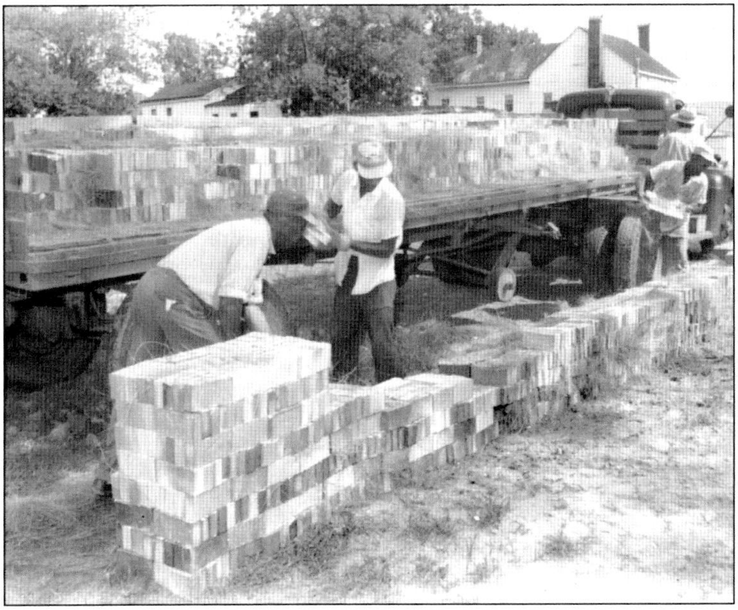

Luke P. Martin Jr., the son of Union Civil War veteran Luke Martin, was the lead brickmason during the restoration of Tryon Palace. Martin worked on 50 other historic buildings and taught vocational classes in area schools for students and military veterans.

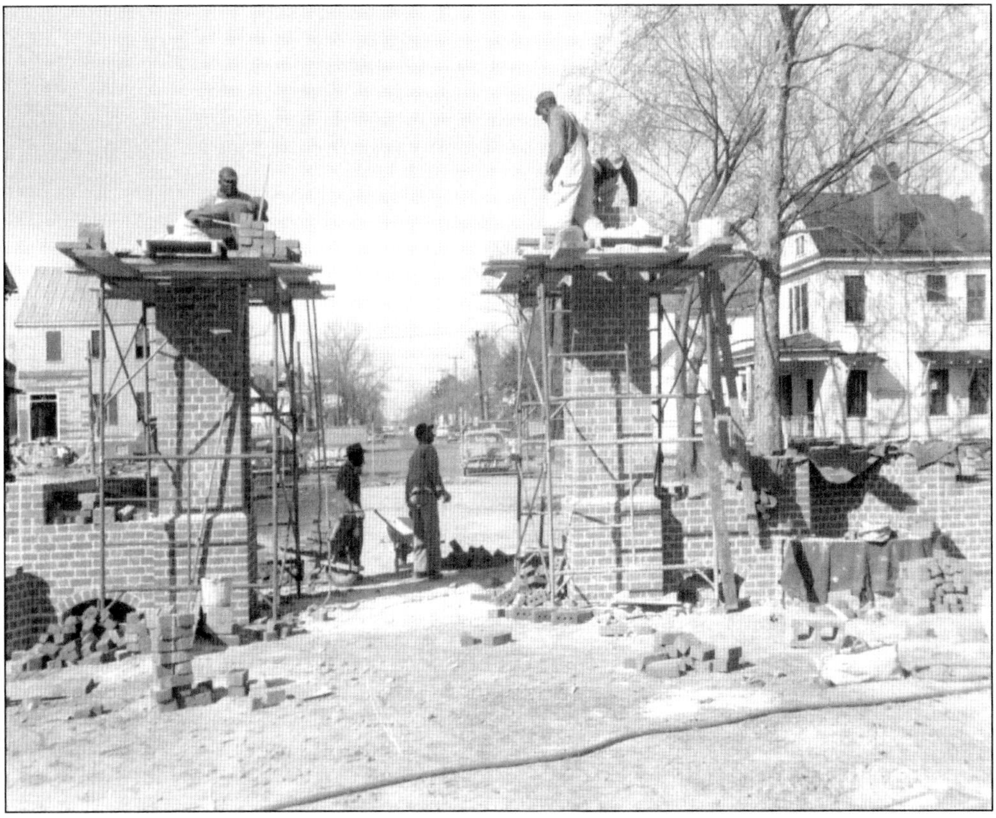

Although there was a lack of archeological evidence to suggest the exact shape or form of the gates and fences around the palace, the decision was made to include them. Initially, the fence in front of the palace was to be made of milled steel, but the Tryon Palace Commission voted to have it made of wrought iron, which is a more authentic and durable material.

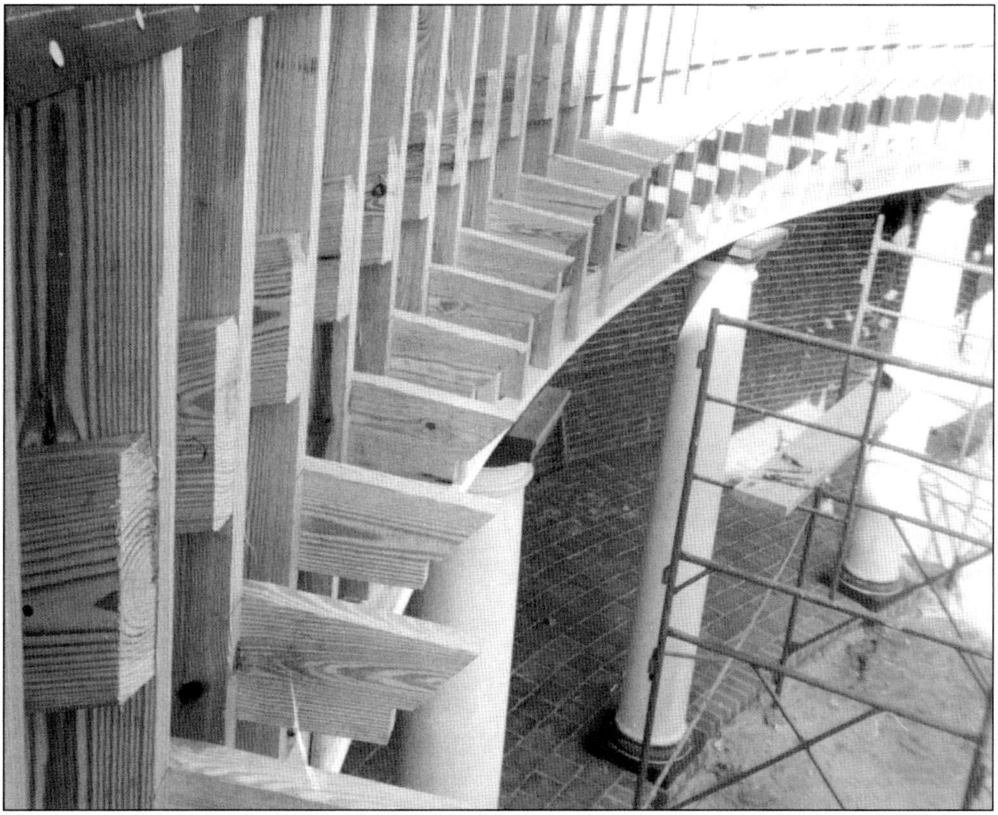

Work on the palace progressed quickly, beginning with the kitchen office and restoration of the stable office. Once the main building was nearly complete, final construction began on the colonnades that connected the three areas. The columns were put in place—where the pedestals had been added during construction of the masonry—before the roof was added. This photograph shows work being completed on the colonnade roof.

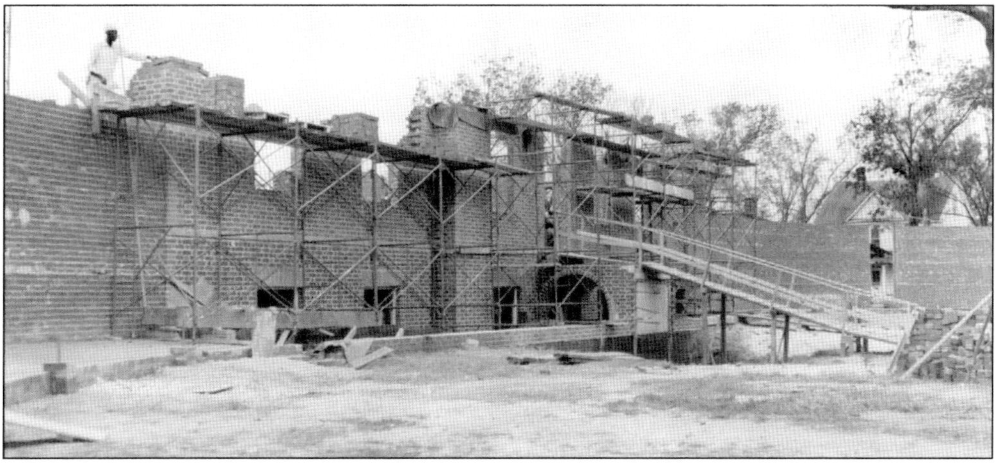

The back wall of the colonnades was completed as the main building was constructed. Workers had to build scaffolding around where the front stairs of the palace would be located in order to complete the facade of the building. A ramp led up to the front door entrance and into the main floor.

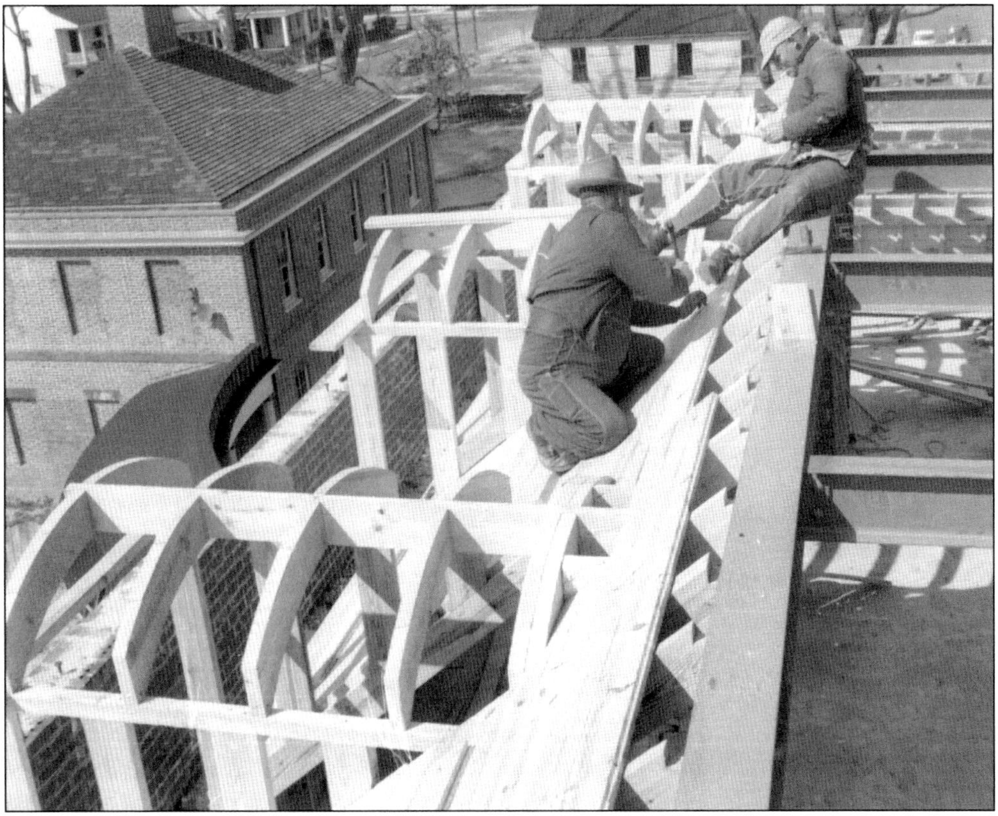

When the palace was first constructed, workers added dormers on all four sides of the main building. Research later revealed that these dormers were not part of the original building and they have since been removed. The photograph shows two men working on the dormers on the roof of the main building.

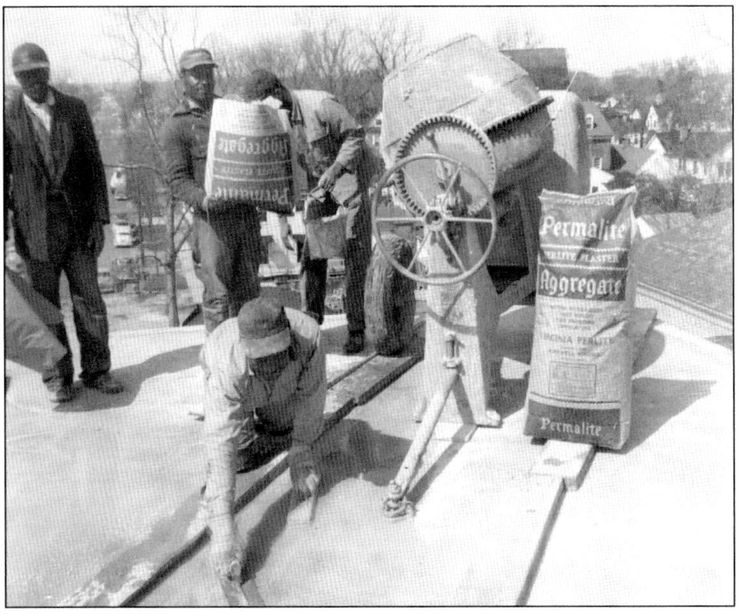

Before the final roofline was constructed, workers laid a slab of Permalite concrete. Produced by the Virginia Perlite Company, Permalite is an aggregate used to make lightweight structural concrete. In the 1950s, lightweight structural concrete could be anywhere from one-third to two-thirds lighter than regular concrete, making it ideal for insulating and fireproofing.

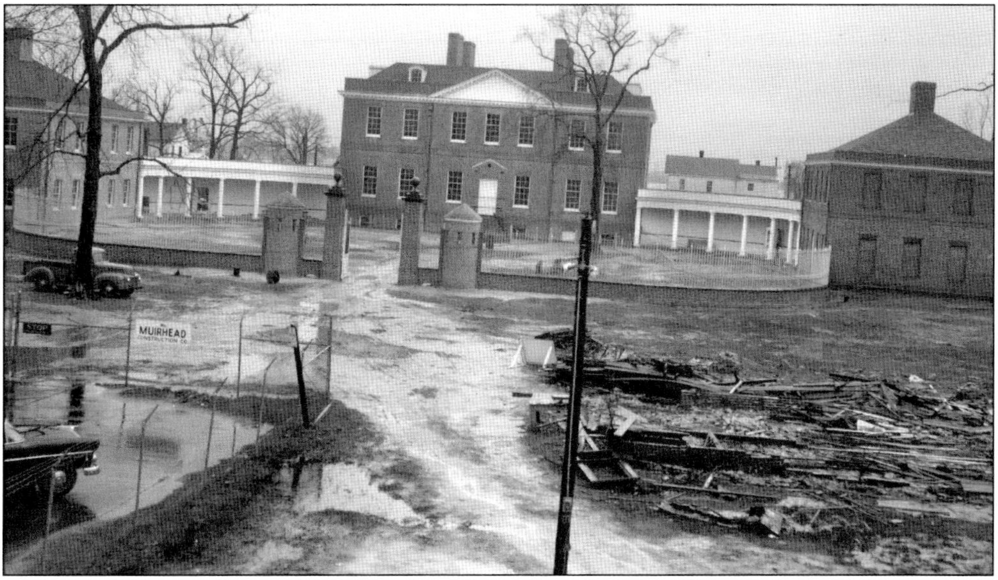

The William Muirhead Construction Company, of Durham, North Carolina, was in charge of the Tryon Palace Restoration. The completed exterior restoration of the building is visible in the background of this image. The remnants of construction material and demolished buildings are still visible in the foreground; work on the front gardens had not yet begun at this point.

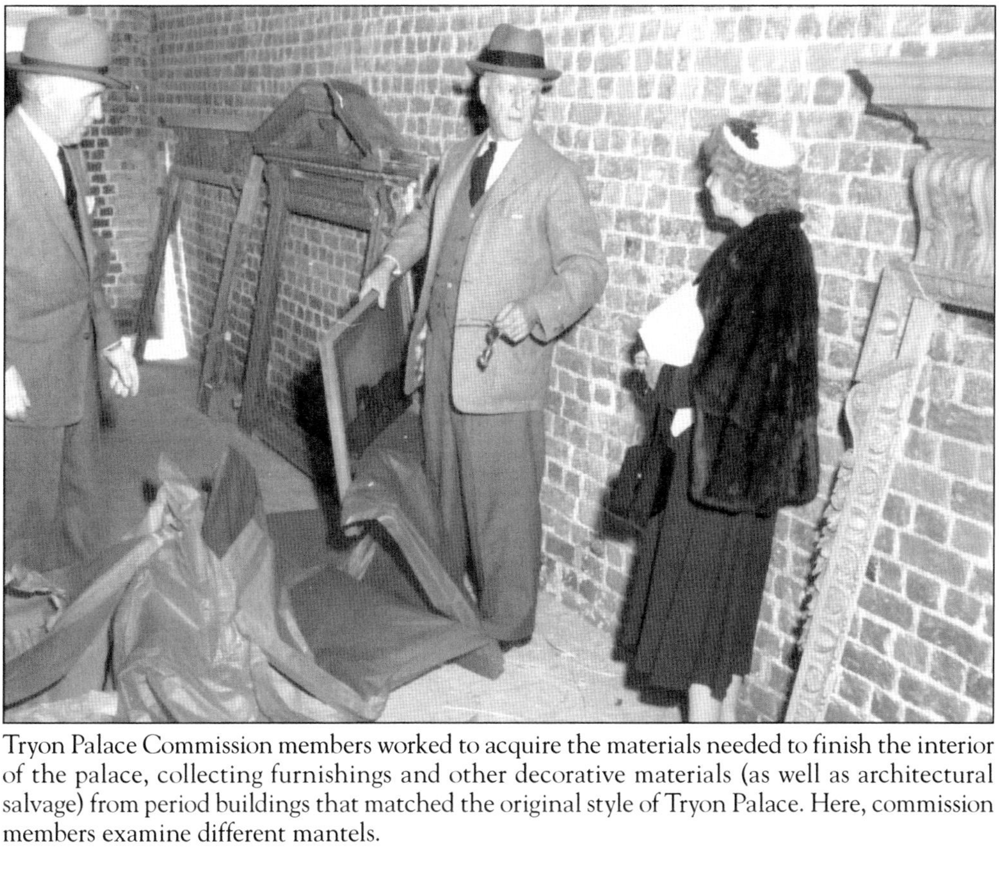

Tryon Palace Commission members worked to acquire the materials needed to finish the interior of the palace, collecting furnishings and other decorative materials (as well as architectural salvage) from period buildings that matched the original style of Tryon Palace. Here, commission members examine different mantels.

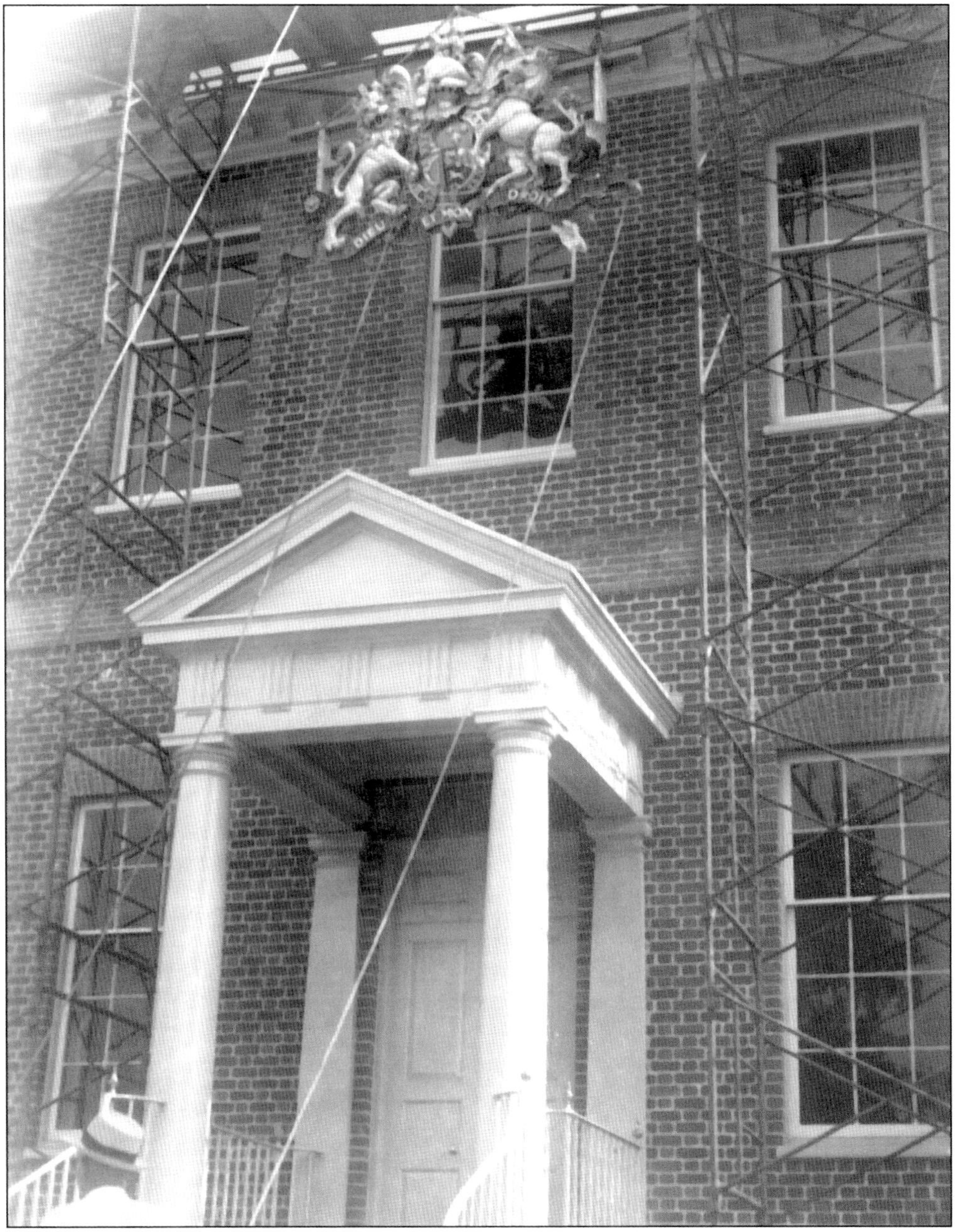

In July 1957, workers raised Tryon Palace's coat of arms into place on the palace pediment. The coat of arms bears the royal seal of King George III. To the left are the golden lion and Tudor rose (representing the English Crown), and to the right are the chained white unicorn and thistle (representing Scotland). In the center is a heraldic device that represents the king's claims in England, Scotland, Ireland, France, and Hanover. The buckled belt wrapped around the shield (or heraldic device) represents the Order of the Garter, and the motto on the belt is *Honi soit qui mal y pense* ("Shame on him who thinks this evil"). Underneath the figures is the royal motto, *Dieu et mon droit* ("God and my right"). The royal seal, which was originally erected by Royal Governor William Tryon, remained in place even after Josiah Martin fled office and the building was taken over by the state government.

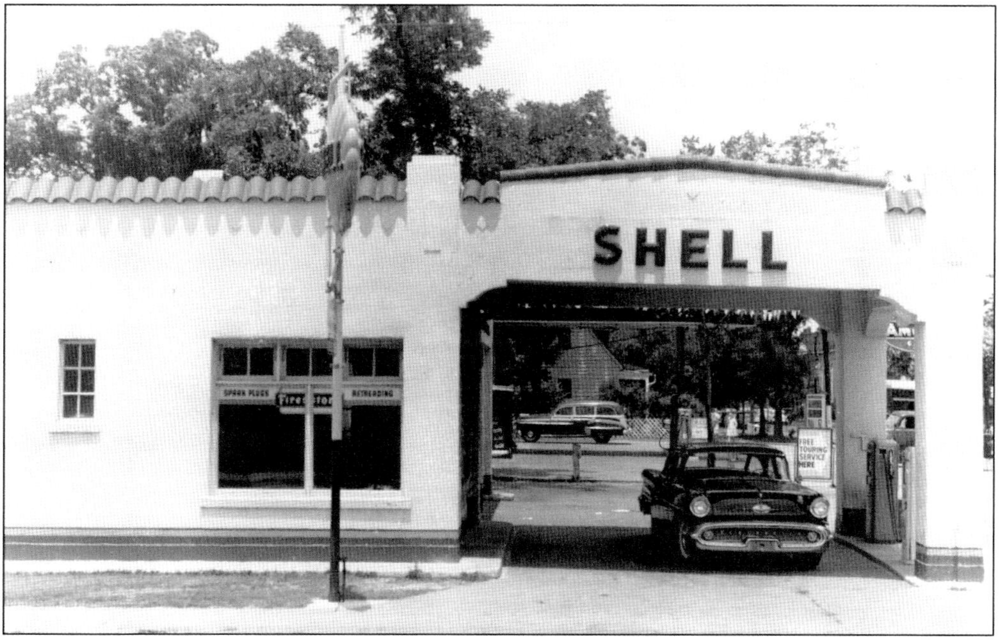

A Mission-style Shell Oil station on Pollock Street (above) served travelers and locals for many years before it was acquired by Tryon Palace. The tile roof and shaped parapet—designed in homage to Spanish Mission architecture in the southwestern United States—were featured on many early 20th-century gas stations. In the late 1950s, the former service station was transformed into Tryon Palace's visitor center and gift shop (below), but a few hints remain—including the diamond panel still visible on the former support pier—of its architectural origins. Now known as the Waystation, this satellite visitors' facility is located next to the Gertrude Carraway Garden.

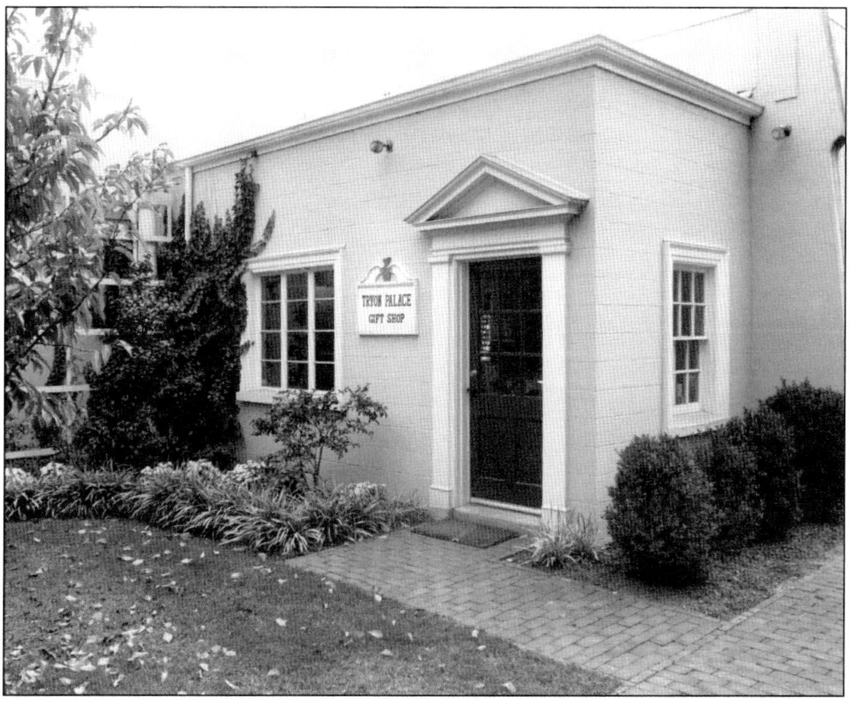

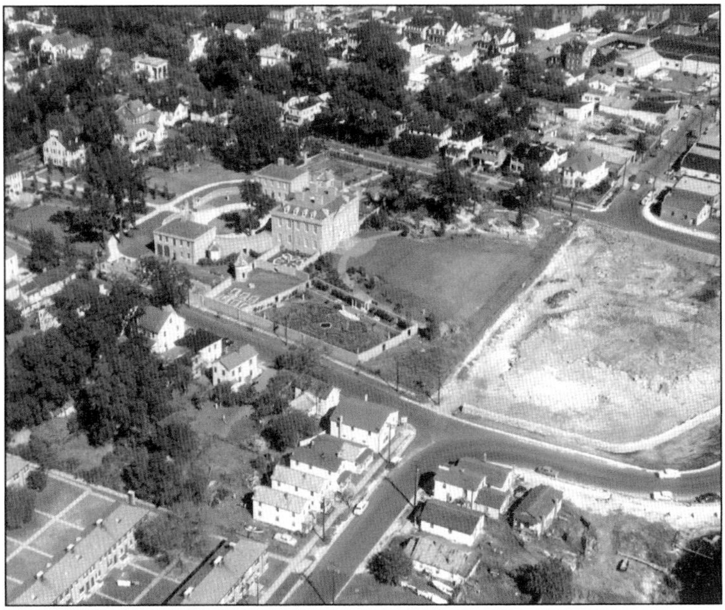

This aerial photograph, taken by local photographer S.C. Sweeney in October 1959, shows the palace gardens under construction—three walled gardens visible in the center, and the kitchen garden behind the palace. The landscape garden known as the "Wilderness," a wooded area meant to emulate an English country house's picturesque wooded preserve, is adjacent to the kitchen garden.

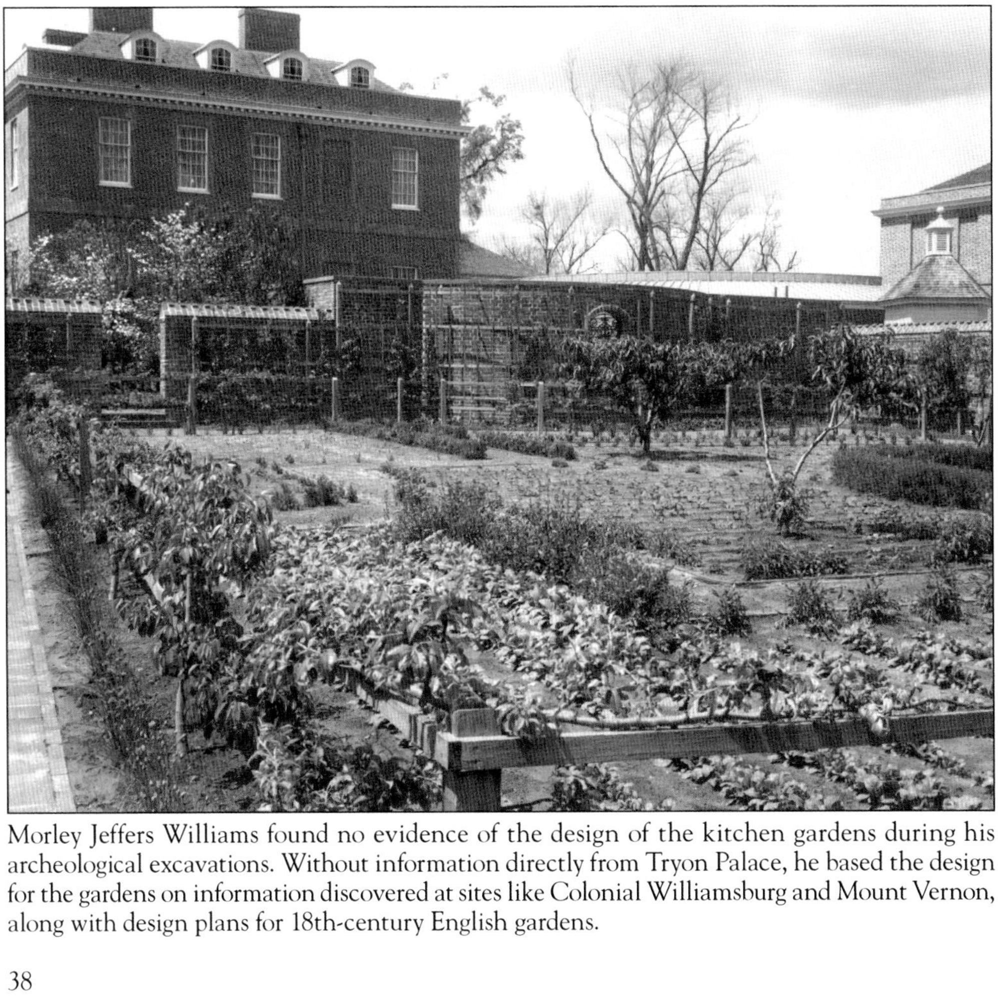

Morley Jeffers Williams found no evidence of the design of the kitchen gardens during his archeological excavations. Without information directly from Tryon Palace, he based the design for the gardens on information discovered at sites like Colonial Williamsburg and Mount Vernon, along with design plans for 18th-century English gardens.

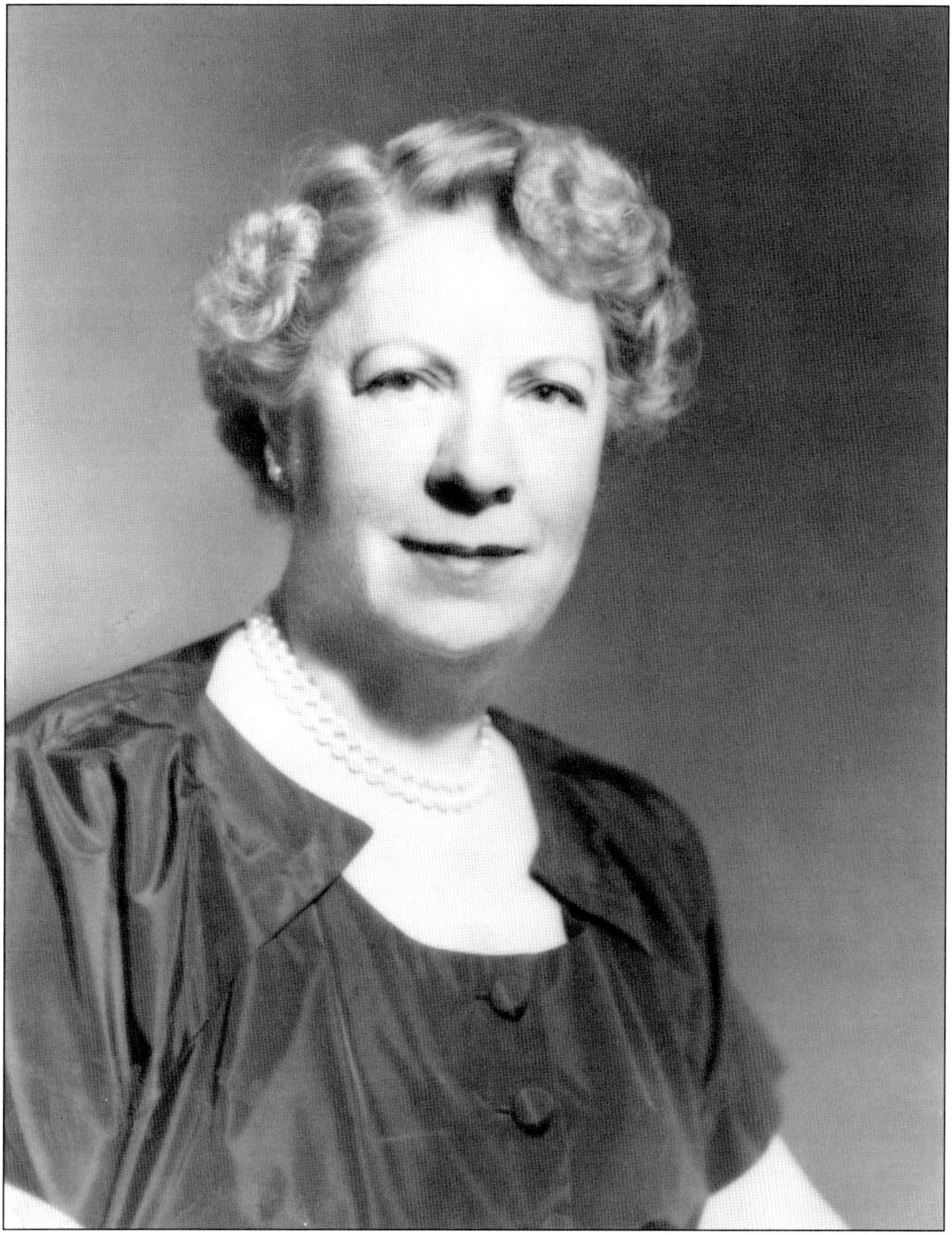

Gertrude Sprague Carraway (1896–1993) was a not only a major force in Tryon Palace's restoration but also in the development and progress of New Bern itself. A teacher, journalist, and indefatigable leader in the Daughters of the American Revolution (DAR), Carraway worked with regional, state, and national entities to find Tryon Palace's original plans and secure the site for reconstruction. Carraway began serving as palace director by 1962 and trained numerous guides to relay the palace's history and decorative arts in a natural and compelling way. As she put it, "We could get a Victrola to say the same thing over and over . . . that is what I used to emphasize with the hostess . . . they just spout. You can get a little machine to do that. The main thing is the personality."

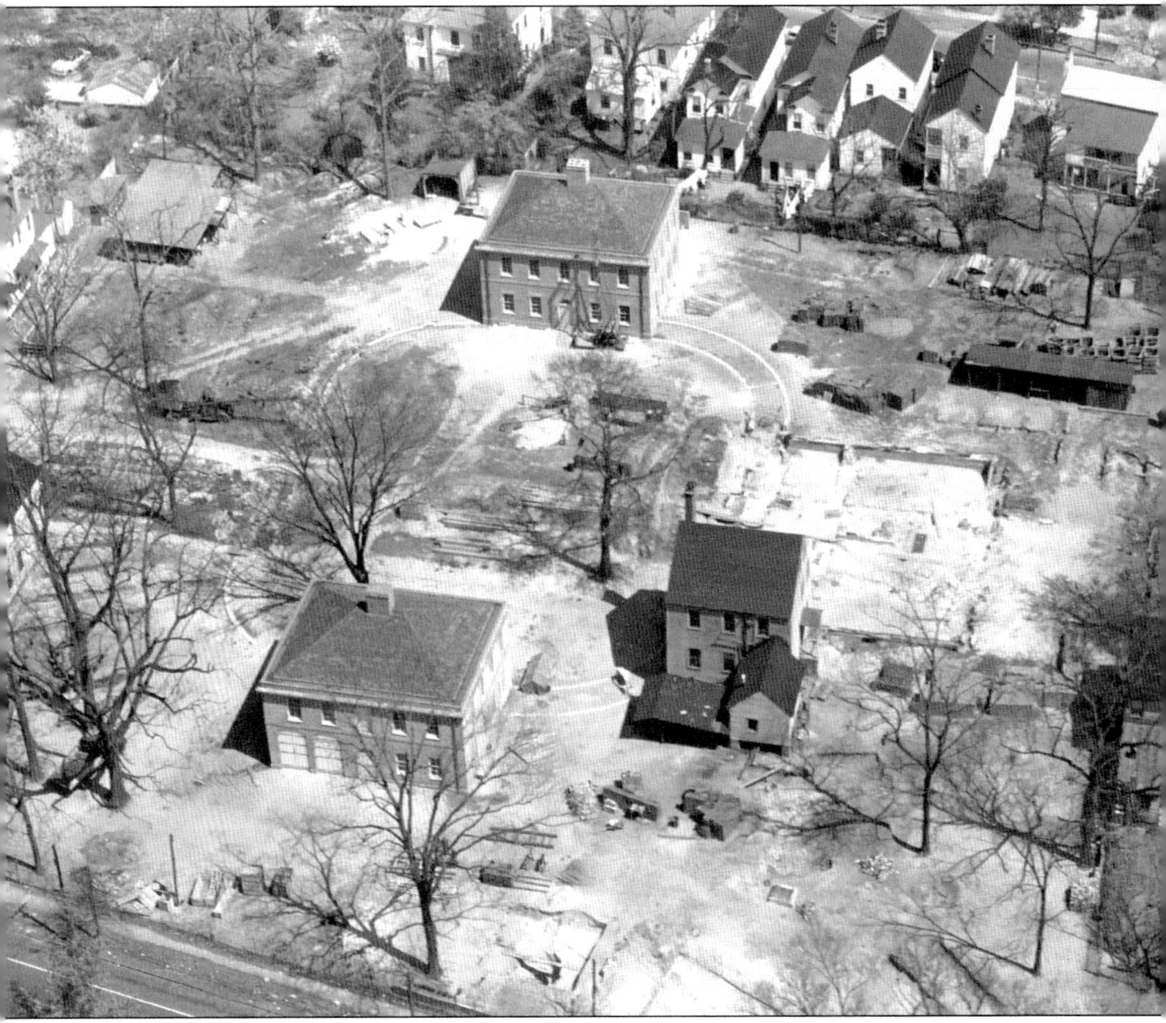

This partial aerial photograph was taken before construction began on the main building of Tryon Palace. The stable office (visible in the foreground) has been restored, and the kitchen office (visible in the background) has been reconstructed. The excavated foundation of the main building is visible to the right of these two buildings. This scene is not a familiar view of the palace; there are no gardens, and the houses crowd near the stable and kitchen offices—all of this would change in less than 10 years. This photograph also shows the great deal of change that had already taken place. For example, George Street no longer runs down the center of the site connecting the George Street Bridge with other local thoroughfares, and some buildings had already been demolished.

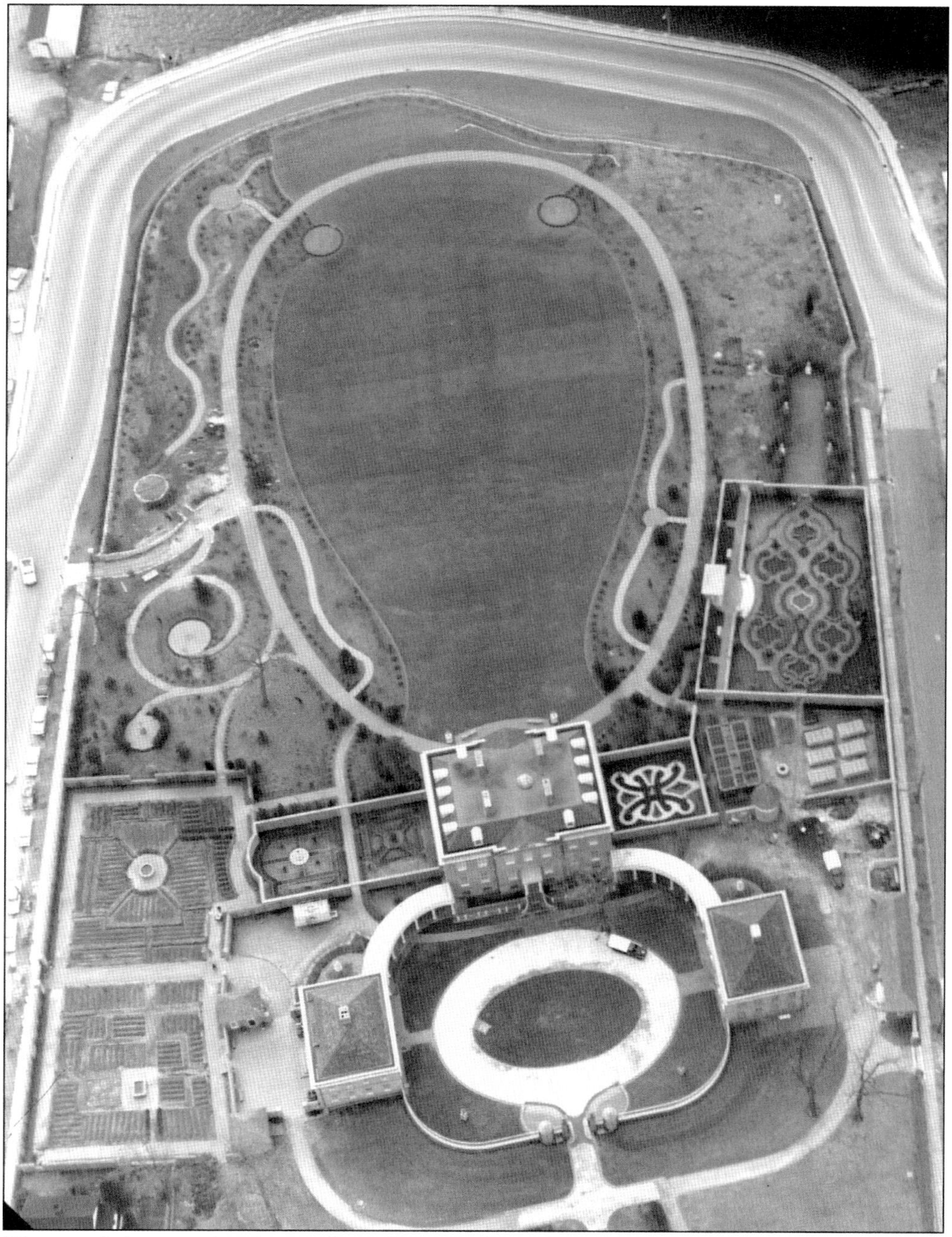

This aerial photograph, taken in the early 1960s, shows the completed restoration of Tryon Palace and grounds. Winding pathways and carefully sculpted gardens are clearly visible from above. The "Wilderness" landscape garden stretches from the rear of the kitchen gardens to the base of the south lawn overlooking the Trent River. The oval-shaped south lawn is bordered by pathways and the formal gardens. Most of the formal gardens are complete, but there is still space behind the Latham Garden, where new gardens would be created and extend to the Trent River. Although work crews were still finalizing the area behind the stable office at the time this photograph was taken, this view resembles the layout of the gardens today.

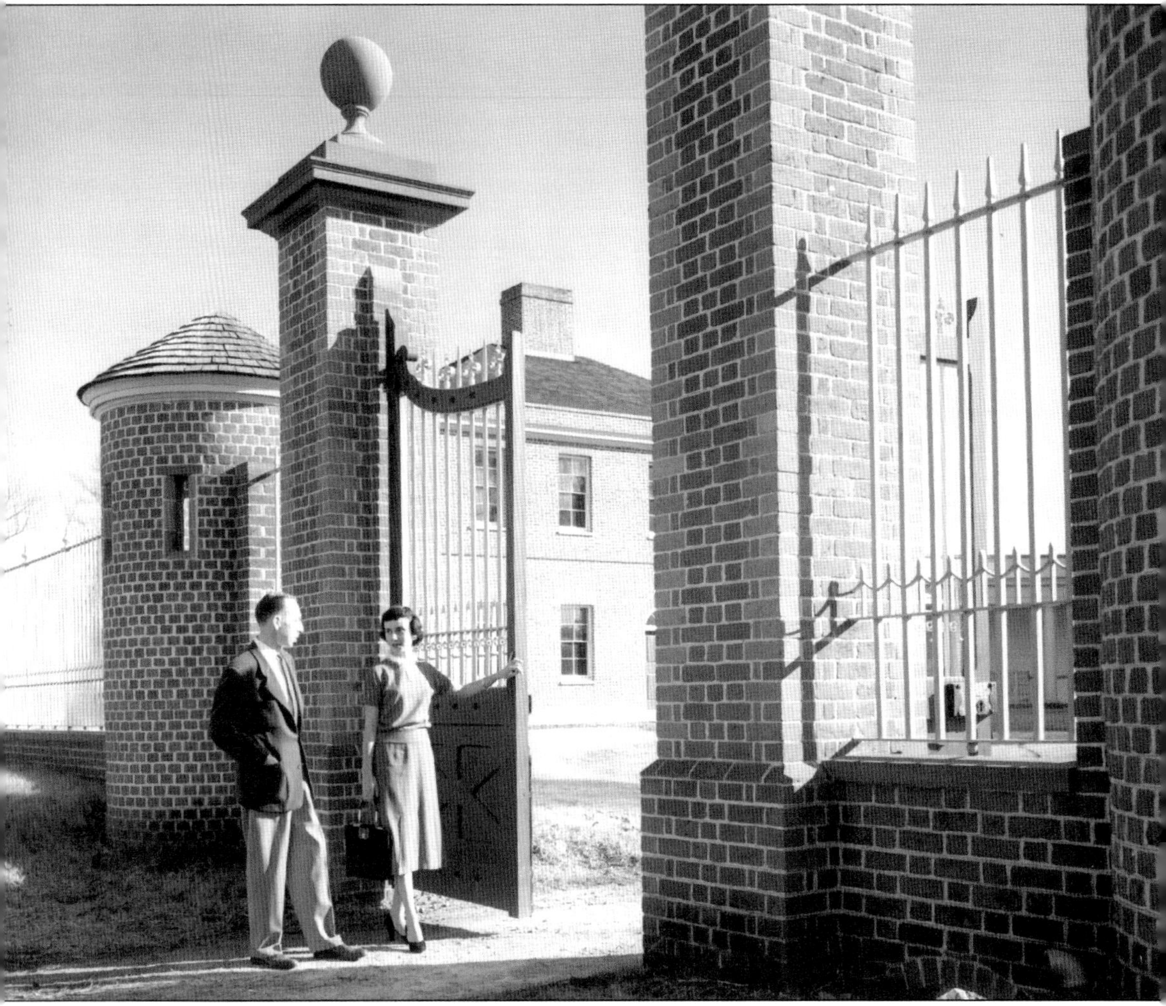

In 1957, the Tryon Palace Commission hired Gregor Norman-Wilcox as curator of decorative arts to manage the furnishing of the palace. He worked on several of these projects throughout his career, including the furnishing plans for the Hugo Reid Adobe in Los Angeles. Norman-Wilcox spent a year in New Bern with his wife, Grace A. Steen, a specialist in Oriental art. This photograph shows the married couple entering the newly completed gates of Tryon Palace. Norman-Wilcox was born Gregor Norman Humphreys in 1905 and graduated from the Cleveland School of Art. He worked briefly as an interior designer in Cleveland before moving to Los Angeles, where he joined the Los Angeles County Museum of Art in 1931. He remained in that position for the rest of his career, taking sabbaticals to work on special projects like Tryon Palace.

Three

The Palace Opens

After nearly 10 years of construction, the palace was ready for its grand opening in 1959. The celebratory events—which began on Wednesday, April 8, and continued until the public opening on Friday, April 10—included a ribbon-cutting ceremony, military band concert, gala dinner, and other activities. Perhaps the most notable thing about the event was that the opening celebrations marked the first time in over 150 years that the North Carolina General Assembly met in New Bern. The collective vision of the Dreamers was a success, and the community gathered together to celebrate the restoration of Tryon Palace. Over the next decade, the palace had several more openings as the gardens and grounds were expanded and new inaugural programming was instituted. One of the most touching events was the opening of the Latham Garden in 1961. Named in honor of Maude Moore Latham, who spearheaded the restoration of the palace, the gardens are a constant reminder of her dedication to Tryon Palace. Tryon Palace also held its inaugural Decorative Arts Symposium in 1969; the event was held annually for 40 years (until 2009); these symposia united the general public and top scholars in the fields of material culture and the decorative arts.

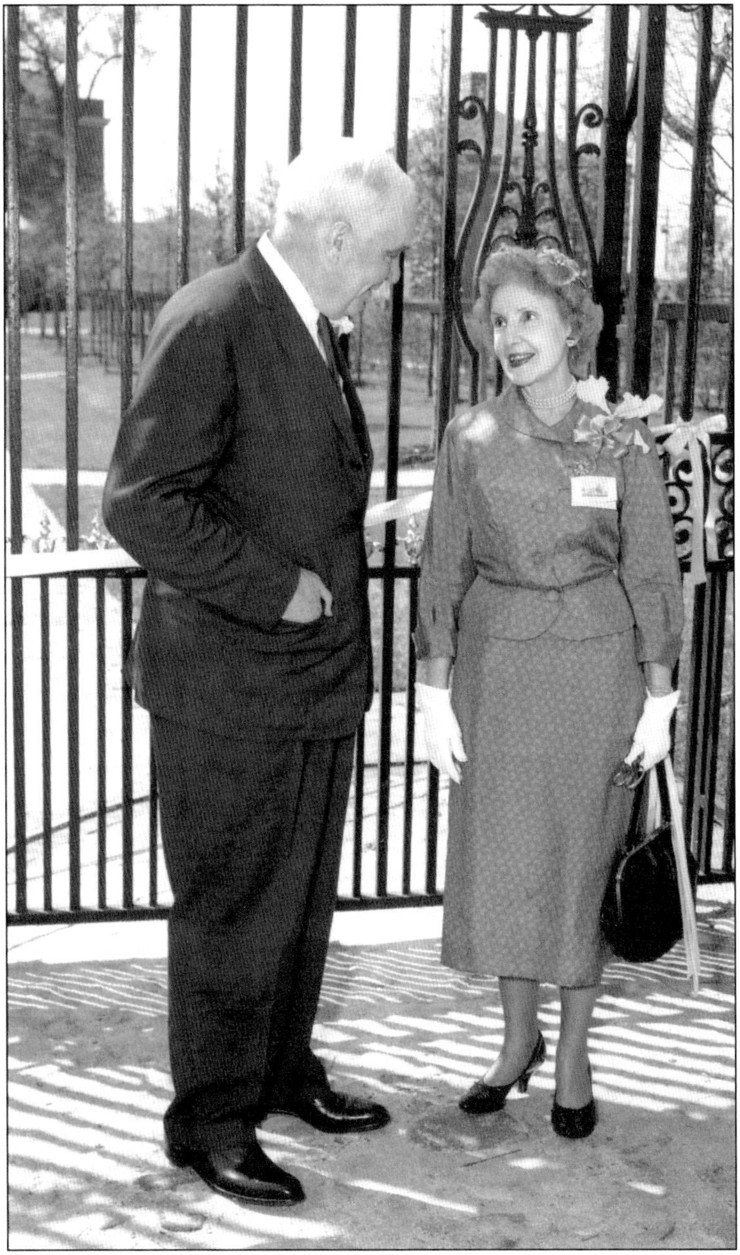

Tryon Palace's grand opening began on April 8, 1959, with a 19-gun salute by 12 Marines from Camp Lejeune. The day's ceremonies included several events surrounding the opening of the palace, its transition to the care of the State of North Carolina, and celebrating the historical significance of New Bern to the state government. As a part of these activities, May Gordon Latham Kellenberger, chairman of the Tryon Palace Commission, presented Gov. Luther Hartwell Hodges with a key to Tryon Palace, officially handing the building over to the care of the State of North Carolina from the care of the Tryon Palace Commission. Kellenberger and Hodges are shown in this image. The presentation of the palace key was followed by a ribbon-cutting ceremony held at the front gate of the palace. After the ribbon-cutting ceremony, state legislators entered the palace to convene the 1959 North Carolina General Assembly.

The 2nd Marine Aircraft Wing Band, from Cherry Point, played from the front lawn during the grand opening ceremony on April 8, 1959, as visitors eagerly awaited their chances to see the completed palace for the first time. Since its opening, Tryon Palace has proudly continued to host military bands for special events and concerts.

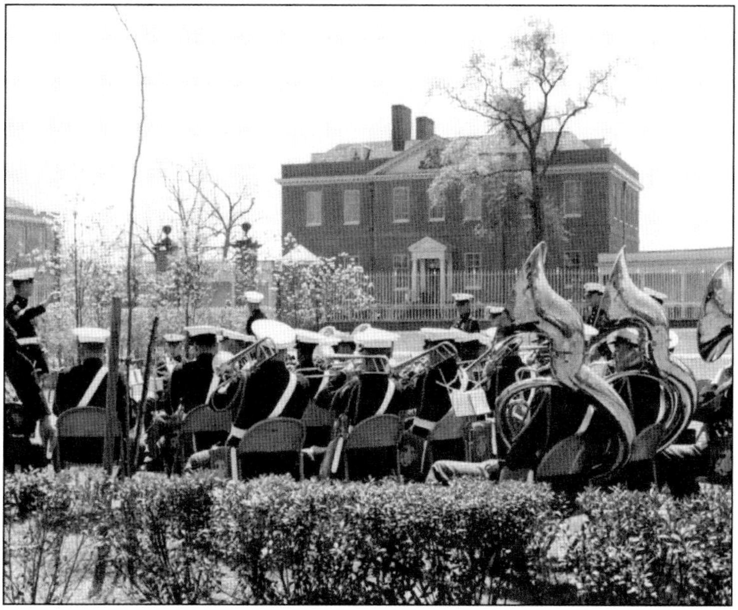

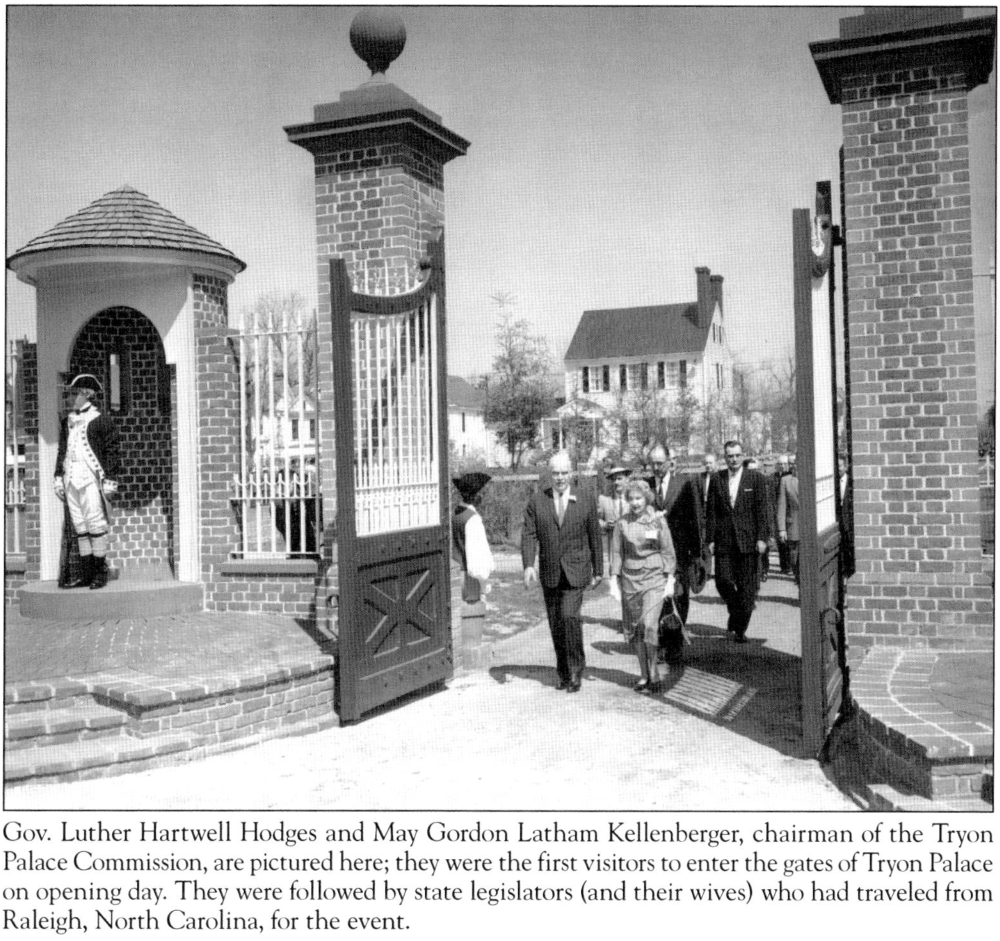

Gov. Luther Hartwell Hodges and May Gordon Latham Kellenberger, chairman of the Tryon Palace Commission, are pictured here; they were the first visitors to enter the gates of Tryon Palace on opening day. They were followed by state legislators (and their wives) who had traveled from Raleigh, North Carolina, for the event.

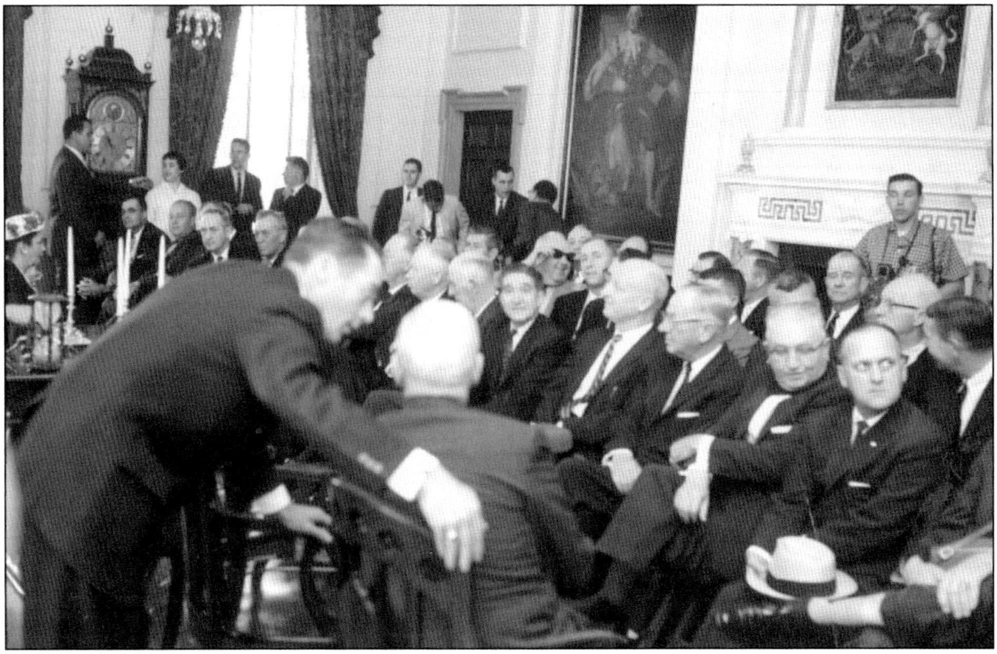

For the first time in more than 150 years, the North Carolina General Assembly convened in Tryon Palace's council chamber. The 1959 General Assembly met at Tryon Palace; according to witnesses, the senate met in the council chamber, and the house met in the cellar. This was the first time the legislature had convened at the palace since 1793.

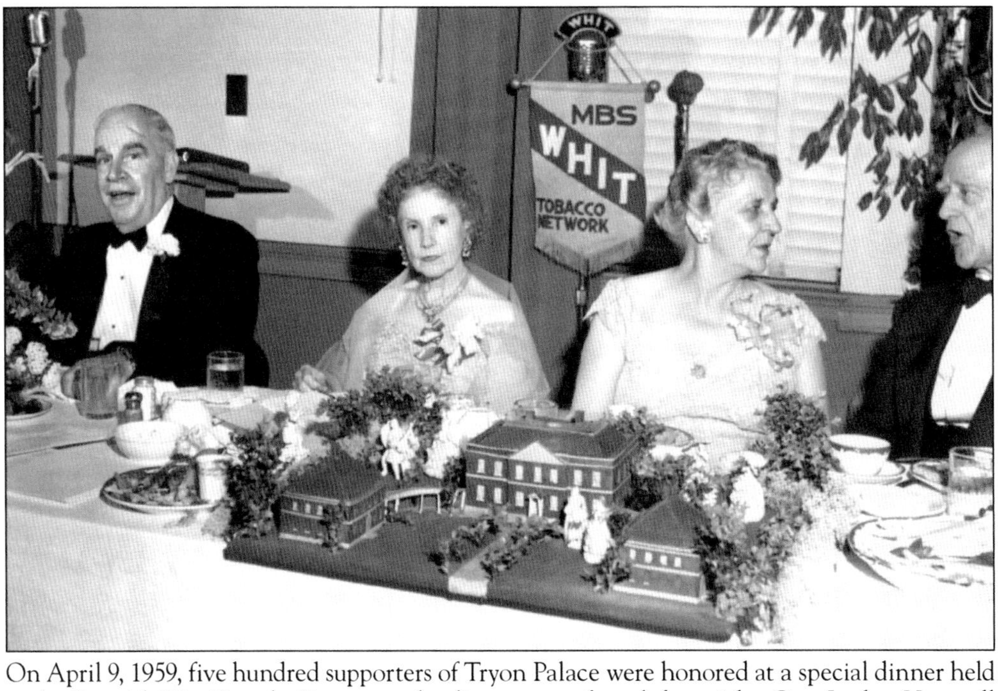

On April 9, 1959, five hundred supporters of Tryon Palace were honored at a special dinner held at the Scottish Rite Temple. Present at the dinner were, from left to right, Gov. Luther Hartwell Hodges, May Gordon Latham Kellenberger, and the governor's wife, Martha Blakeney Hodges. During the dinner, Governor Hodges gave a speech praising the restoration.

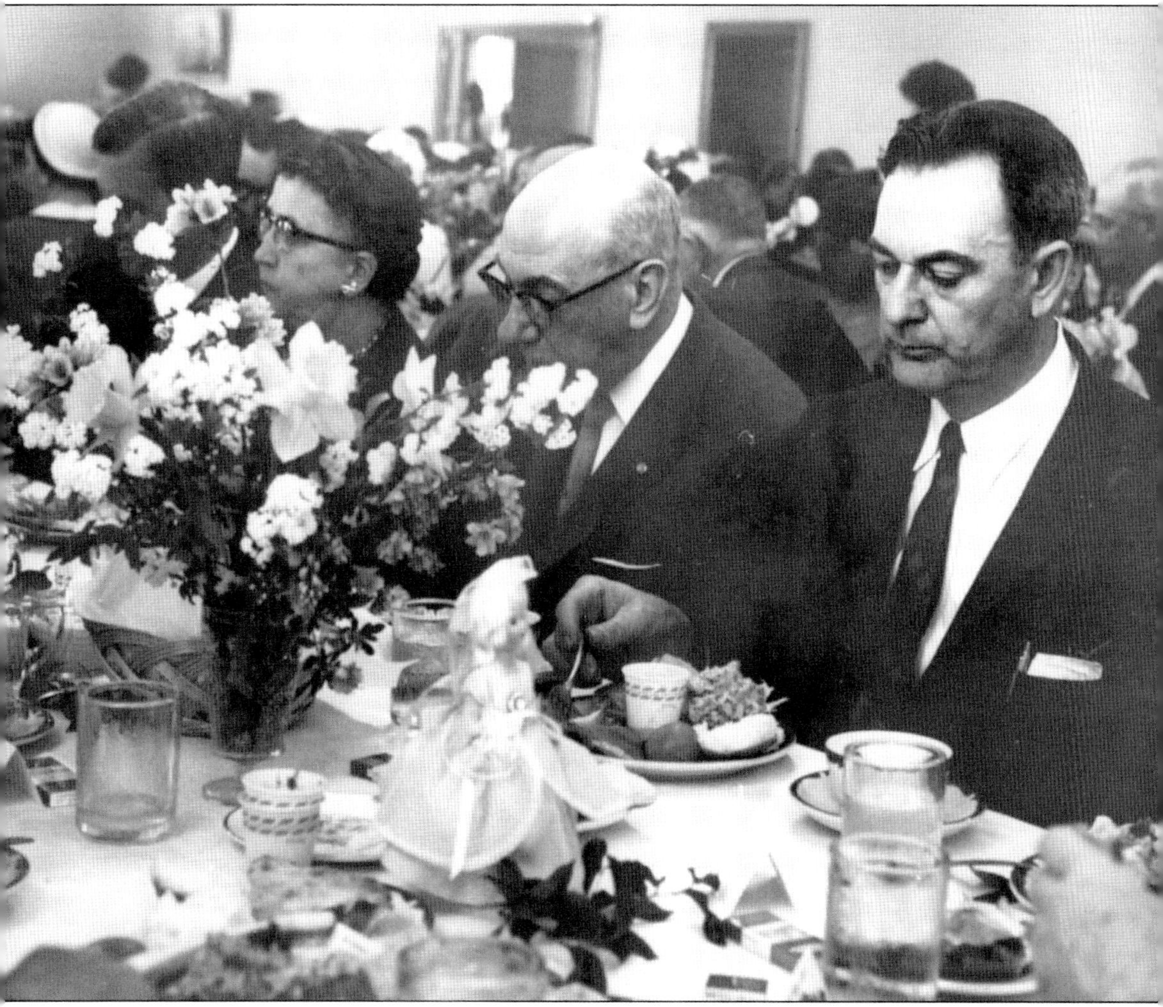

Alexander "Sandy" Hawkins Graham (1890–1977), seated center, was one of the 500 guests at the Scottish Rite Temple dinner on April 9, 1959. A Hillsborough native with ties to New Bern, Graham came from a distinguished political family and served the state in a number of capacities from 1921 until 1957. During these years, he worked to improve the state's infrastructure and was named the head of North Carolina's State Highway and Public Works Commission from 1945 to 1949 and again from 1953 to 1957. He was involved in the early efforts to secure the palace property and was also on the North Carolina State Highway Commission during the construction of the new bridge at Union Point, which replaced the George Street Bridge. Although Graham retired in 1957, he remained active in his church and took on many philanthropic endeavors.

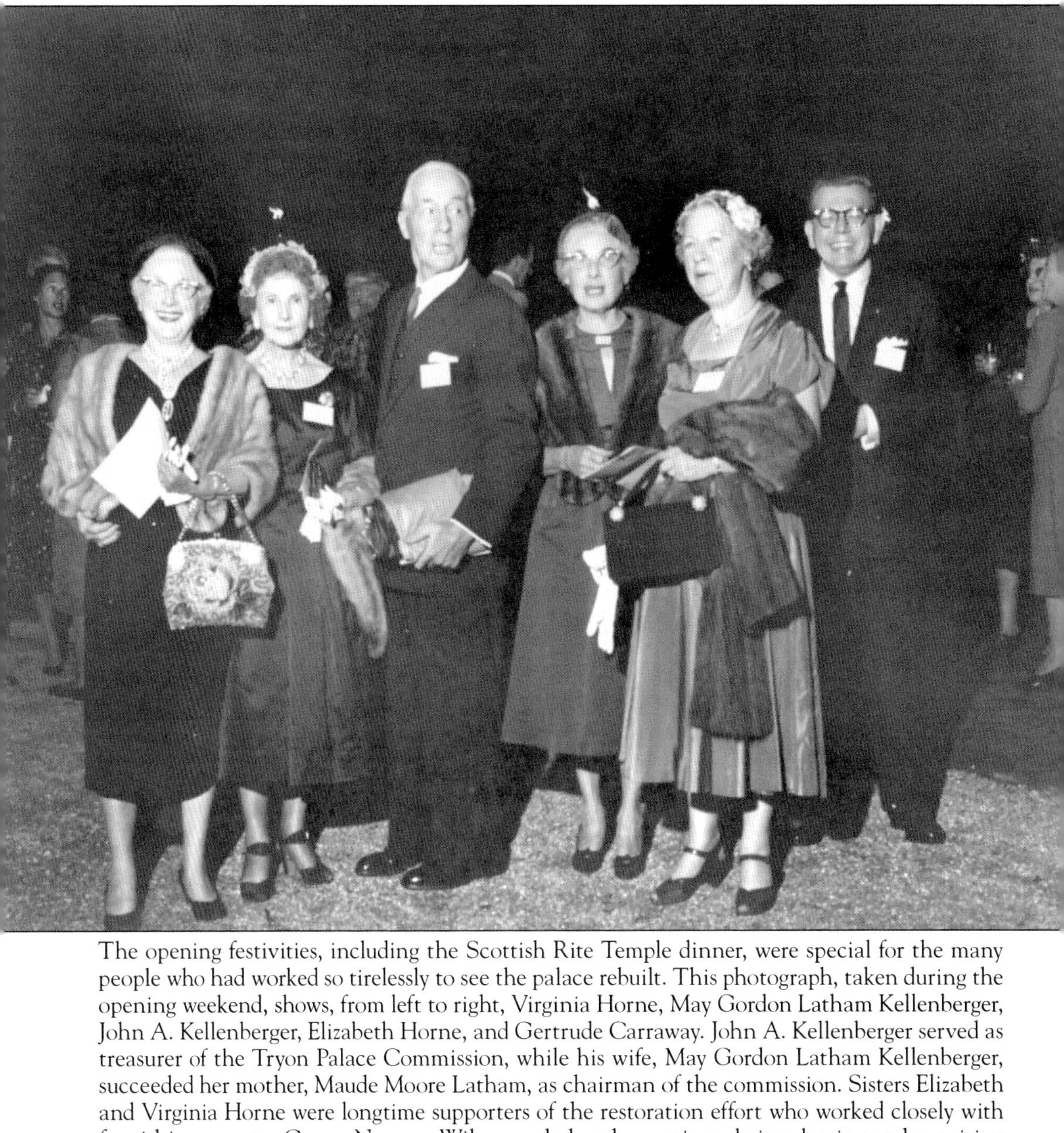

The opening festivities, including the Scottish Rite Temple dinner, were special for the many people who had worked so tirelessly to see the palace rebuilt. This photograph, taken during the opening weekend, shows, from left to right, Virginia Horne, May Gordon Latham Kellenberger, John A. Kellenberger, Elizabeth Horne, and Gertrude Carraway. John A. Kellenberger served as treasurer of the Tryon Palace Commission, while his wife, May Gordon Latham Kellenberger, succeeded her mother, Maude Moore Latham, as chairman of the commission. Sisters Elizabeth and Virginia Horne were longtime supporters of the restoration effort who worked closely with furnishings curator Gregor Norman-Wilcox and played an active role in selecting and acquiring furnishings for the palace, including several gifts from the North Carolina Daughters of the American Revolution and Daughters of the American Colonists. Carraway became the first director of Tryon Palace.

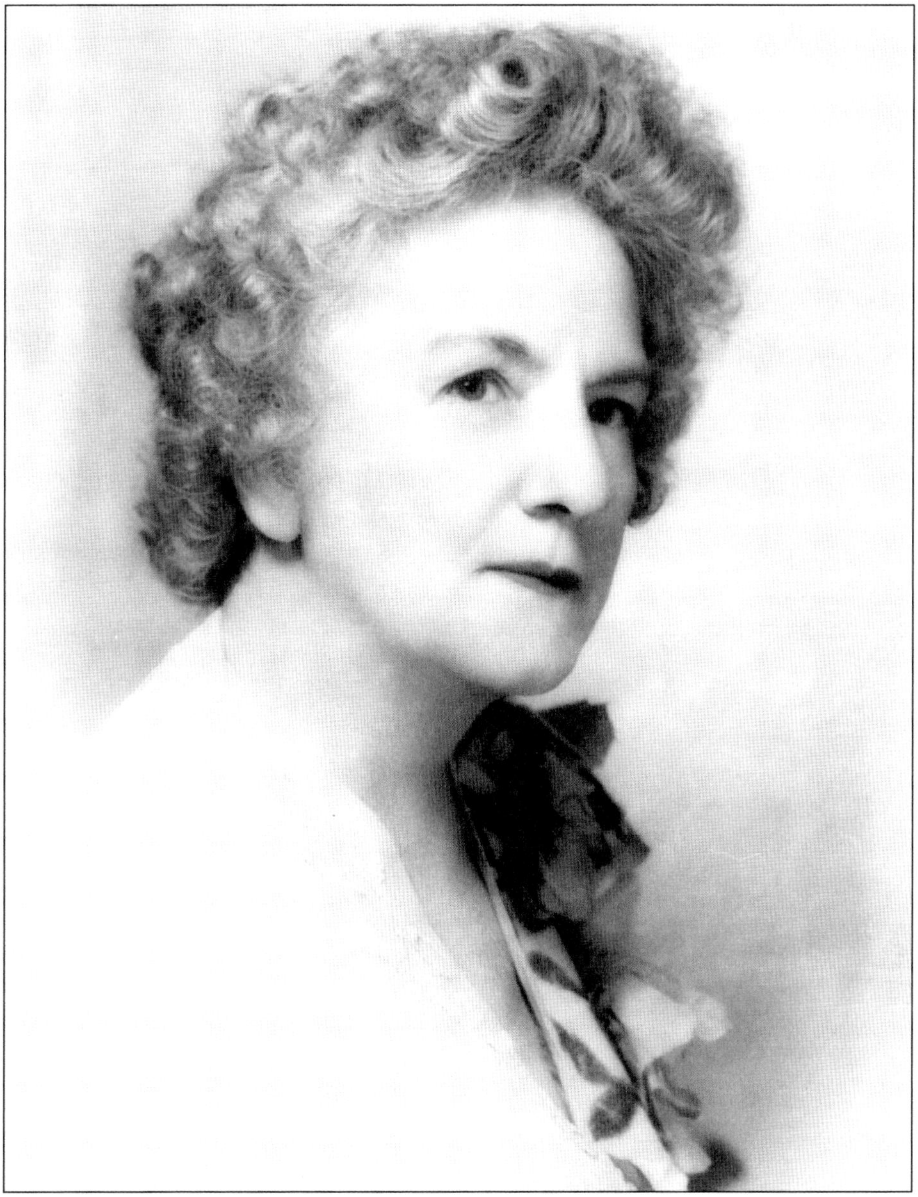

Maude Moore Latham was born in New Bern on December 16, 1871. Educated and well-traveled, she spent her life advocating for the arts and historic preservation. Latham's crowning achievement was the reconstruction of Tryon Palace. A longtime supporter of the project, she began publicly campaigning for the palace in 1939 by financing the publication of *Old Homes and Gardens of North Carolina*, in which Dr. Archibald Henderson emphasizes the importance of restoring the palace. She continued her advocacy, and in January 1944, Latham established the Maude Moore Latham Trust Fund, dedicating $100,000 towards the project. The trust was created with the understanding that the state would purchase the land, and she would ensure that the palace was restored. In 1945, the North Carolina General Assembly set aside funds to purchase the land and appointed the members of the Tryon Palace Commission, which elected Latham as chairman. Latham continued to contribute to the trust, giving the remainder of her estate—$1,115,000—to the Tryon Palace Commission in 1951. The Latham Garden is named in her honor.

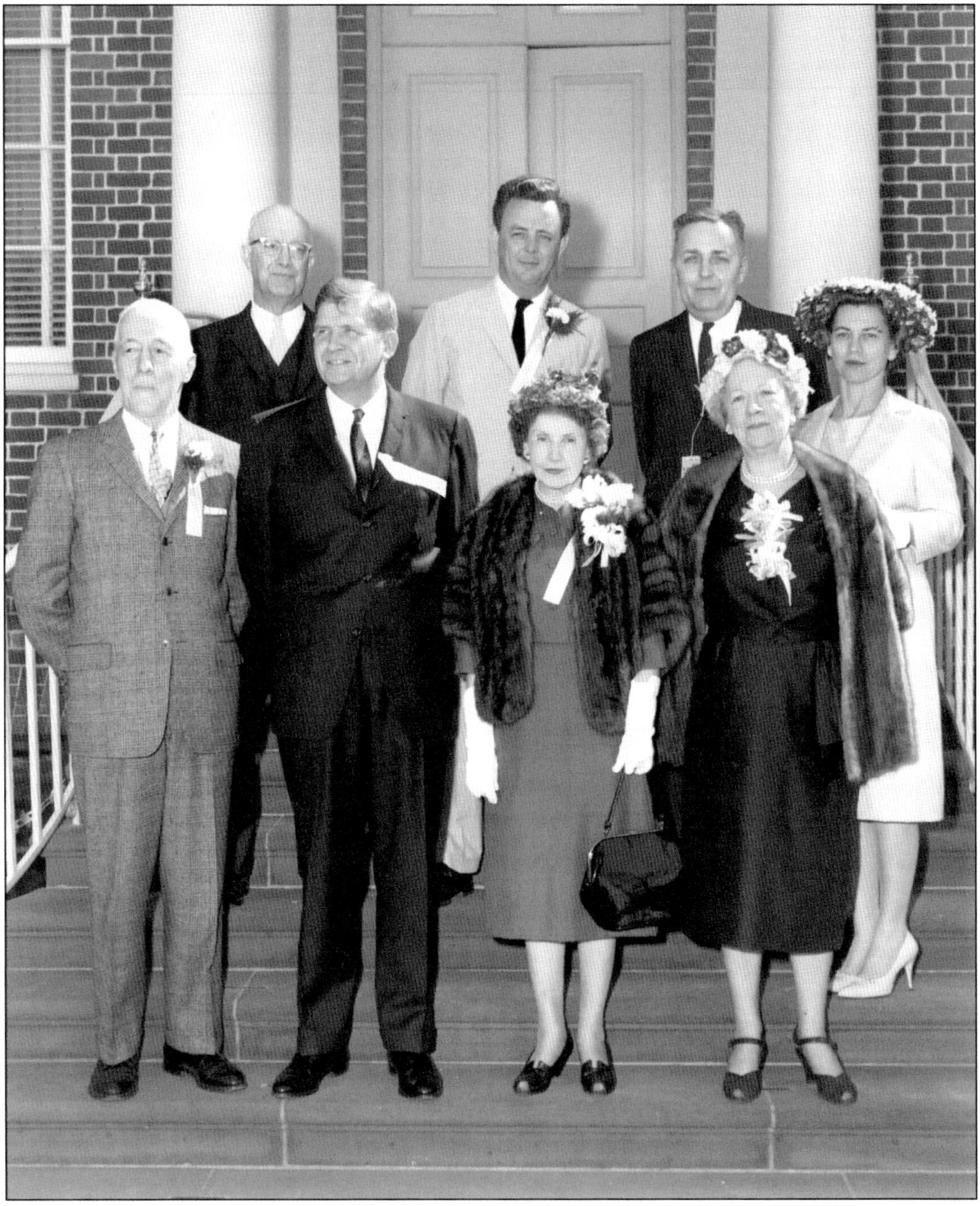

This group photograph was taken on the palace steps on April 8, 1961, during the dedication of the Latham Garden. From left to right are (first row) John A. Kellenberger, Gov. Terry Sanford, May Gordon Latham Kellenberger, and Gertrude Carraway; (second row) "Libby" Ward, Hargrove "Skipper" Bowles, New Bern mayor Robert L. Stallings Jr., and his wife, Margaret Hay Stallings. Sanford (1917–1998), who served as North Carolina's governor from 1961 to 1965, advocated for improvement in education and for the arts. In 1961, Sanford appointed Bowles (1919–1986) to head the North Carolina Department of Conservation and Development. Bowles later served in the North Carolina General Assembly as a representative (from 1967 to 1969) and then as a state senator (from 1969 to 1972). Robert L. Stallings Jr. later served as head of the Tryon Palace Commission and was instrumental in Kay Williams being appointed director of Tryon Palace in 1983.

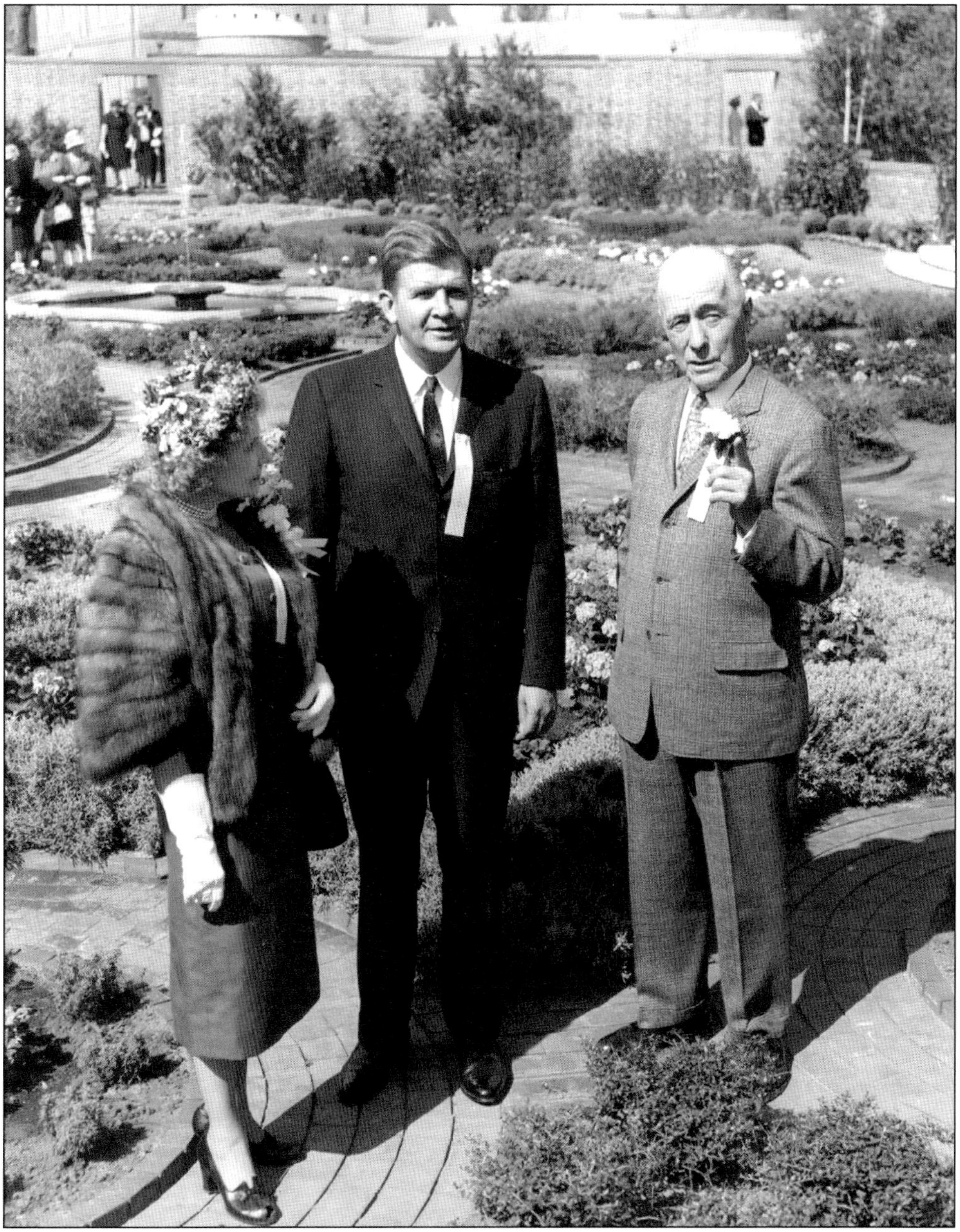

At the Latham Garden dedication ceremony, held on April 8, 1961, the Kellenbergers (Maude Moore Latham's daughter and son-in-law) escorted North Carolina governor Terry Sanford around the garden. This photograph shows the three of them: May Gordon Latham Kellenberger (left), Sanford (center), and John A. Kellenberger. Before they toured the gardens, Sanford and May Kellenberger were among the day's speakers. In his speech, Sanford praised Maude Moore Latham's dedication and work to restore Tryon Palace as the "most magnificent single gift that has been presented to the people of North Carolina." During her remarks, Kellenberger spoke of her mother, saying, "I feel that her spirit hovers over us and that she silently gives her approval to our work. One of my greatest joys is believing, with all my heart, that, were she here, she would be highly pleased with all that has been done."

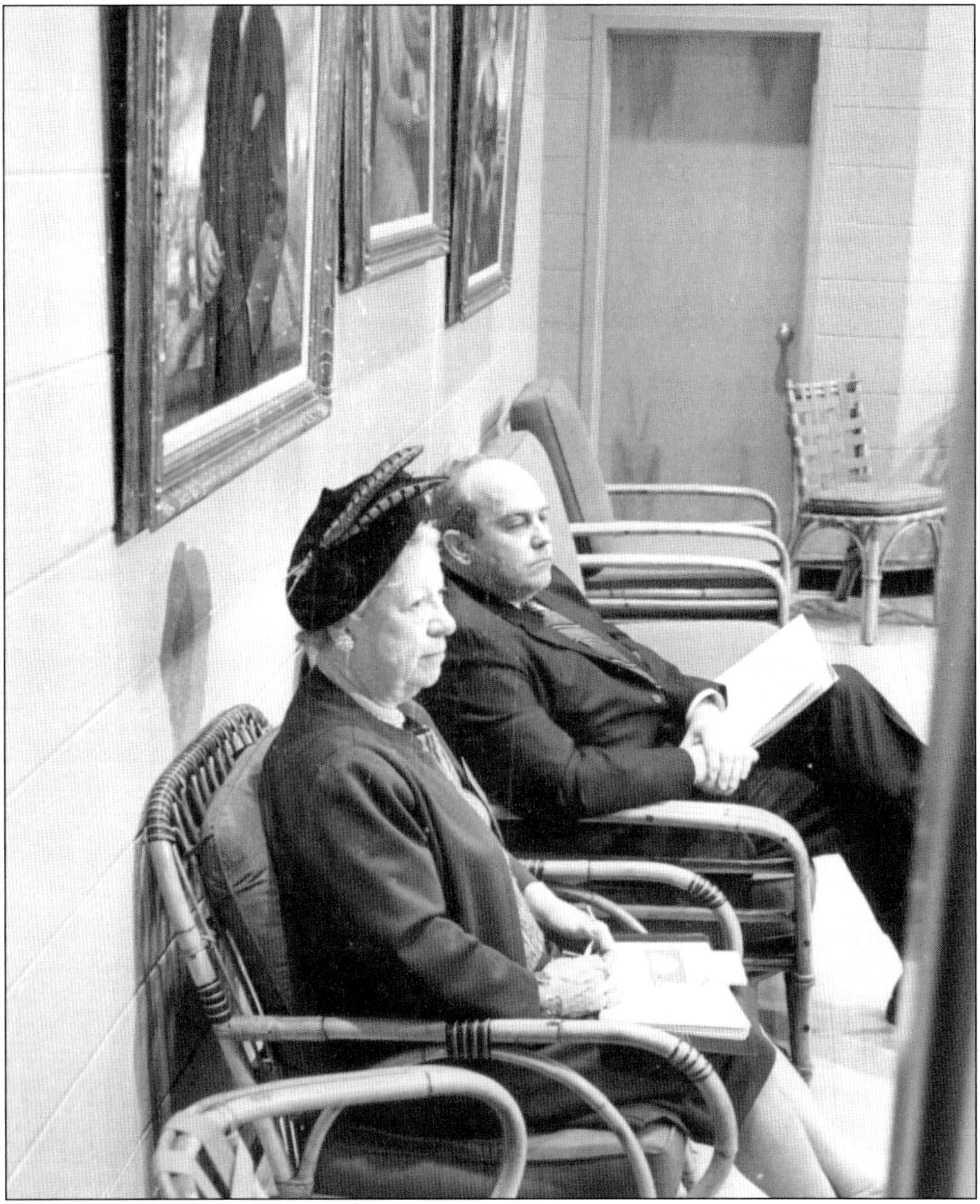

Tryon Palace's first Decorative Arts Symposium was held on March 4 and 5, 1969. Organized in conjunction with East Carolina University's Division of Continuing Education, the theme for the first year was "Tryon Palace and 18th-Century Decorative Arts." Participants were asked to register by February 14, 1969, and fees for the event were $25. The event was publicized across the country, including in *Preservation News*, which is produced by the National Trust for Historic Preservation. Over 160 people attended the event, and some people had to be turned away due to lack of space. The success and popularity of the symposium led to it becoming an annual event for the next 40 years. Each year, the organizers selected a different theme revolving around styles of interior decor, different time frames, or even production materials. Examples of later themes include "The Fine Art of Collecting," "Borrowed, Invented and Stolen," and "Recreating the Past We Wanted: New Visions of Old America."

Four

Tryon Palace Comes to Life

Inside the palace and throughout the grounds, the Tryon Palace staff works to interpret the history of the building and the people who once inhabited it. The way in which the palace is interpreted changed over the years after new historical research was conducted. While the architecture and finishes have remained the same, furnishing plans have changed, costumes for the palace hosts have been altered to reflect a greater diversity of social positions, and new additions have been made to the gardens. Looking back over the palace's 50-year history, it is possible to see these changes in interpretation from the early years—when the furnishings were first installed in the palace—to the recent incorporation of produce from the kitchen garden in cooking demonstrations. Every day, historians at Tryon Palace continue to uncover new information that will be used in interpreting and discussing the palace and other properties on the site.

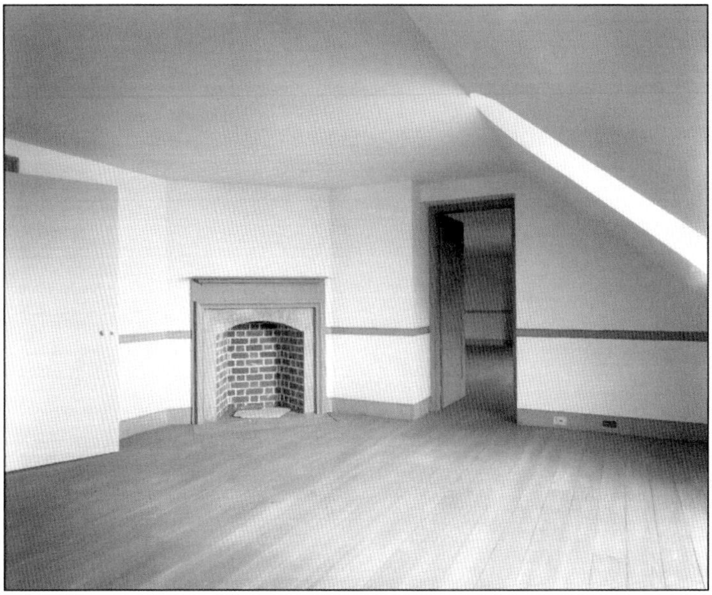

This photograph shows part of the palace attic in 1959. Little historical information remains regarding how the attic was finished. The reconstruction was based on common building materials and styles of the time, along with techniques used in other parts of the palace. The attic remains uninterpreted, since research about its use has failed to provide clear answers.

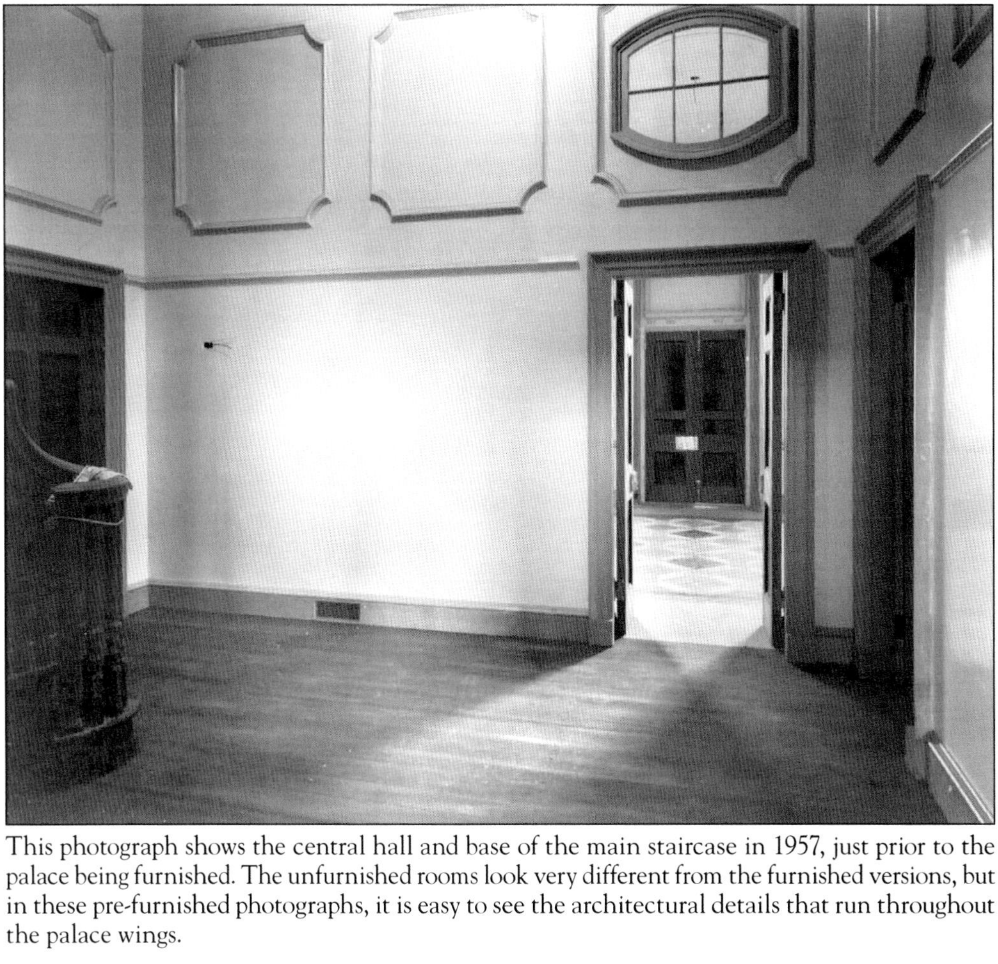

This photograph shows the central hall and base of the main staircase in 1957, just prior to the palace being furnished. The unfurnished rooms look very different from the furnished versions, but in these pre-furnished photographs, it is easy to see the architectural details that run throughout the palace wings.

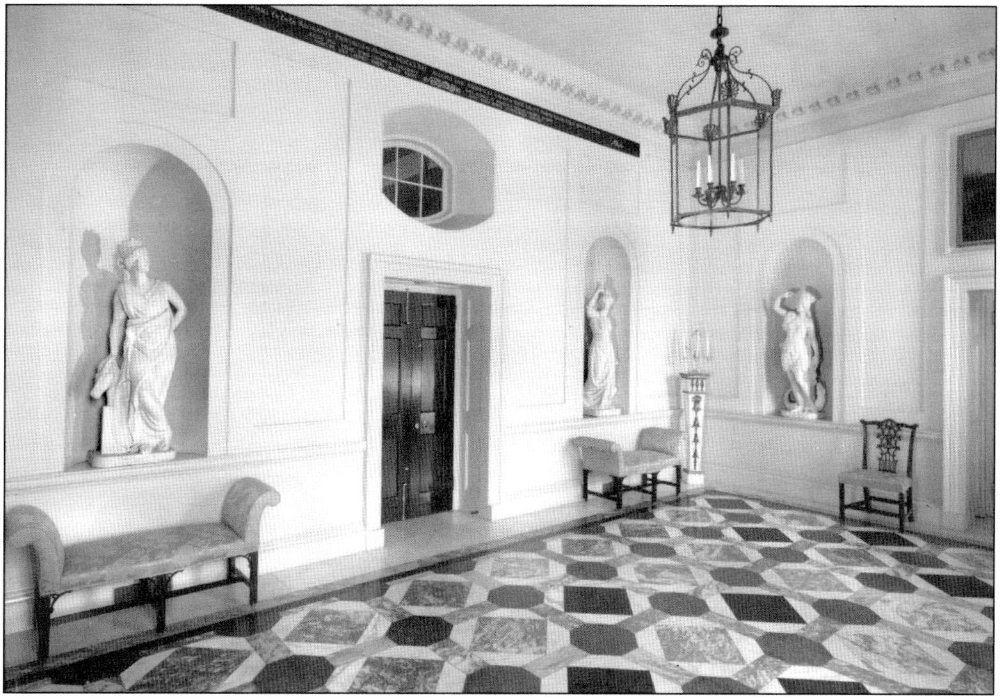

Excavations carried out at the palace beginning in 1952 uncovered evidence that the original marble floor in the entrance hall was constructed of white Italian marble and black Belgian marble. The four marble statues that sit in the niches around the room are the allegorical figures of the four continents (or the four quarters of the globe)—Africa, the Americas, Asia, and Europe.

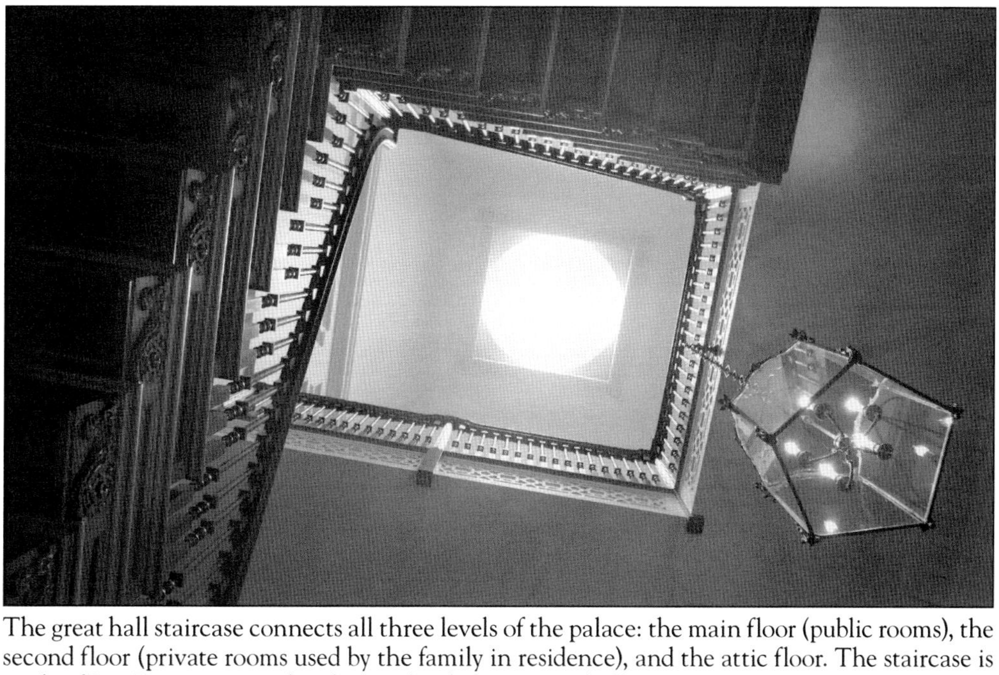

The great hall staircase connects all three levels of the palace: the main floor (public rooms), the second floor (private rooms used by the family in residence), and the attic floor. The staircase is made of San Domingo wood and pegged walnut steps with illumination coming from the skylight dome in the roof.

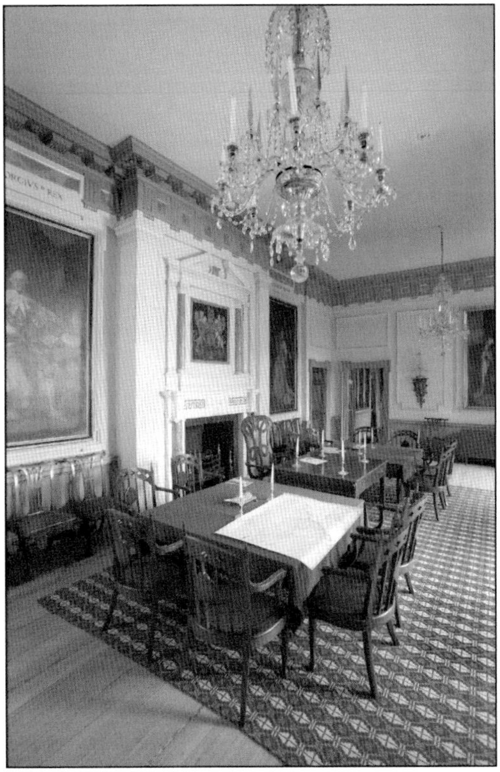

It is important to remember that Tryon Palace was built as a private residence and a government building in the state's first permanent capital. The assembly room, located on the first floor of the palace, was used for meetings of the colonial and, later, state assemblies. This room could also be used for dancing when the resident family hosted a ball.

John Hawks's two sets of plans for this room make it unclear whether it is supposed to be the dining room or the drawing room. When the restored palace first opened in 1959, this room was interpreted as a dining room; however, a 1783 letter from Hawks to Don Francisco de Miranda indicates this room was, in fact, the drawing room; it has since been reinterpreted.

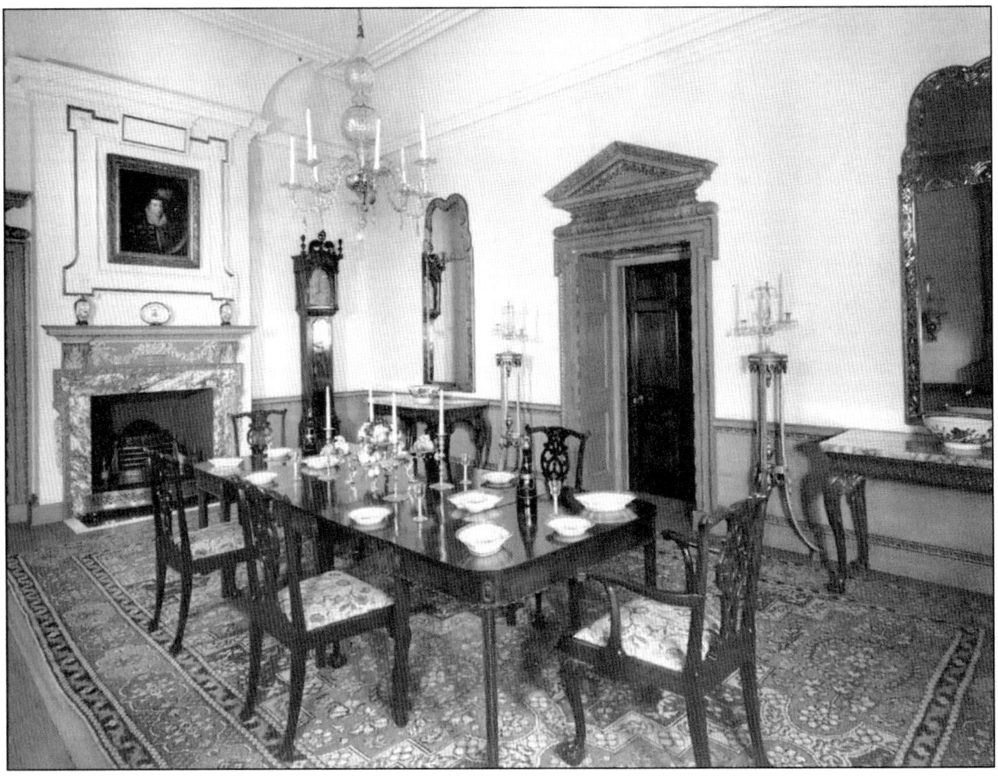

This photograph shows one of the private second-floor rooms that would have been used by the Tryons, Martins, Caswells, and Nashes for family meals while state business was conducted on the main floor. The room's decor reflects the style of the Tryon and Martin families more so than the Caswell and Nash families.

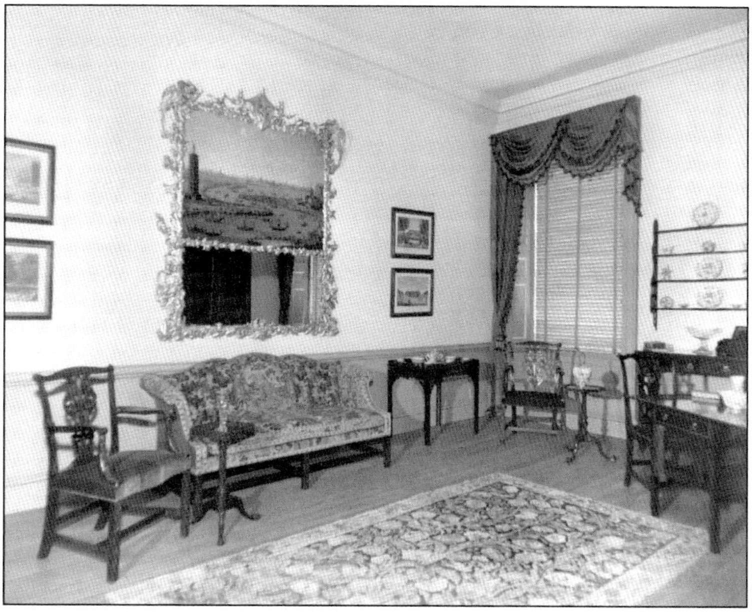

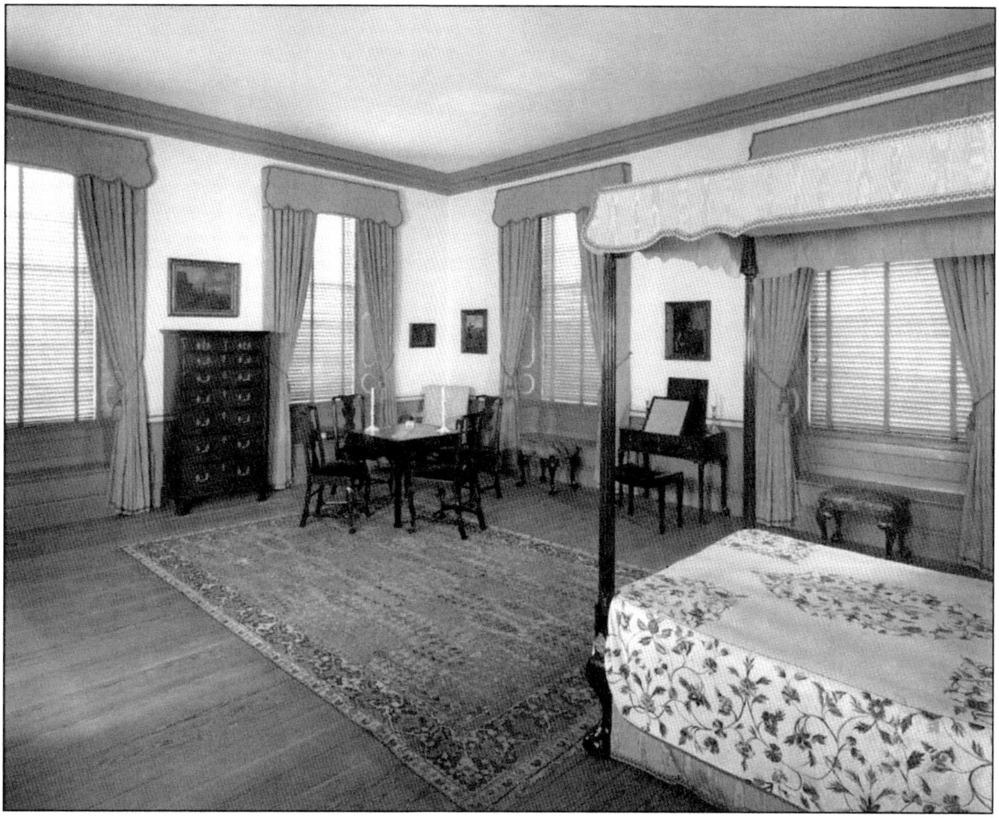

This photograph shows one of the guest bedrooms, located among the second-floor private rooms, with windows looking over the front of the palace grounds and gardens near the west wing. This bedroom is decorated in a style reminiscent of that used by the family of Josiah Martin and includes several prints and paintings of Antigua, where his family had a plantation.

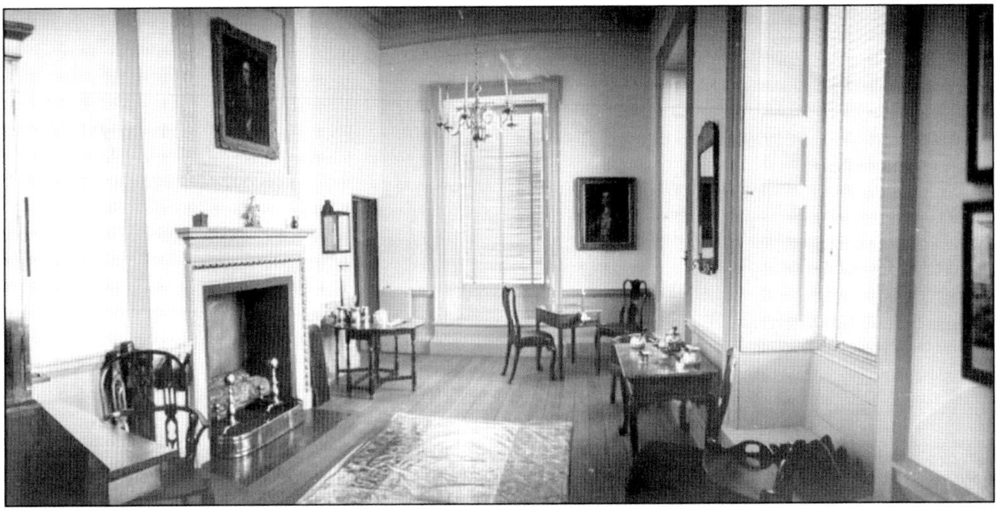

This 1959 photograph shows the servant's hall located to the right of the main foyer. While many household tasks, such as cooking and laundry, were performed in the kitchen office, select members of the staff needed to remain on duty within the main house to meet the immediate needs of the residents; the servant's hall provided them with an area to wait within the house while remaining unseen.

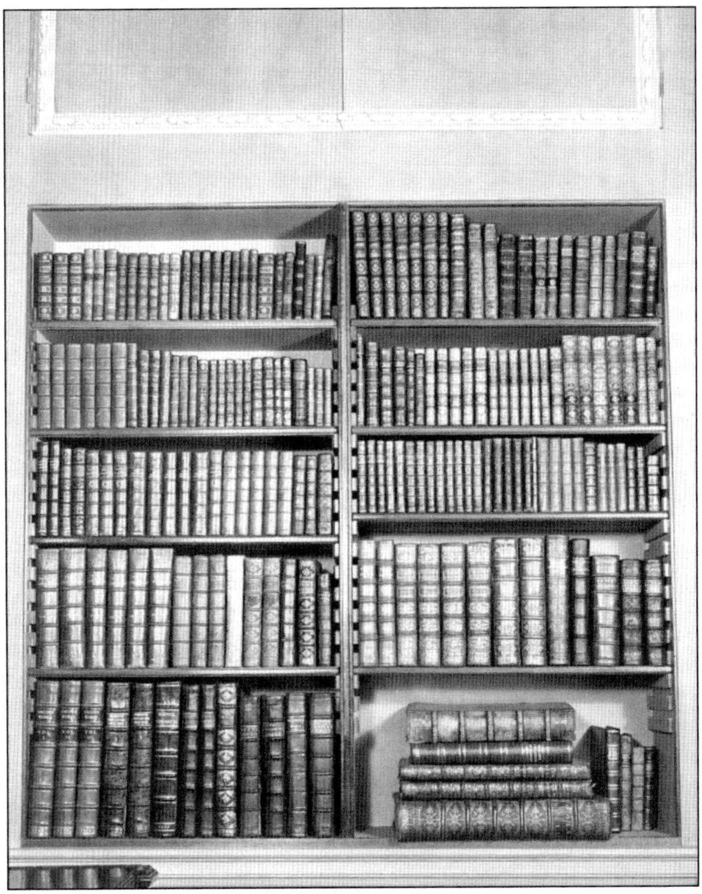

Royal Governor William Tryon had an extensive book collection at the palace. When he was appointed to New York, he took the collection with him, and it was subsequently destroyed. Fortunately, Governor Tryon filed a claim with the British government for the loss of his collection, and based on that inventory, Tryon Palace has been able to recreate his book collection with many of the same editions.

Since its restoration, Tryon Palace has been located near three military bases and welcomed visits from military personnel. This early-1960s photograph shows Pvt. Hubert J. Johnson, of Chattanooga, Tennessee, and Pvt. Thomas H. Kennemer, of Lacy Springs, Alabama. Both were in the 1st Infantry Training Regiment at Camp Lejeune and took rare vacation leave to visit the palace.

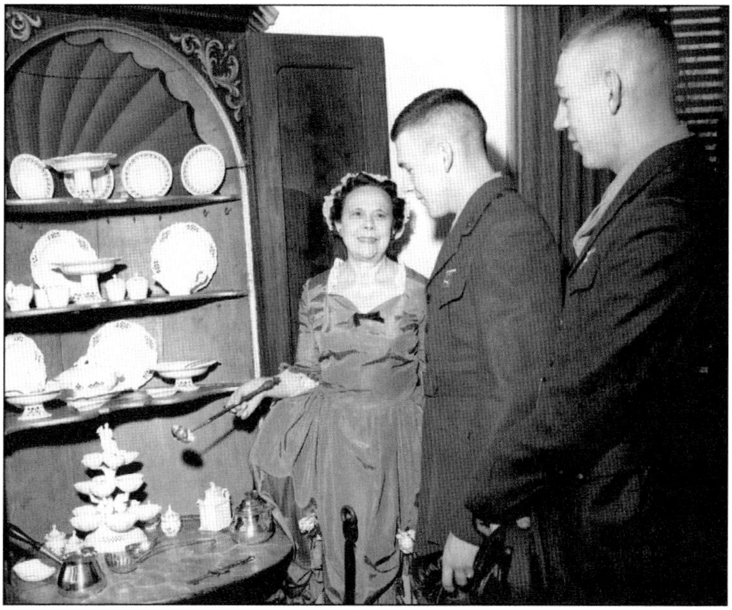

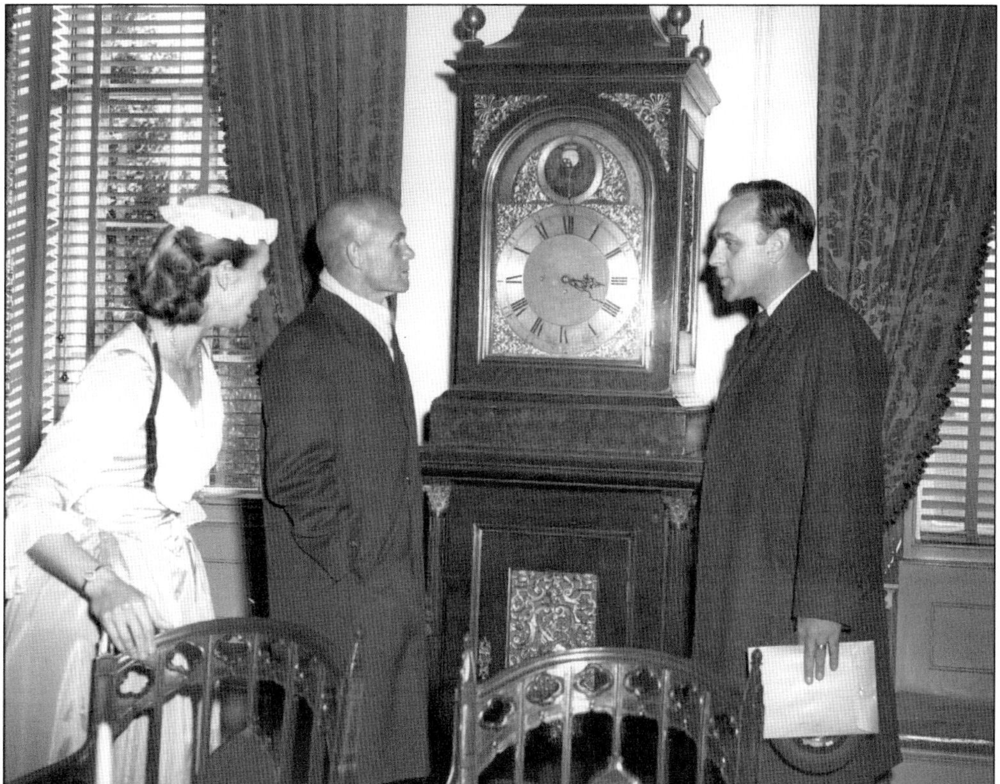

During its first few years, many visitors came to Tryon Palace to witness the beauty of the 18th century. On December 17, 1963, the future met the past when astronaut Lt. Col. John Glenn visited the palace after speaking to the New Bern Chamber of Commerce. Pictured here are palace hostess Mrs. Ray C. Ipock (left), John Glenn (center), and Congressman David Henderson.

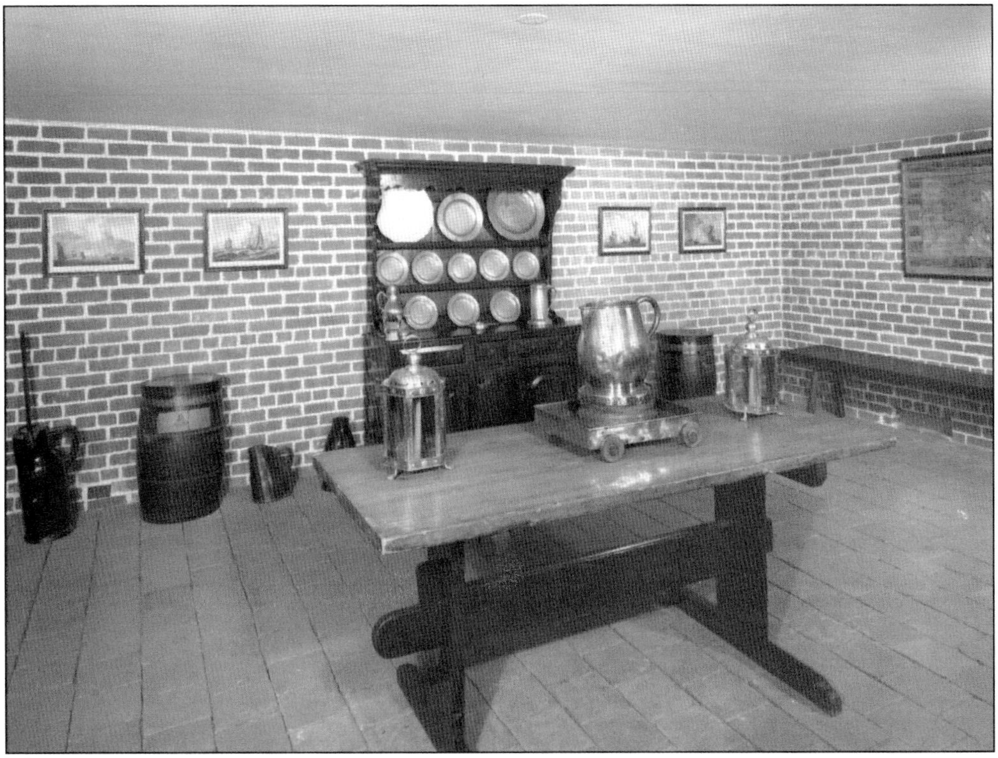

These two photographs show an early interpretation of the basement level at Tryon Palace. Research shows that the basement (or cellar) level was used by the butler and housekeeper, who lived on-site. The area may have been living quarters, a work area, or some combination of the two. When the basement was first interpreted, the focus was on the area as a work space, showing storage and preparation space for the housekeeper and a wide range of hunting accoutrements for the butler. The original brick foundation of the palace, uncovered during excavations, is visible at the back of the butler's workspace.

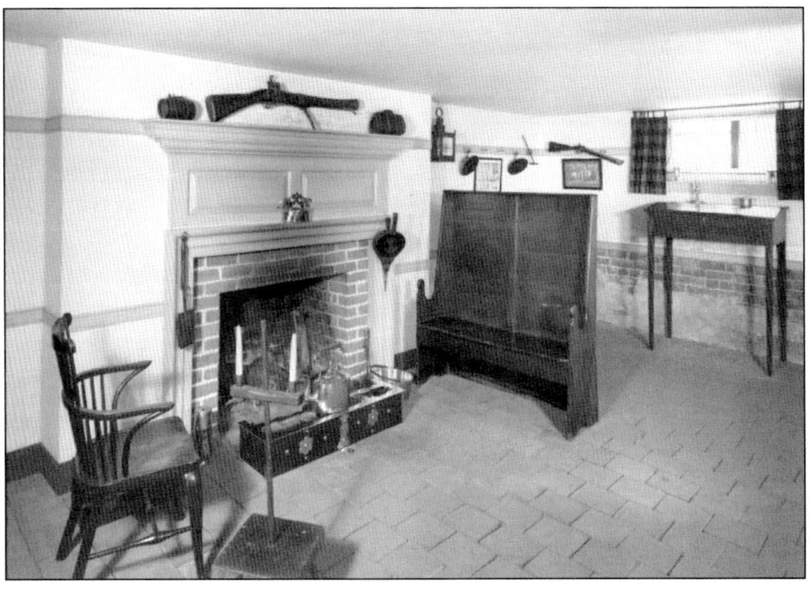

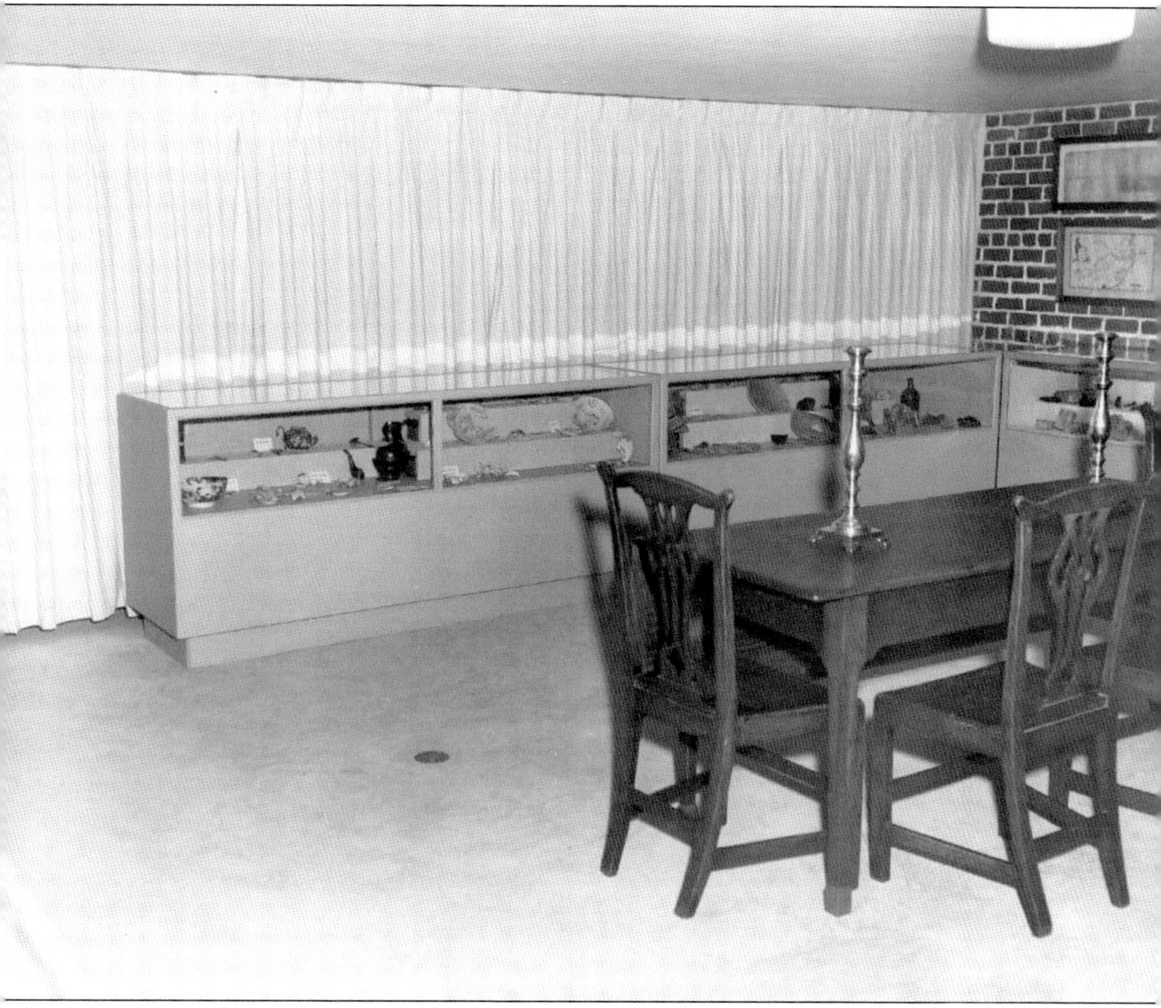

The earliest exhibits at Tryon Palace were situated on the basement level of the main building. This photograph depicts one of the first exhibits, which centered on the archeological excavations that took place before the reconstruction of the palace. Those excavations uncovered a wide range of materials, including pottery fragments, window glass fragments, nails, hinges, locks, and other building materials. Those materials played a key role in locating appropriate pieces for furnishing the main house and kitchen office. After the reinterpretation of the basement level, the exhibit was removed, and the archeological artifacts were placed in storage to be used in further research. The palace has an extensive archeological collection from original excavations conducted before the palace was reconstructed and smaller digs completed since then. In 2010, a few pieces were incorporated into a permanent exhibit at Tryon Palace's North Carolina History Center about the archeology of the palace.

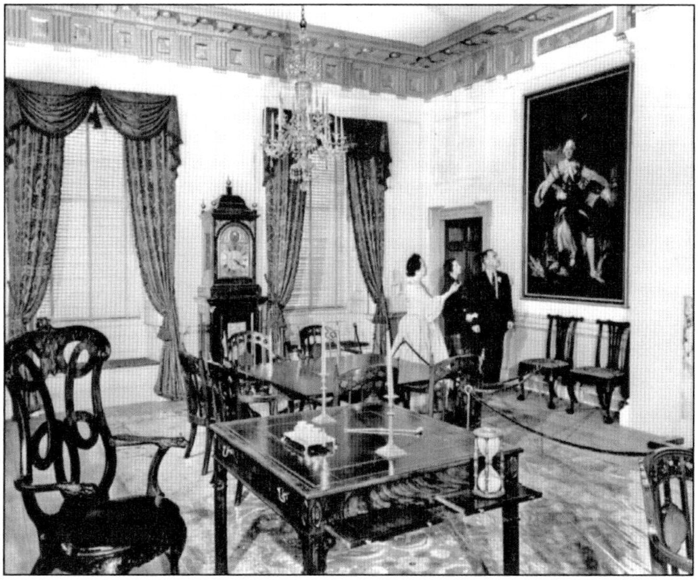

In the 1960s, hostesses guided visitors through Tryon Palace as they explored the decorative arts of the 18th century. Of particular note were the paintings in the council chambers that depict King George III and his wife, Princess Charlotte of Mecklenburg-Strelitz, who ruled Great Britain when the palace was first built in 1770.

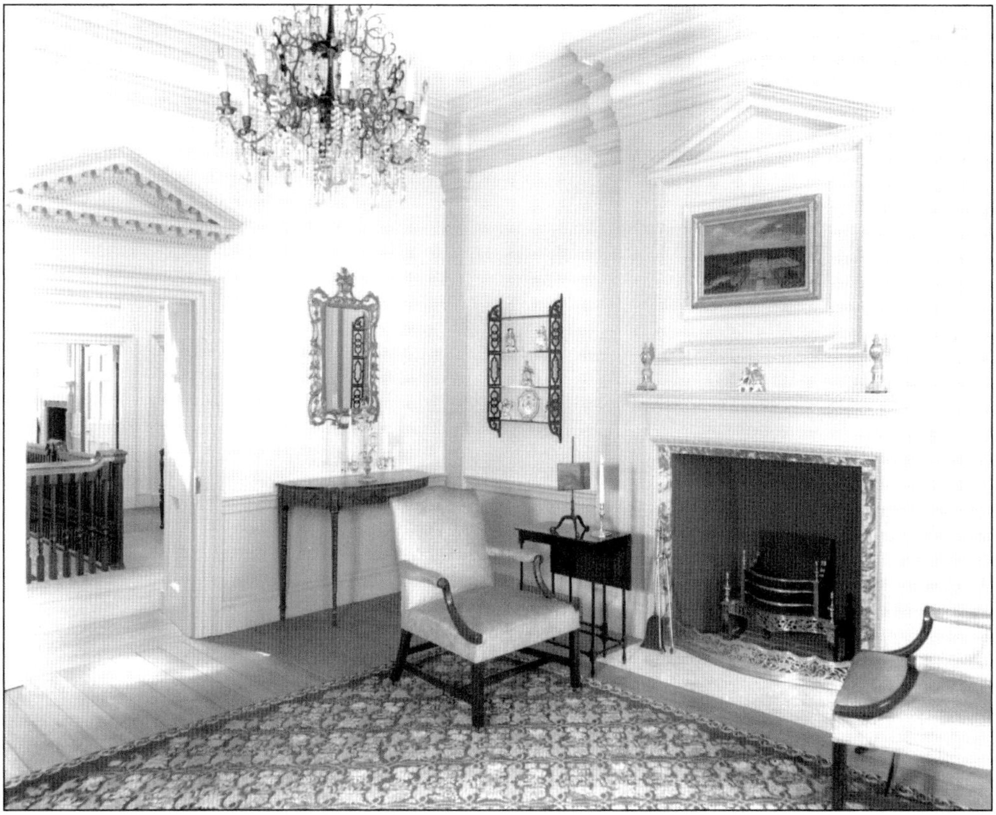

The palace's rooms have long been popular for their rich beauty. Before Tryon Palace officially opened, the upstairs sitting room was selected for Helen Comstock's 1958 book, *The 100 Most Beautiful Rooms in America*. She describes it as "quietly formal" and states that the room's "handsome English panelling" came from Teddesley Hall, Penkridge, Staffordshire. The room was photographed by John Baxter for the book.

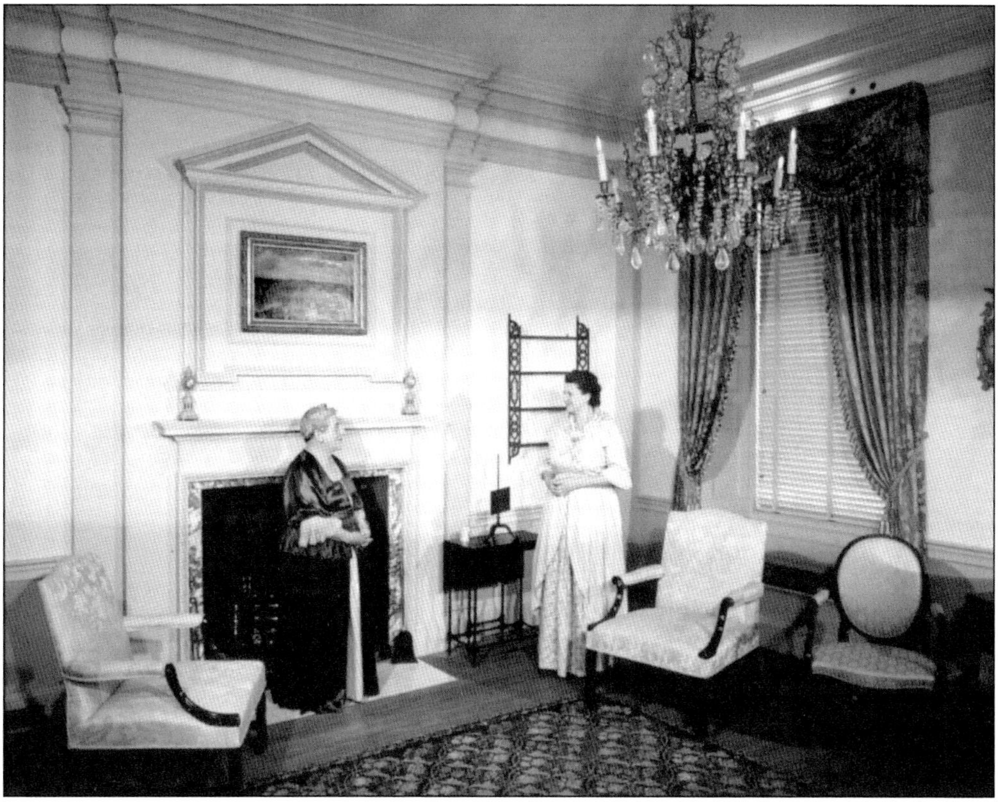

In this 1960s photograph, two unidentified palace hostesses pose in Tryon Palace's upstairs sitting room. This was used as a publicity image to promote the restored building and the period furnishings. The details of the room are clearly visible, including the large windows that would have filled the room with light, extensive crown molding, and wood paneling.

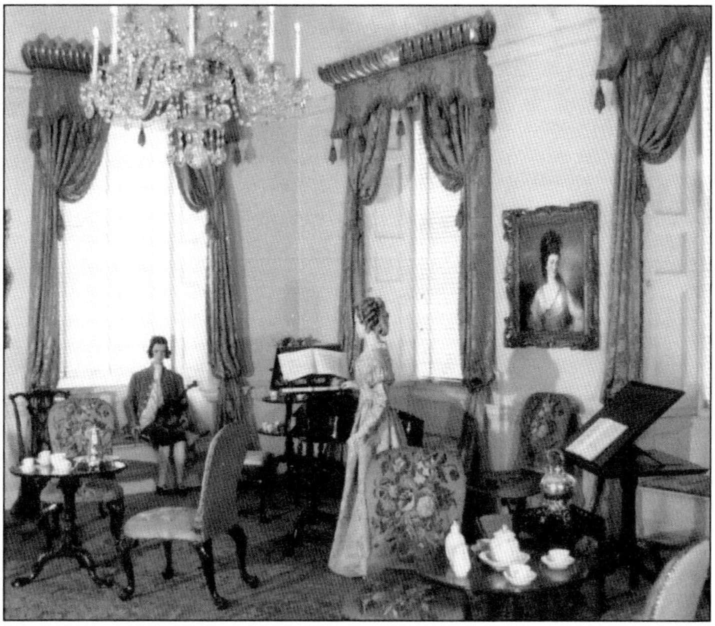

The two mannequins who occupied the palace's parlor were acquired in 1965 by Virginia Horne. The purpose of the mannequins was to showcase a few of the period costumes in the Tryon Palace collection. The female mannequin is dressed in the gown worn by Mrs. Eunice Kelly at the George Washington Ball in 1791, while the male mannequin is dressed in a costume donated by Mrs. Carroll P. Rogers.

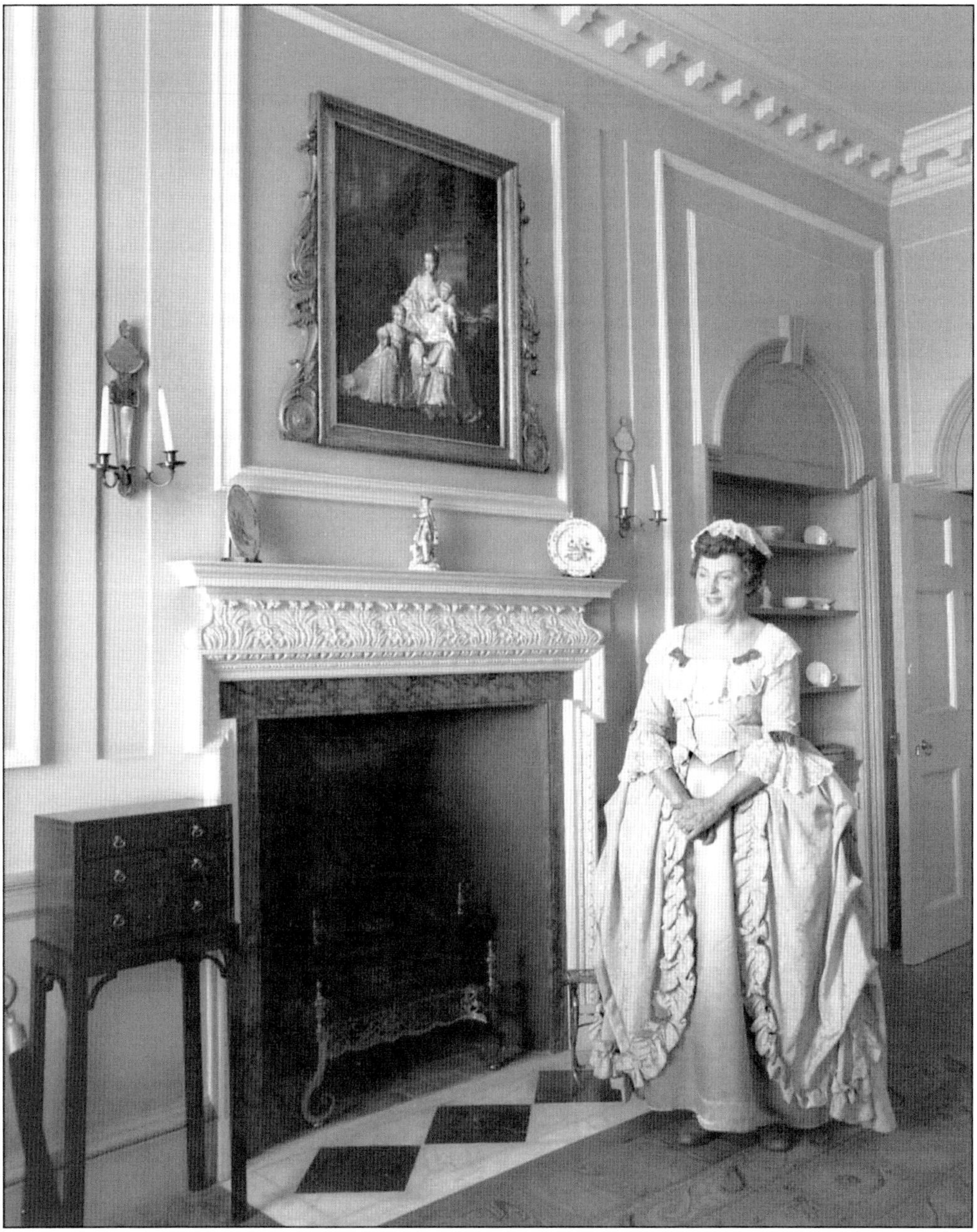

Training for Tryon Palace hostesses began two years before the building opened. In 1957, when the Tryon Palace Commission purchased the Dixon House, palace director Gertrude Carraway quickly began classes on US history that were designed to train local women to become guides. The classes started on January 15, 1957, and there were 16 lessons. The house could accommodate 125 students, and Carraway ended up having to turn women away. The first guides and hostesses received special lectures from Elizabeth and Virginia Horne, May Kellenberger, and William G. Perry, architect of the restoration. As director, Carraway maintained a rigorous training program for hostesses and guides, regularly updating them about new research and findings. She was known for randomly quizzing guides on different topics—from colonial history to the restoration—to ensure they were well versed in the subjects.

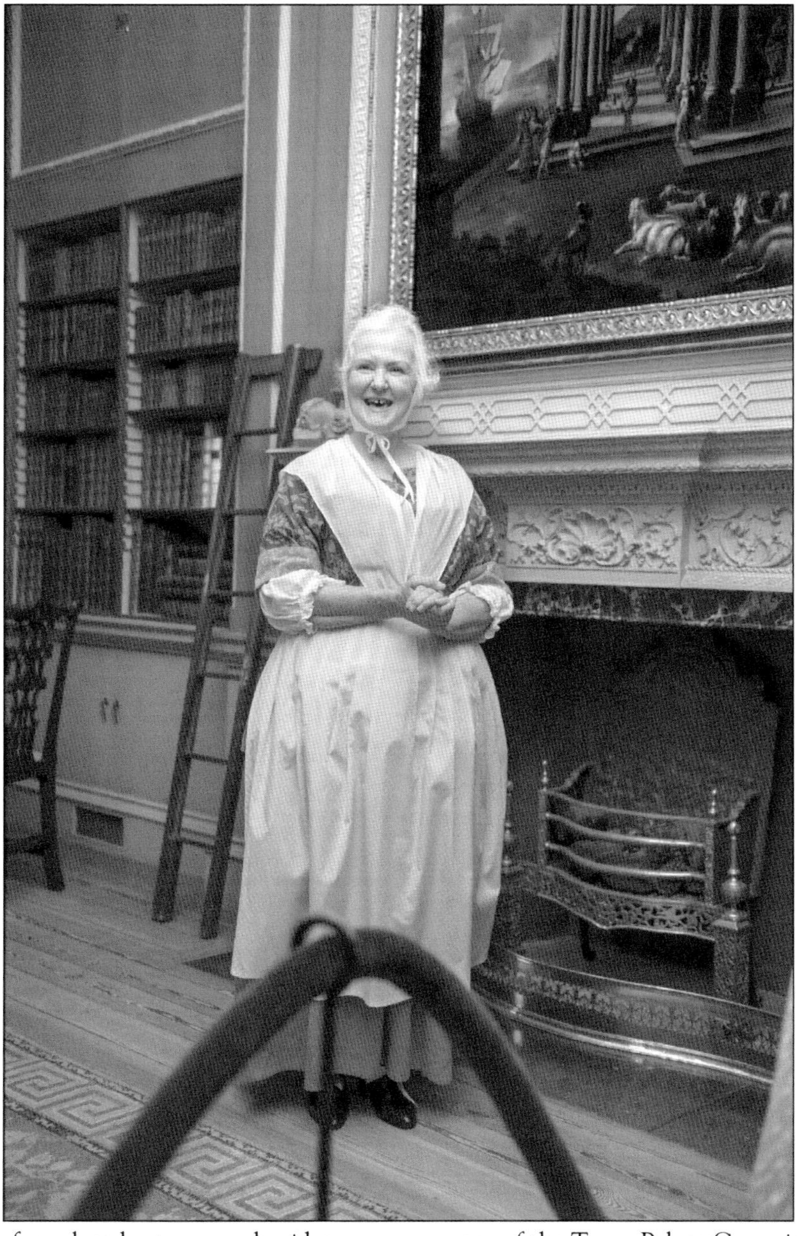

Costumes for palace hostesses and guides were a concern of the Tryon Palace Commission long before Tryon Palace opened. At a 1957 commission meeting, the costumes committee reported its findings from a recent trip to Colonial Williamsburg, presenting the commission with a list of concerns such as climate, income of the hostess, and durability of the costumes. The first costumes compromised on historical authenticity but were made of durable and affordable materials. As the interpretation of the palace has changed, so have the costumes for the palace's hostesses and guides. Materials shifted from man-made to natural, including wool, linen, and cotton. Buttons and laces replaced zippers, and caps were made. The biggest change has been the types of dresses worn. Initially, the hostesses all wore fancy dress as would have been worn by affluent ladies for special occasions. However, fancy dresses were eventually reserved for balls, and guides began wearing day dresses (and even lower-class clothing) for their work in the palace.

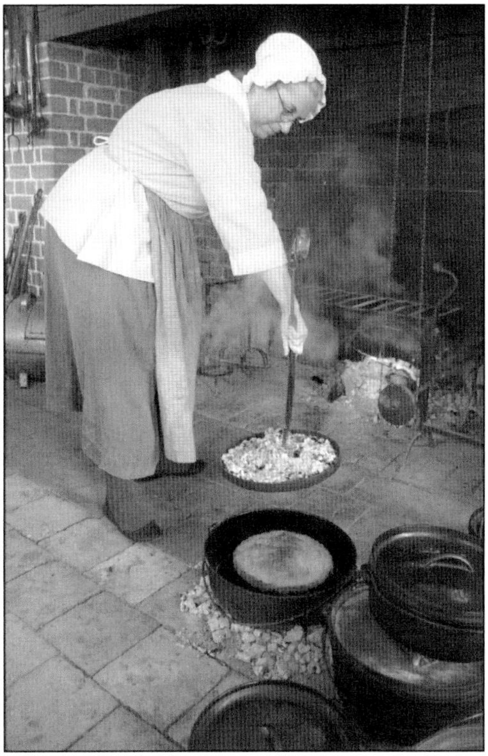

The reconstructed kitchen office has several work areas that would have been used by the staff to prepare meals for the household, repair linens, and eat their own meals. Half of the first floor is taken up by a large kitchen with an open hearth used for cooking. Every day, a costumed interpreter, such as Susan Quarles (pictured), demonstrates how to prepare meals on an open hearth.

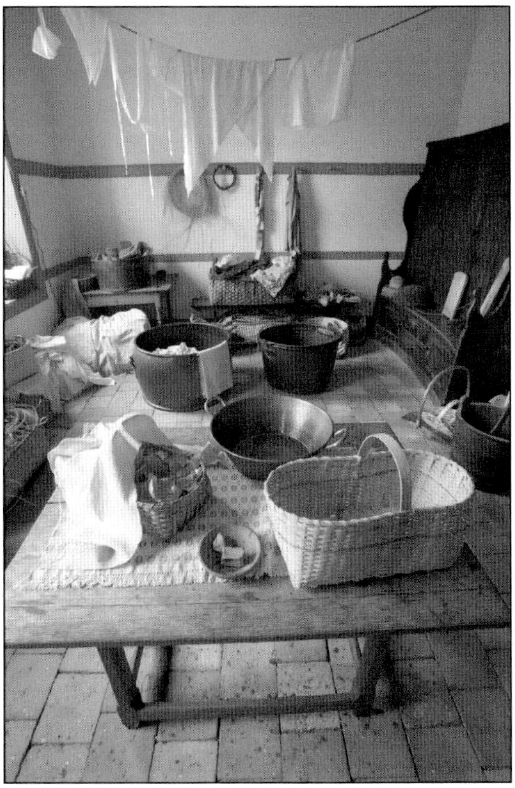

The remaining half of the kitchen office's first floor would have been used by staff to wash, dye, and mend linens. In the 18th century, laundry was an intensive process that required carrying water into the kitchen area, heating it, hand-washing the linens, and line-drying them. If any linen needed to be dyed, workers used natural materials (such as onion skins).

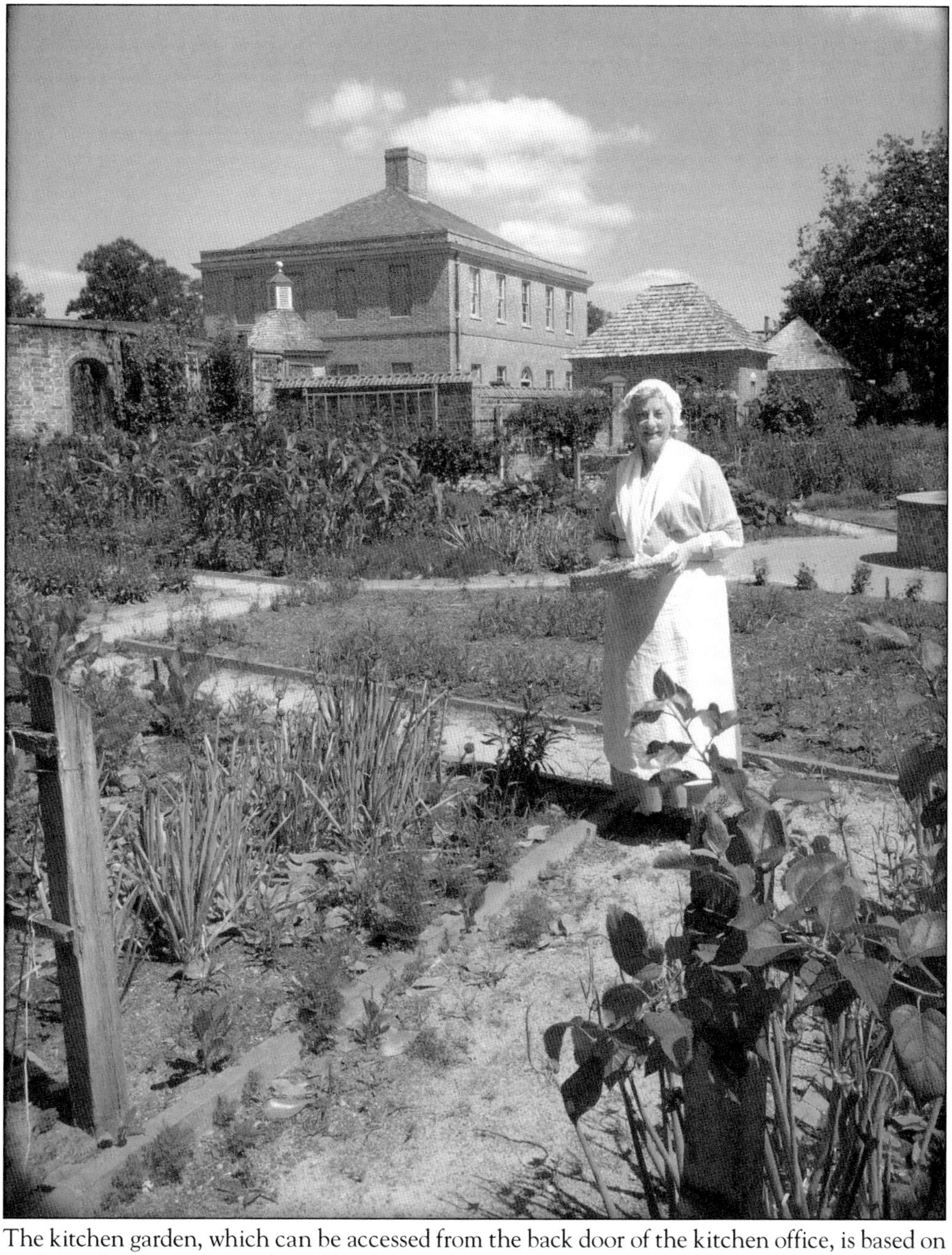

The kitchen garden, which can be accessed from the back door of the kitchen office, is based on traditional 18th-century colonial kitchen gardens on large estates. These gardens were tended by staff and located adjacent to the home's kitchen on a small plot of land that would not require draft animals to plow. These gardens were tightly planted and designed to make the most efficient use of space by providing the household with produce from the beginning of spring into early winter. Plants grown in these gardens would have been used in food preparation and for medicinal purposes. Examples of some plants commonly found in kitchen gardens include sage, pumpkins, squash, artichokes, and celery. Costumed interpreters at Tryon Palace, such as Jan Conaty (pictured), use produce from the kitchen garden in their kitchen demonstrations.

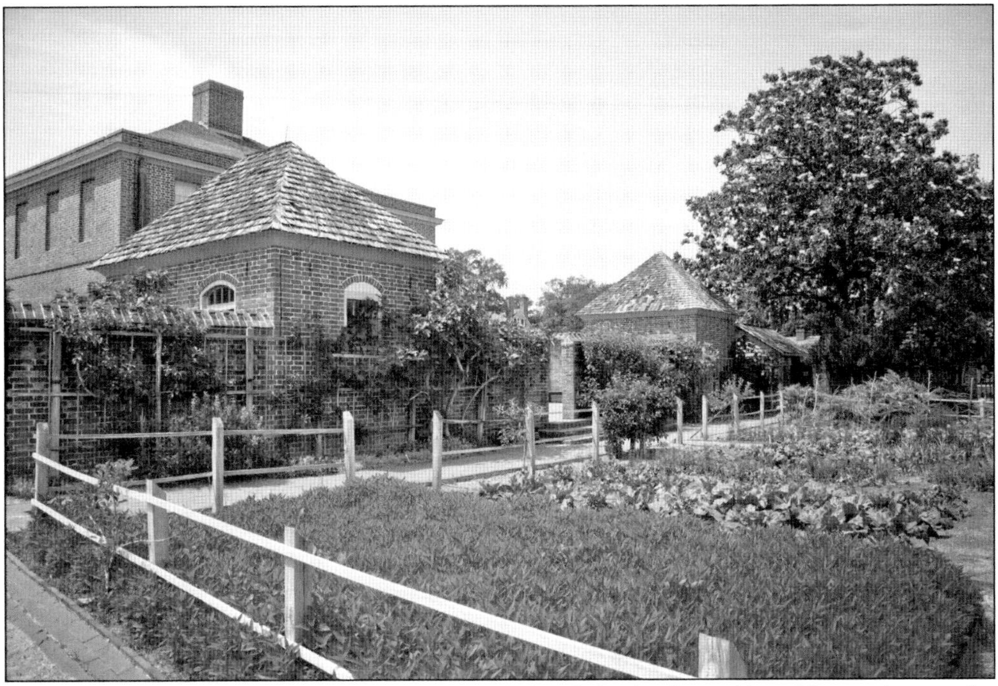

The kitchen garden at Tryon Palace is located behind the kitchen office. The garden can be accessed through a small paved courtyard with two storage sheds. Even though it is the least formal garden on the property, the kitchen garden features a larger space and luxury vegetables, such as artichokes. As a utilitarian garden, it features fruits, vegetables, and herbs that would have been used by colonial cooks. Designed to provide produce almost year-round, the kitchen garden continually has new plantings and fresh vegetables being harvested for use in the kitchen office.

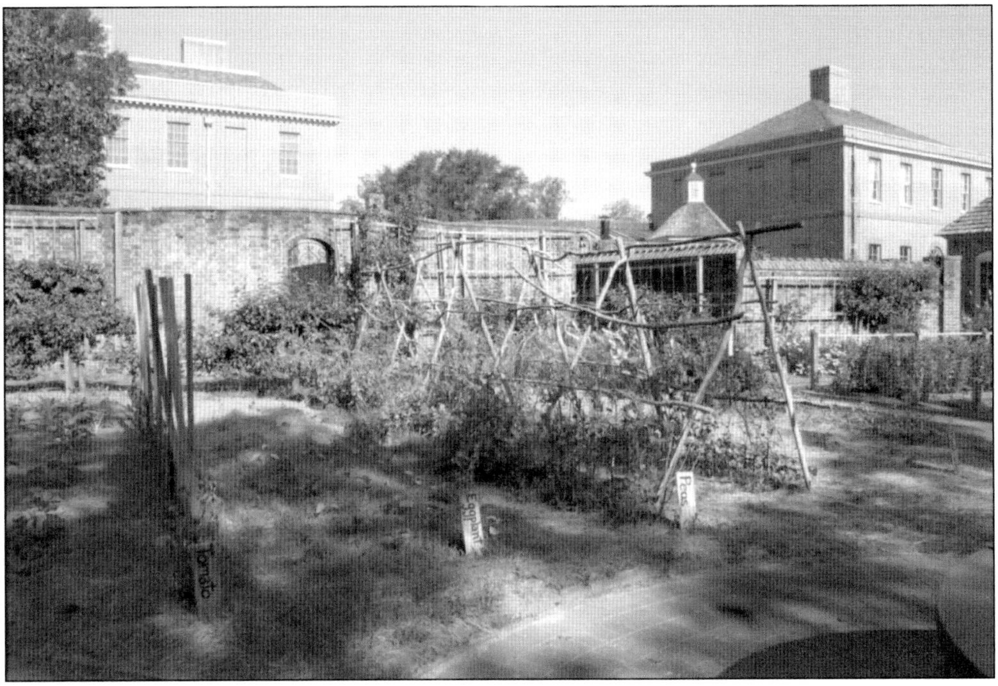

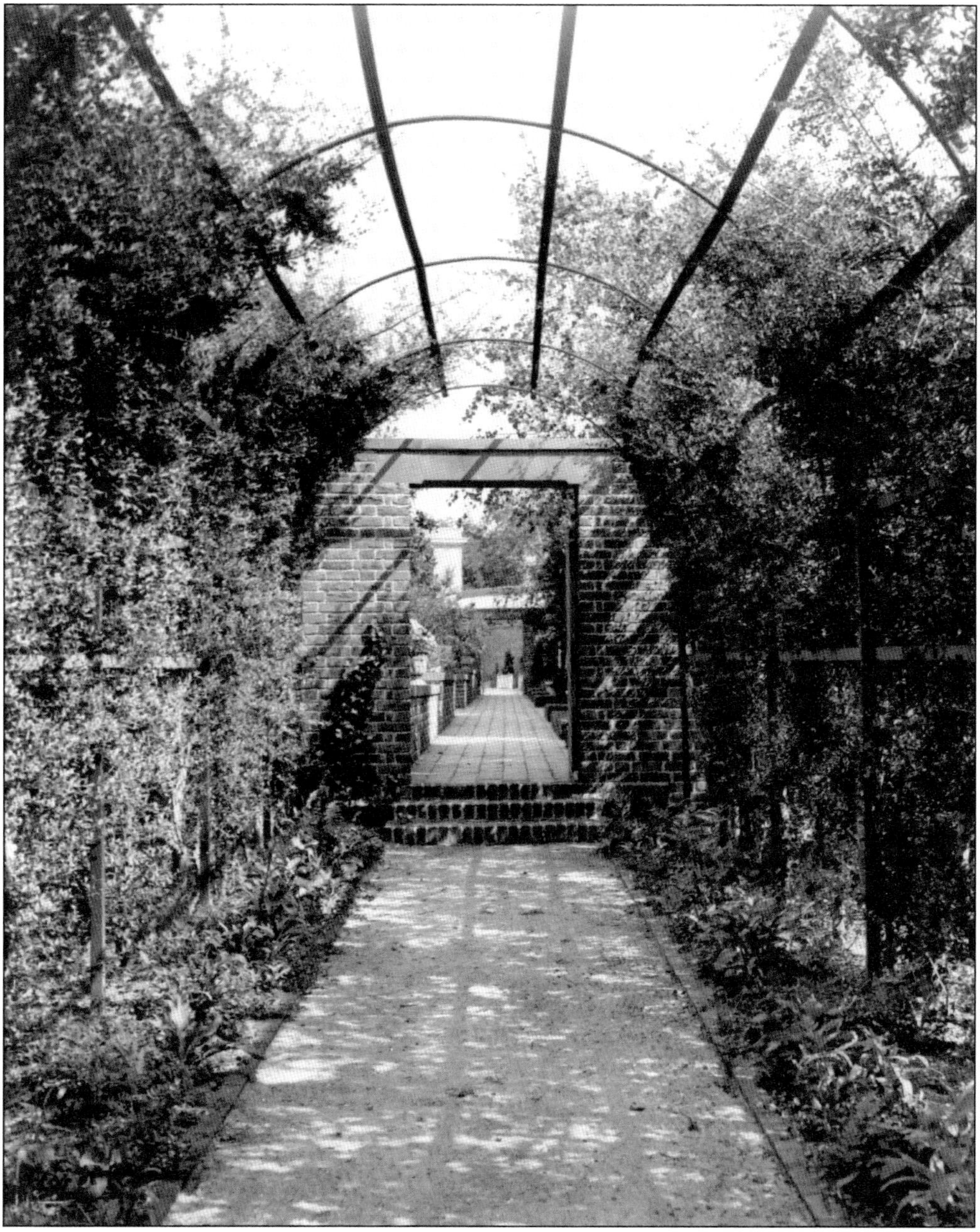

The Pleached Allée is part of the formal gardens to the west rear of Tryon Palace. The shaded path connects the Green Garden to the Trent River, providing visitors access to the other formal gardens, including the Latham Garden and the Hawks Allée. The technique of pleaching is used to train trees and shrubs into fences and archways. First developed during the Middle Ages and used by farms to strengthen fences, the technique remained in use through the 18th century. Pleaching is labor-intensive and did not see wide use in the American colonies as a result; however, as both a government house and a residential estate, Tryon Palace would have had the financial stability and access to trained gardeners to maintain this type of ornamental garden. This photograph shows the Pleached Allée, made of yaupon holly, as it begins to form the overhead archway.

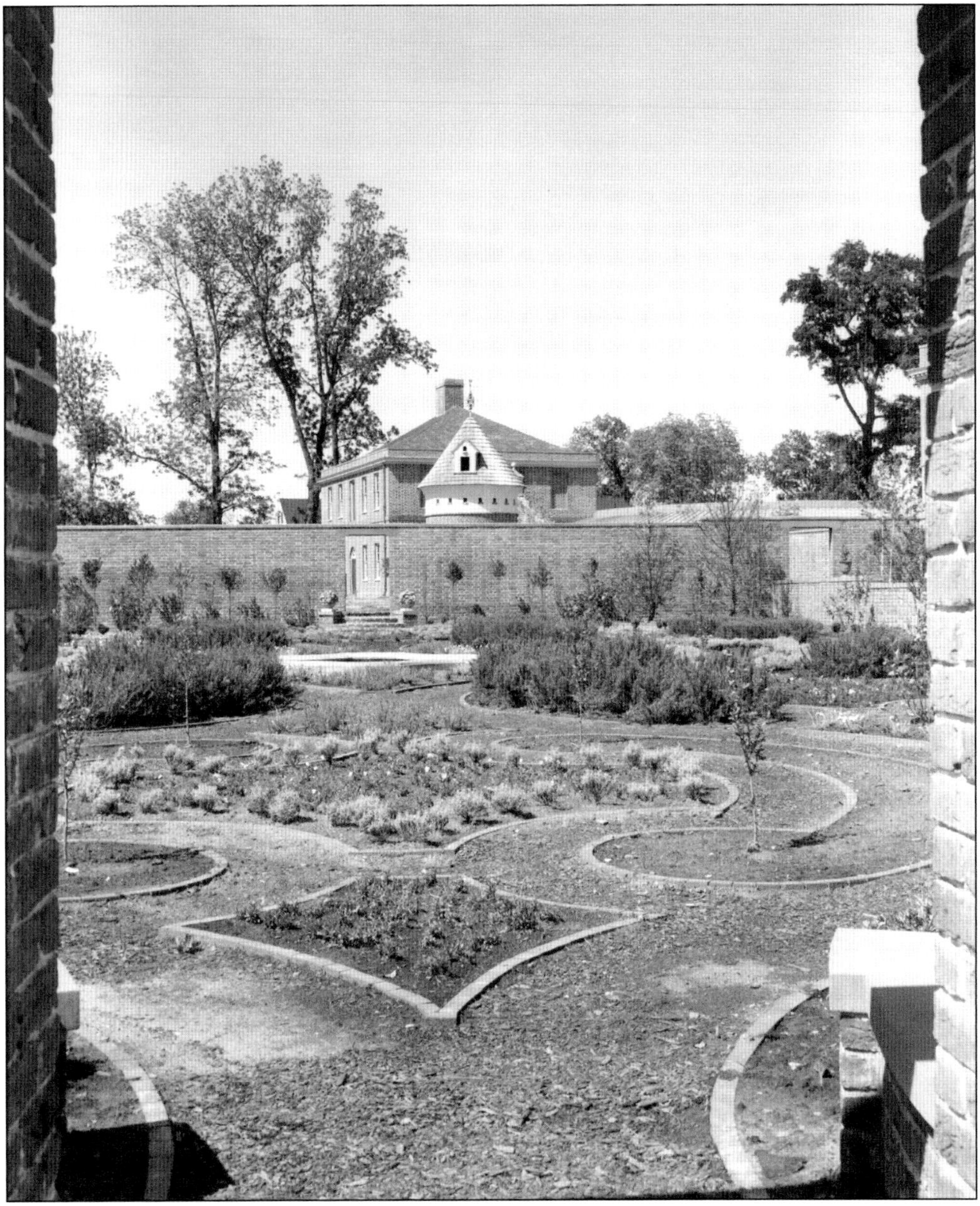

During the reconstruction, Tryon Palace Commission members could not find historical or archeological evidence to suggest what garden patterns existed at the original Tryon Palace. As a result, plans for the formal gardens were based on traditional 18th-century gardens. Symmetrical geometric designs, popular at the beginning and end of the 18th century, incorporated trimmed hedges and flower beds to create a sense of order and beauty. Basic geometric shapes, along with complex knot designs, were commonly used in combination with these gardens. The 18th century also saw the introduction of the more informal landscape garden. Landscape gardens resemble parks, with open spaces, streams or lakes, and one focal feature. Classical monuments were common focal features in 18th-century landscape gardens. At Tryon Palace, these elements were incorporated into a variety of different garden designs, resulting in knot gardens, formal hedge designs, and open lawns.

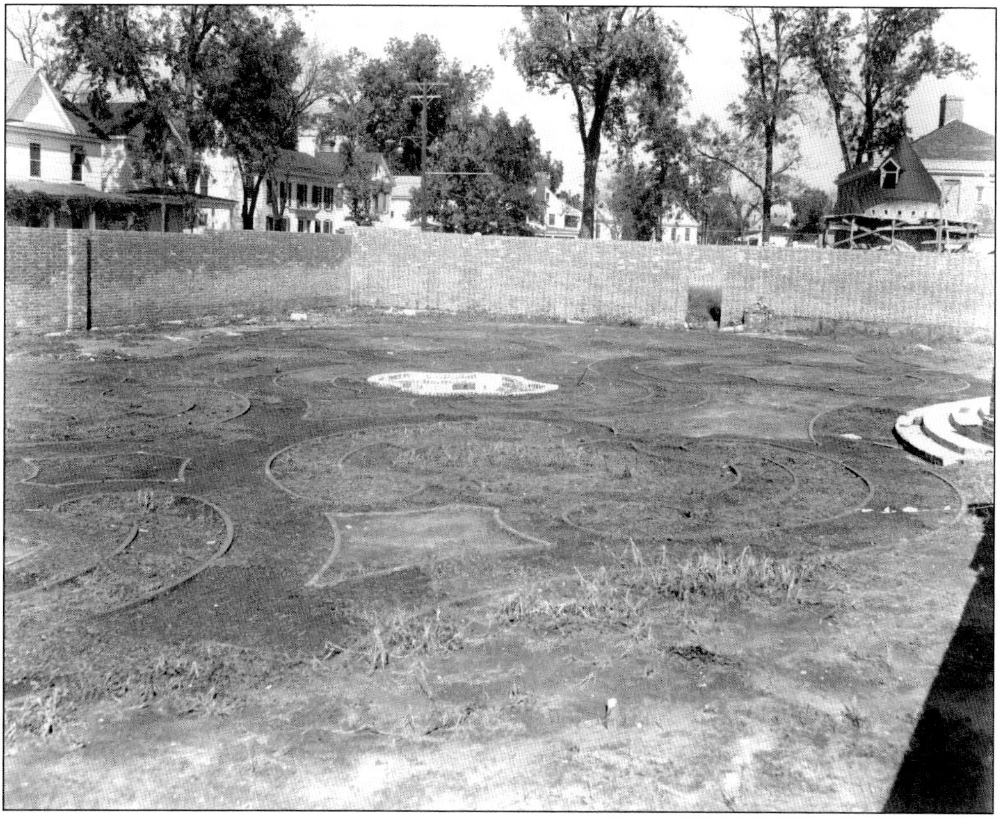

Work began on the formal gardens before construction was complete on the palace. Once the outer walls had been completed, workers began marking the footpaths and flower beds. This first stage resulted in a baroque serpentine pattern appearing on the ground, the second phase involved planting, and the final phase resulted in paved walkways. When the gardens opened, the flowers had started to grow, but it would be several years before they reached the desired size. Having moved into the building when it was first completed, the Tryon family would have enjoyed the gardens under similar conditions.

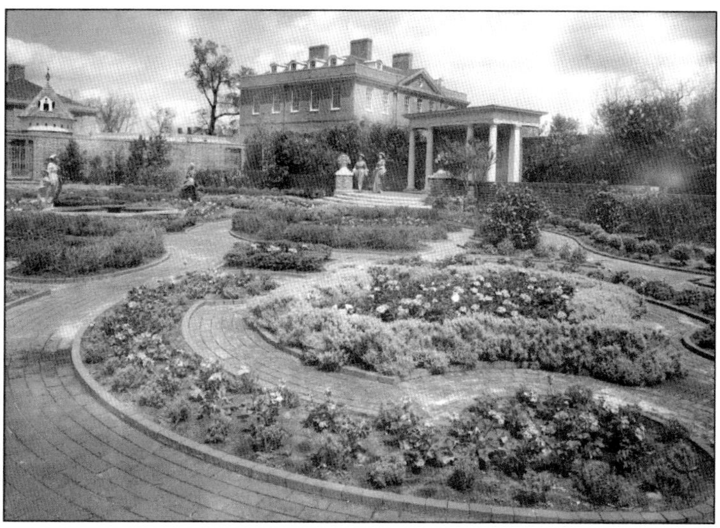

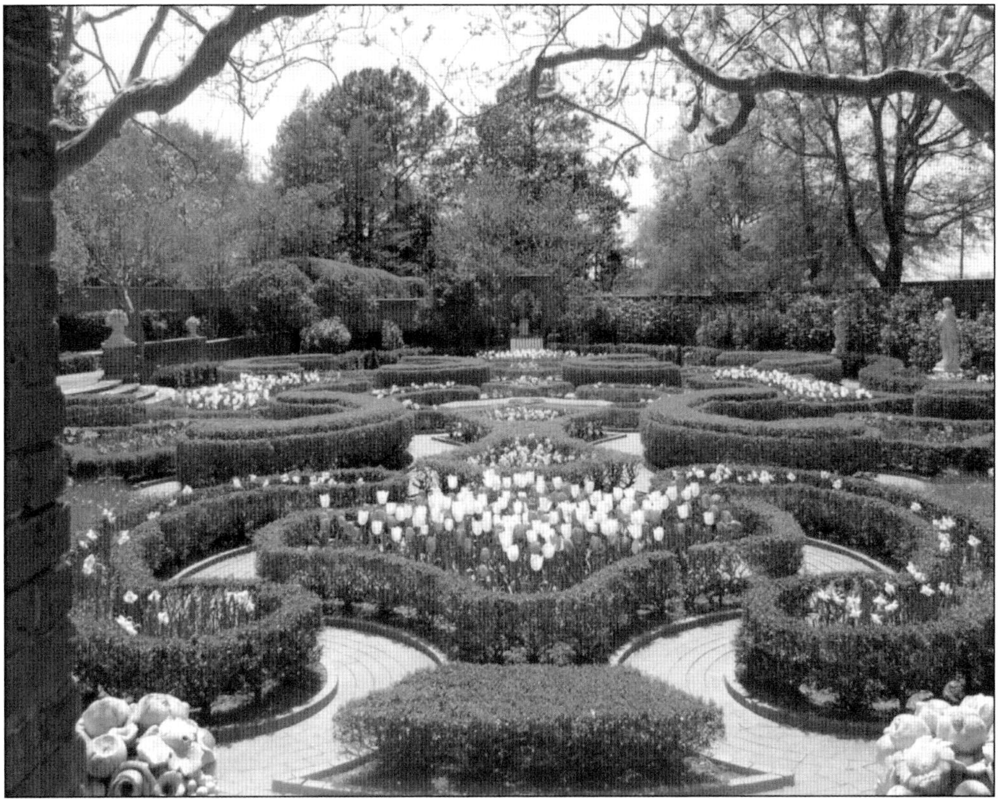

The Latham Garden, located to the west rear of the palace, is a formal garden that combines hedges, footpaths, and seasonal flowers in a traditional parterre garden pattern. This style of garden dates from the 16th century and was popular throughout the 18th century. The hedges are dwarf yaupon holly, a North Carolina native plant, while the flowers are changed seasonally for different varieties, including tulips and chrysanthemums. The four statues around the perimeter of the garden represent the four seasons. The garden is named in honor of Maude Moore Latham, who was the driving force behind the reconstruction of Tryon Palace.

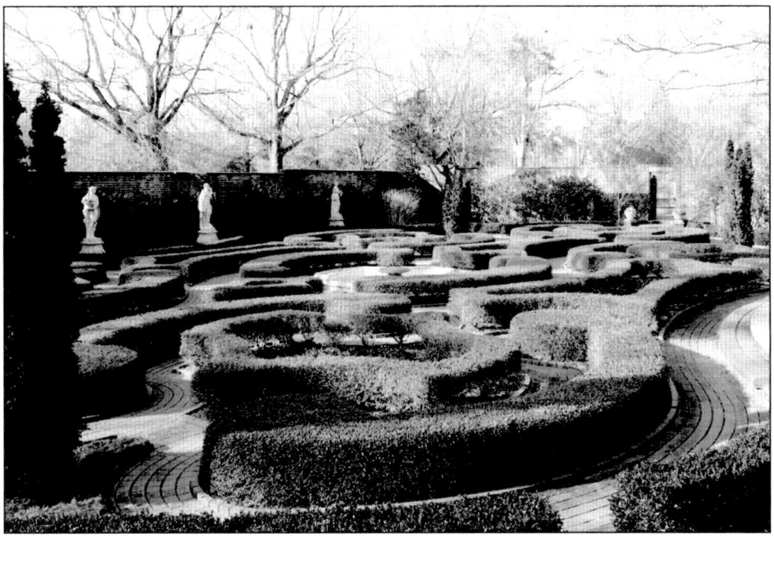

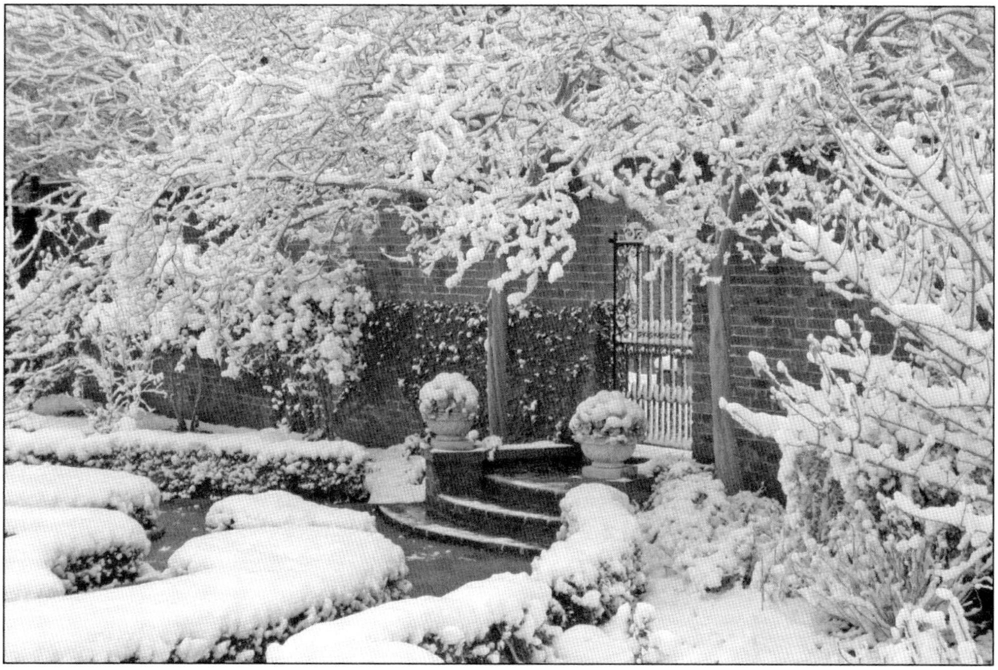

New Bern, North Carolina, enjoys four distinct seasons, and the ornamental gardens at Tryon Palace are as beautiful in winter as in the other three seasons. The snow-dusted hedges offer visitors an opportunity to appreciate the sculptural quality of the gardens, which can often become lost amidst the riotous colors of spring and summer.

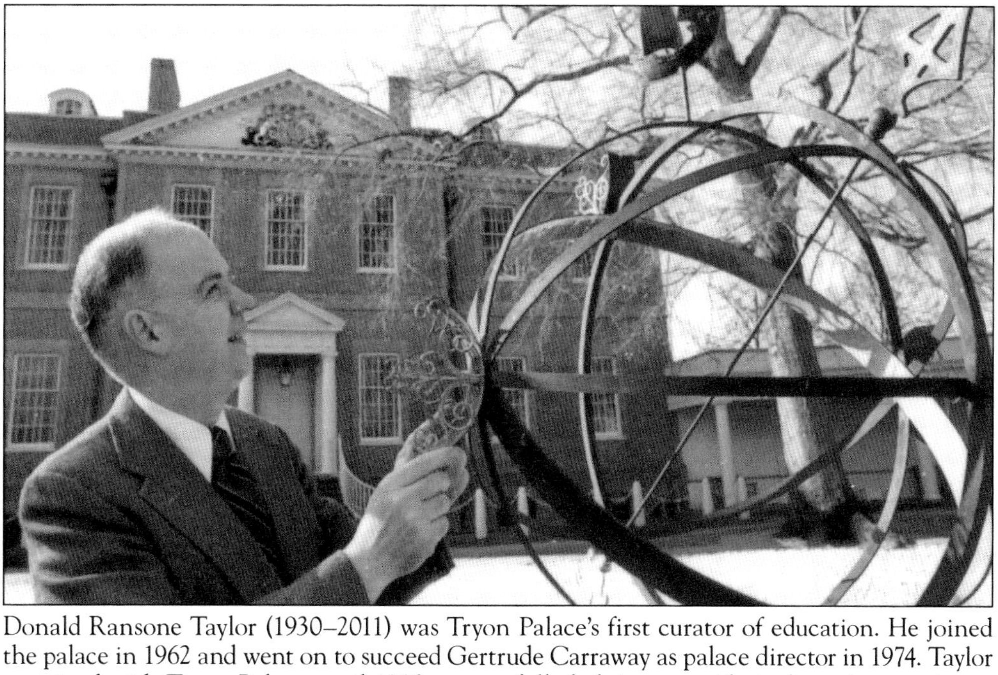

Donald Ransone Taylor (1930–2011) was Tryon Palace's first curator of education. He joined the palace in 1962 and went on to succeed Gertrude Carraway as palace director in 1974. Taylor remained with Tryon Palace until 1983, successfully helping to guide it through several new programs. He left to become director of Virginia's Gunston Hall, a position he held until his retirement in 1992.

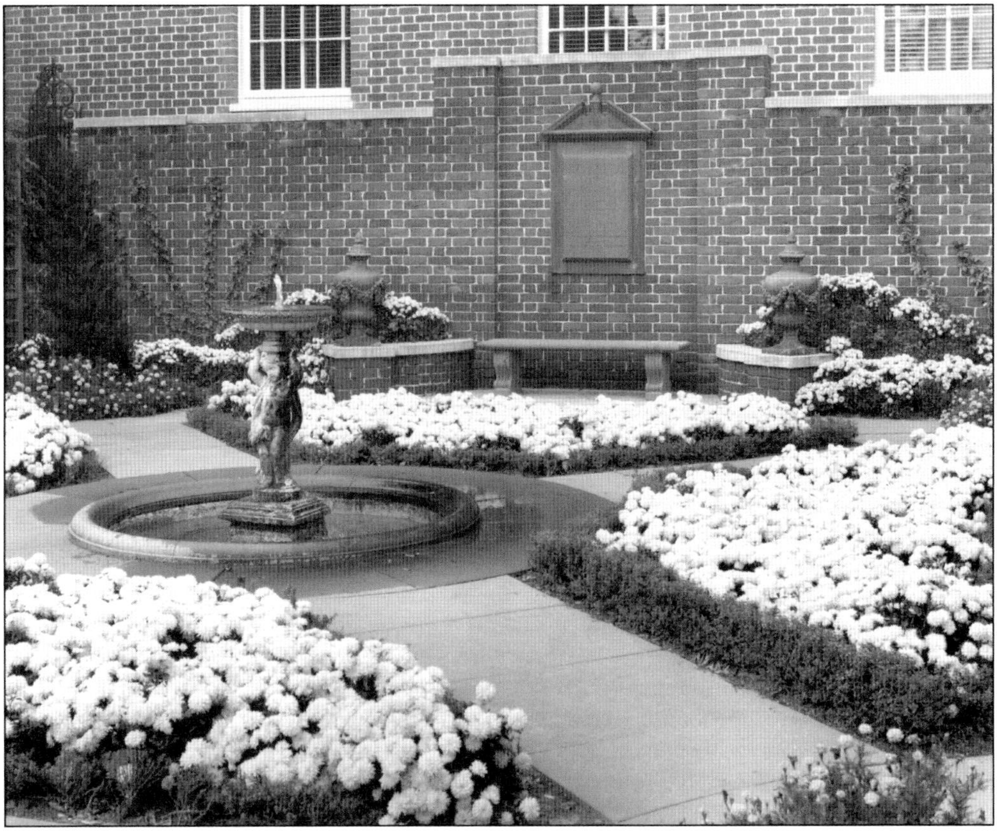

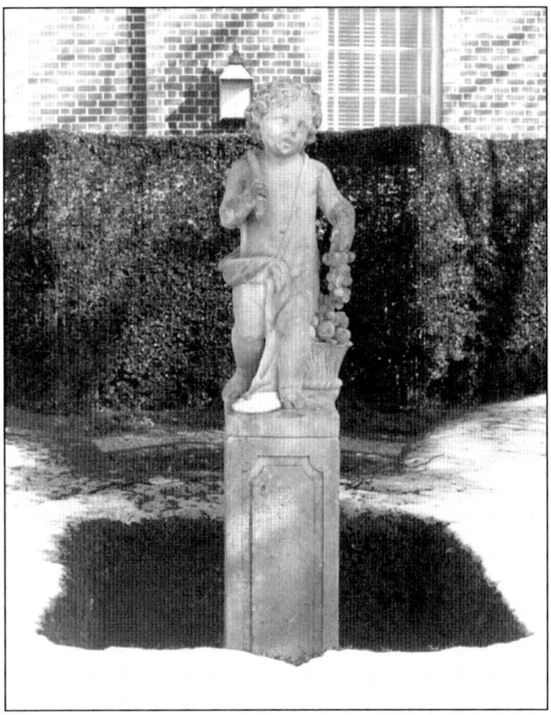

The Kellenberger Garden is located on the east side of the palace in a walled garden visible from the assembly room. The garden includes several traditional 18th-century features, including geometric and symmetrical flower beds, classically inspired sculptures, and trimmed hedges. The flowers are changed seasonally; each fall, chrysanthemums display a rainbow of colors in this garden.

The use of statuary in gardens rose to an unprecedented scale with the introduction of new technologies and materials in the 18th century. The classics became the most popular subject for these sculptures. Ancient mythological and allegorical figures abounded, including the goddess Venus, the four seasons, and the Roman wrestler. This cherub statue appears in the walled Green Garden.

The Kellenberger Garden is named in honor of John A. Kellenberger and his wife, May Gordon Latham Kellenberger. Pictured here, they were two of the original benefactors of the palace reconstruction, and both served on the Tryon Palace Commission. John served as treasurer for the commission, and May took over her mother's role as commission chairman (her mother was Maude Moore Latham).

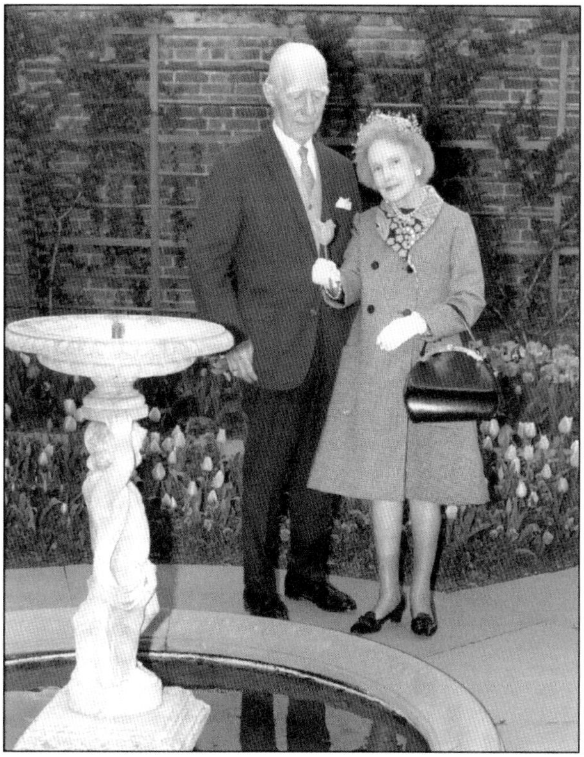

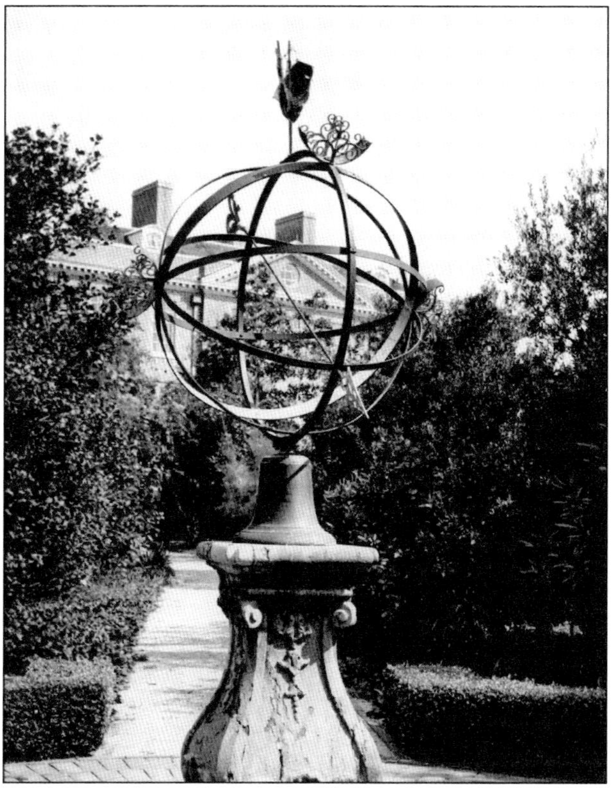

A decorative sundial, traditionally located in the front garden of the palace, is shown here on the west side of the south lawn; it is based on the design for an armillary sphere. Even though clocks and watches were becoming more common, there remained a large interest in sundials during the 18th century. Sundials were used to calculate time and to set household clocks or watches.

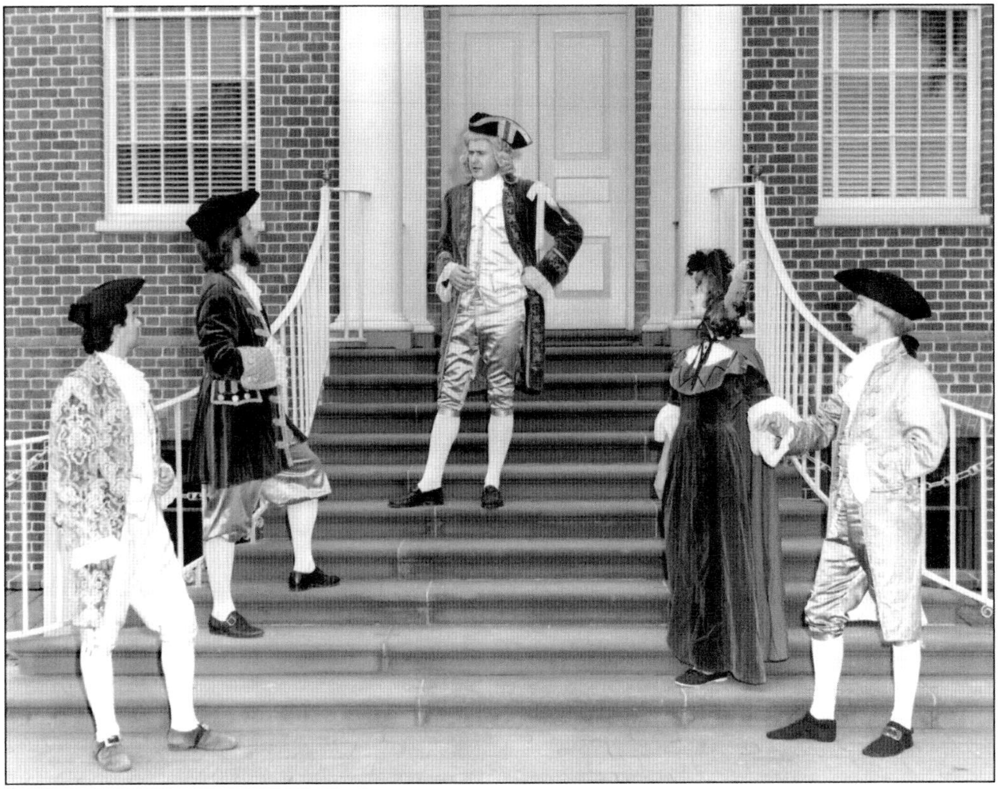

From June 11 through June 25, 1960, playwright Kermit Hunter (1910–2001) presented his drama *The Third Frontier*, which celebrated the William Tryon era of early New Bern, in the New Bern High School Auditorium. Hunter wrote several plays exploring North Carolina's history, including *The Liberty Tree*, *Horn in the West*, and the first edition of *Unto These Hills*. In the photograph below, Gov. William Tryon, played by Ralph Rives (of Enfield), welcomes Polly, a servant girl played by Doris Robbins (of Roanoke Rapids), in a scene from *The Third Frontier* set on the palace lawn.

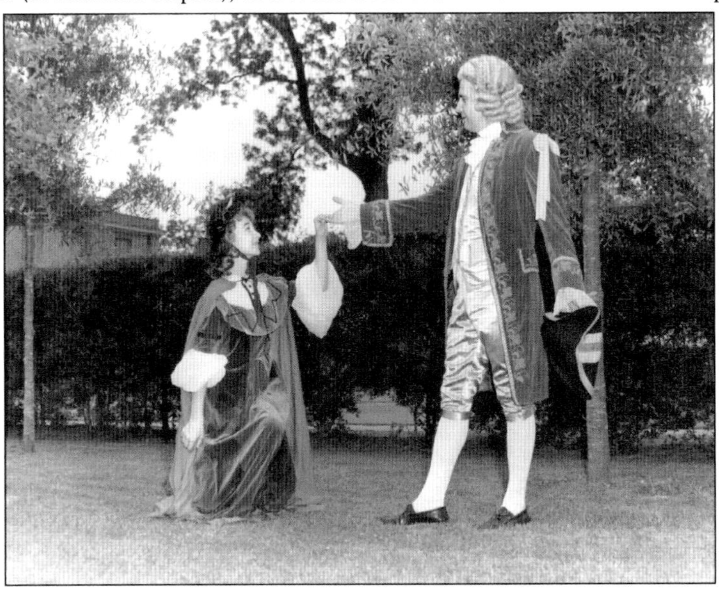

Five

BUILDING A BIGGER STORY

Tryon Palace is more than just the palace and its grounds. During its history, the Tryon Palace Commission has worked diligently to acquire other historic properties that help interpret local history. Among those properties are the Dixon and Daves Houses, which were constructed on palace lots sold after the fire of 1798. These two houses were kept intact during the reconstruction of the palace in the 1950s. The Stanly House, which was moved to its current location in the 1960s, focuses on the prominent Stanly family, who took part in political life from the early American republic through the Civil War. In the 1980s, Tryon Palace took over New Bern Academy, the first publically chartered school in North Carolina, in order to include more information about education in New Bern and life during the Civil War. But there were still more stories to tell, and Tryon Palace wanted to provide historical context for the original 28-year history of the palace that occurred from 1770 to 1798. In the 2000s, construction began on a new history center that would incorporate new interpretative exhibits and provide room for changing exhibits; in October 2010, the North Carolina History Center opened with a focus on regional history.

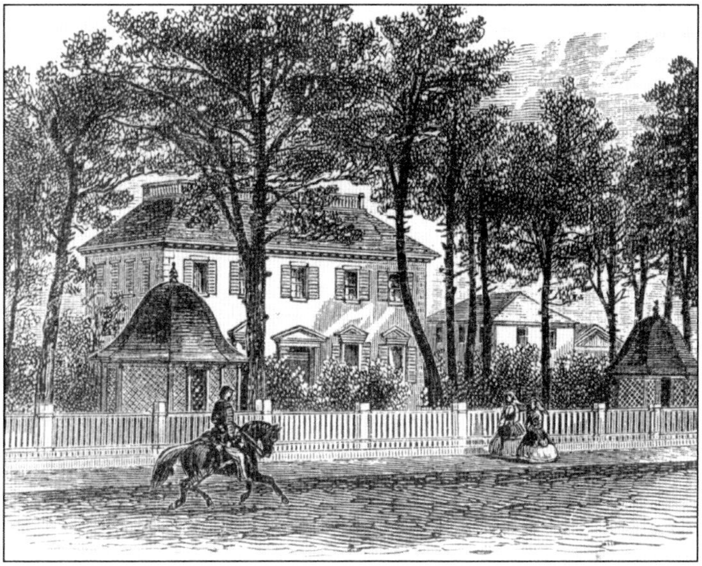

This mid-19th-century engraving depicts the original setting for the John Wright Stanly House, named for John Wright Stanly (1742–1789), who was born in Virginia and came to New Bern in 1772, where he married Anne Cogdell. During the American Revolution, Stanly operated a fleet of vessels for trade and as a privateer. He held several small political offices, but his main focus remained on shipping and distilling.

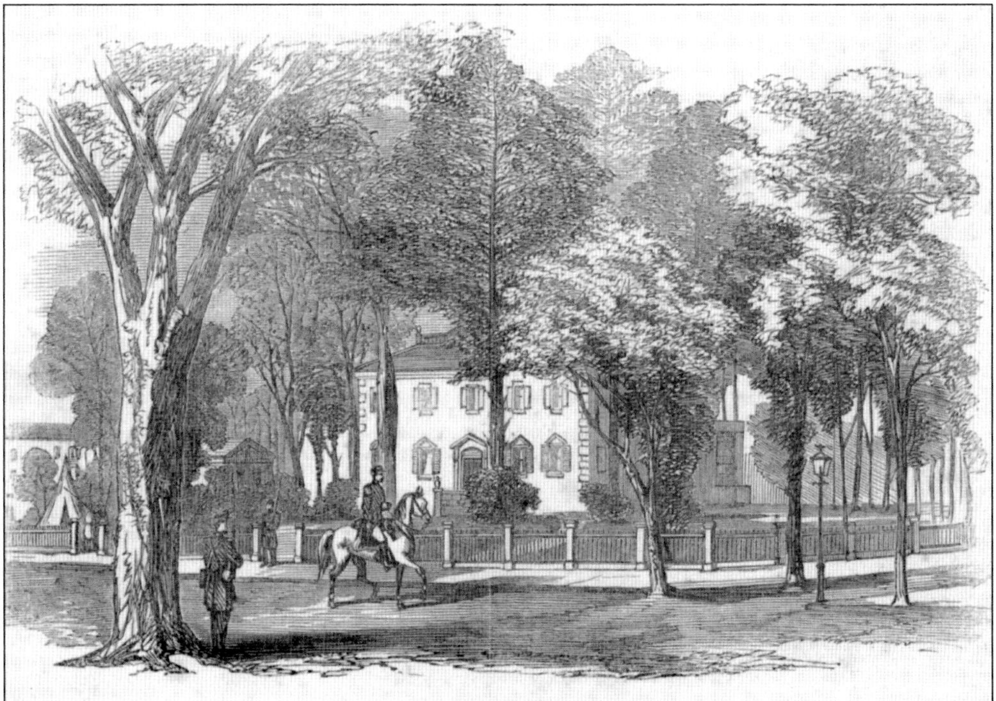

The Battle of New Bern took place on March 14, 1862, and by the time it concluded, New Bern was occupied by Union forces. The John Wright Stanly House, shown in this engraving, became the headquarters for Union general Ambrose Burnside before becoming a convent for the Sisters of Mercy. Edward Stanly, grandson of John Wright Stanly, was born in the house and served as the military governor of North Carolina for the Union until resigning his post in 1863.

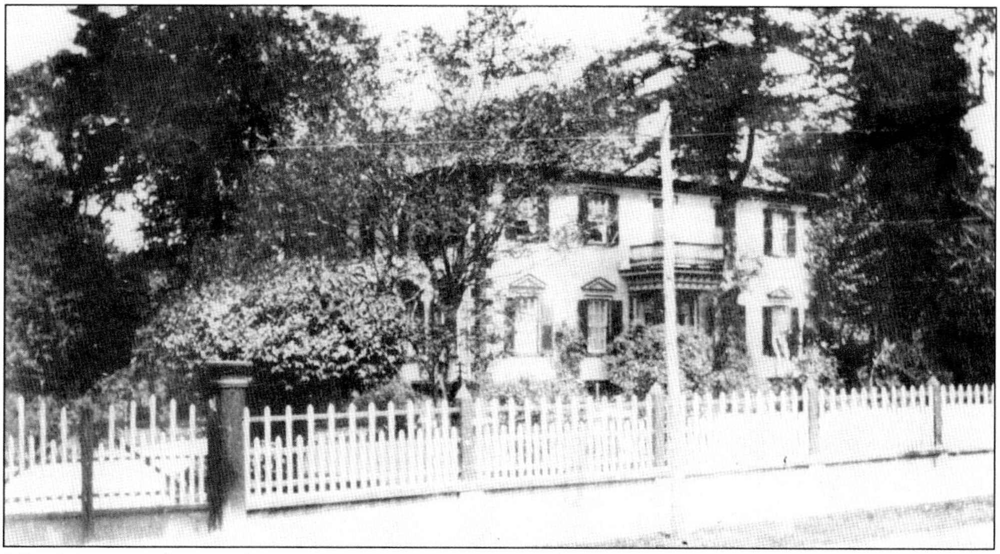

The John Wright Stanly House was originally located at a different New Bern address. When it was constructed, it occupied an entire city block with outbuildings and gardens. This early 20th-century photograph shows the Stanly House at its original location with landscaped front lawns and a modified front door. The additions to the facade were made during the second half of the 19th century.

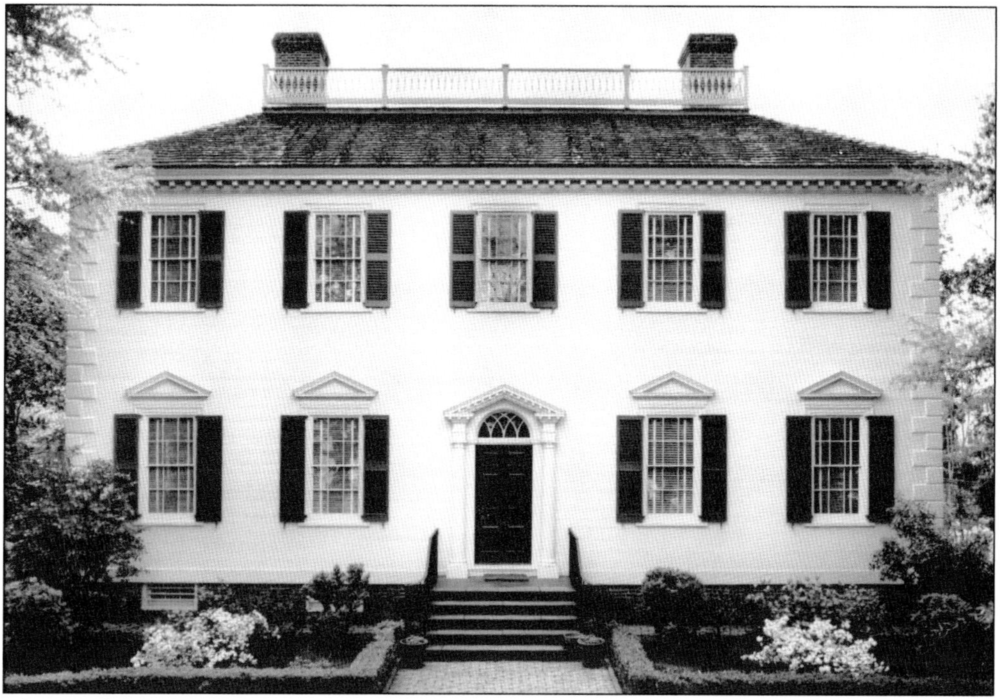

The Stanly House features classic Georgian architecture and is crafted of hand-hewn longleaf pine, however, the exterior is designed to look like stone from the street. The house remained vacant after the deaths of John Wright Stanly and his wife. In 1798, their eldest son, John Stanly, took possession of the house. He served in both the North Carolina General Assembly and the US Congress.

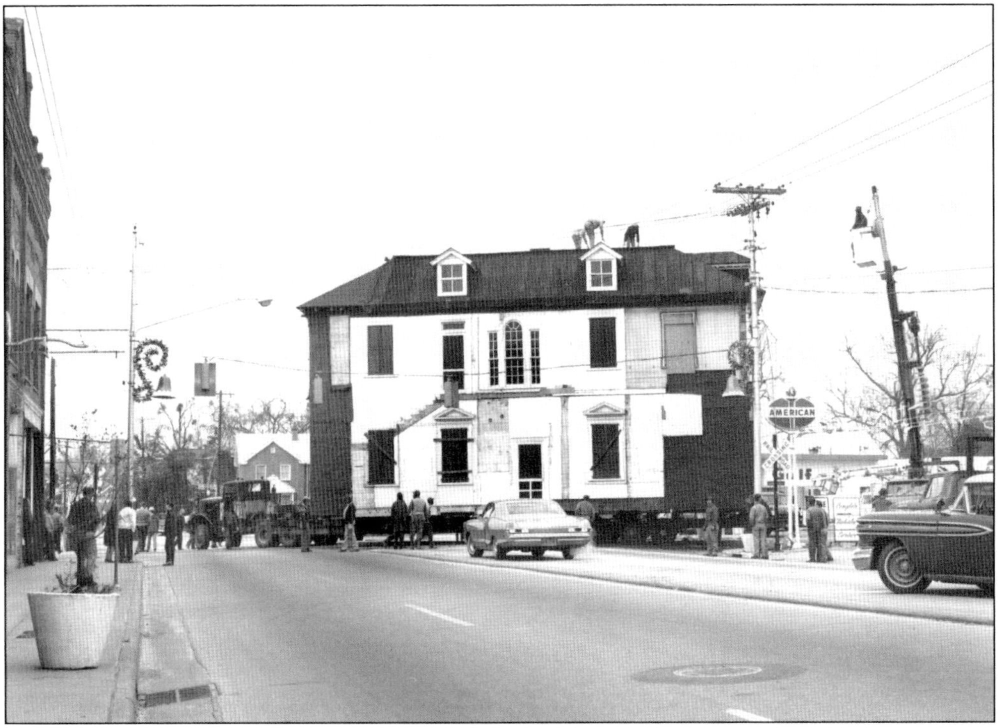

The John Wright Stanly House first served as a private home, but after it was moved to New Street, it served as the town library from 1935 to 1965. When the New Bern Library Association donated the house to the Tryon Palace Commission in 1966, the building was moved several blocks to its current location near the palace on George Street. In order to move the house, the protruding portico and balcony over the front door had to be removed. These details—added during the 19th century—were not restored to the house after it was resettled.

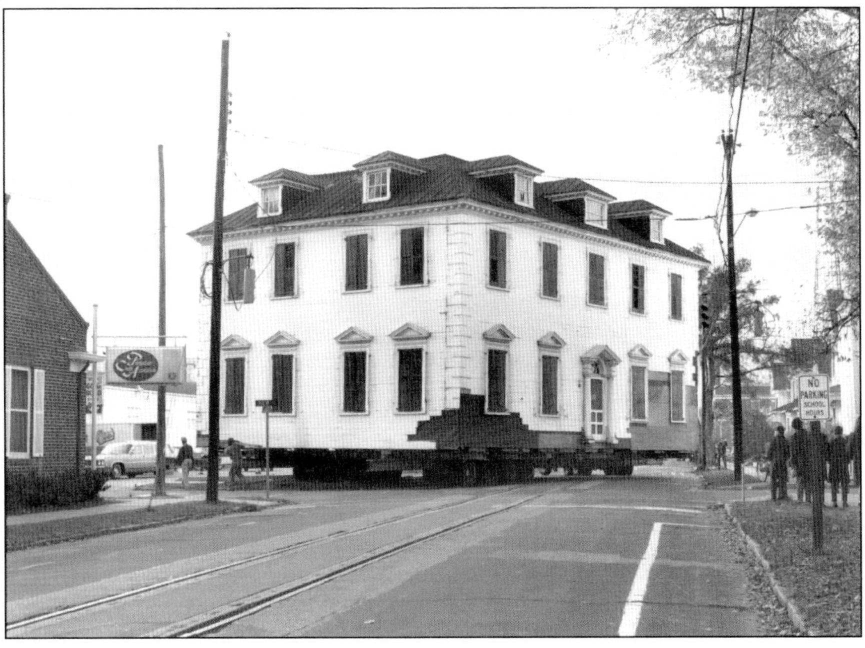

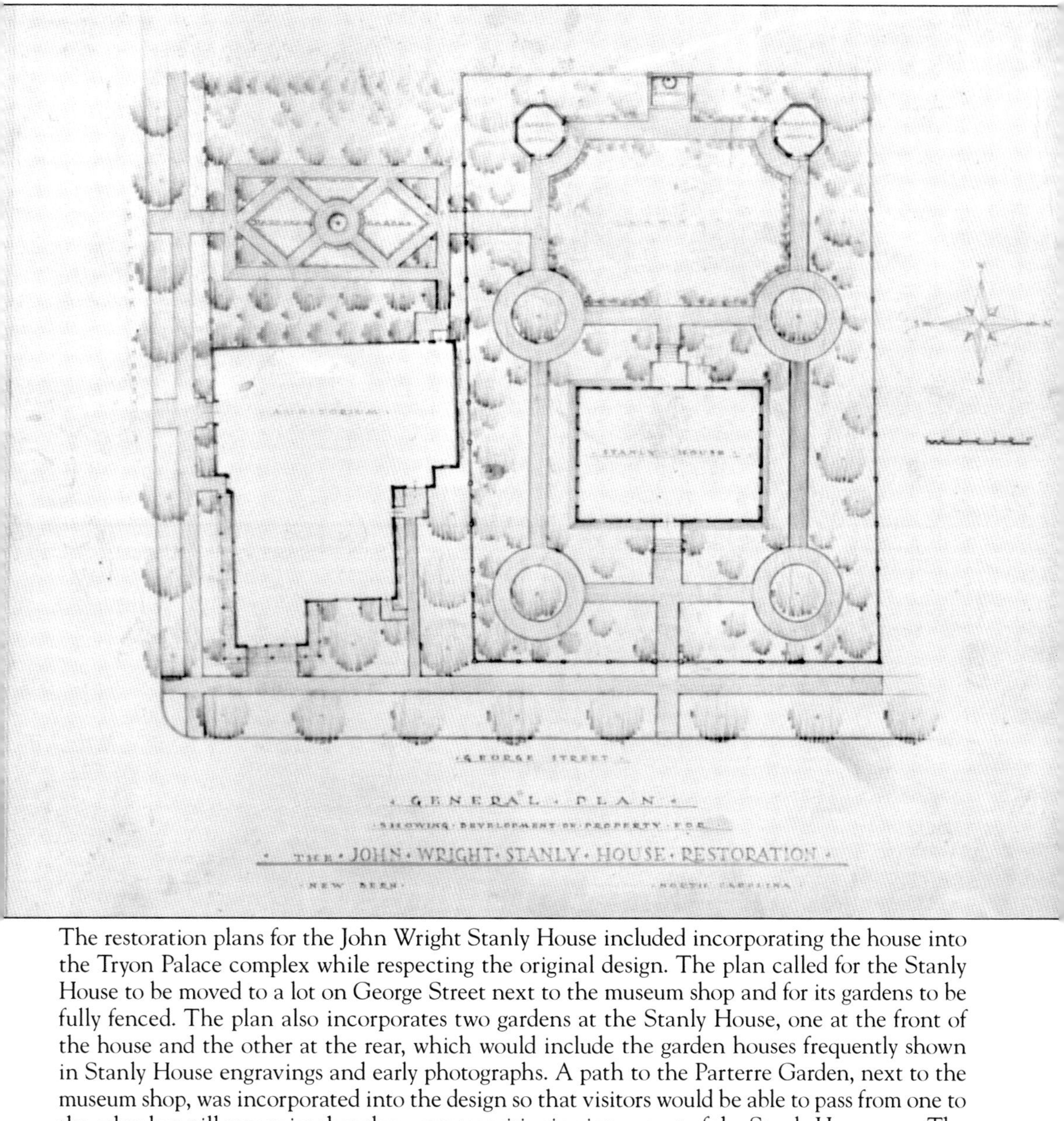

The restoration plans for the John Wright Stanly House included incorporating the house into the Tryon Palace complex while respecting the original design. The plan called for the Stanly House to be moved to a lot on George Street next to the museum shop and for its gardens to be fully fenced. The plan also incorporates two gardens at the Stanly House, one at the front of the house and the other at the rear, which would include the garden houses frequently shown in Stanly House engravings and early photographs. A path to the Parterre Garden, next to the museum shop, was incorporated into the design so that visitors would be able to pass from one to the other but still recognize that they were transitioning into or out of the Stanly House area. The plan was successfully executed, and by 1972, visitors were enjoying tours of the Stanly House.

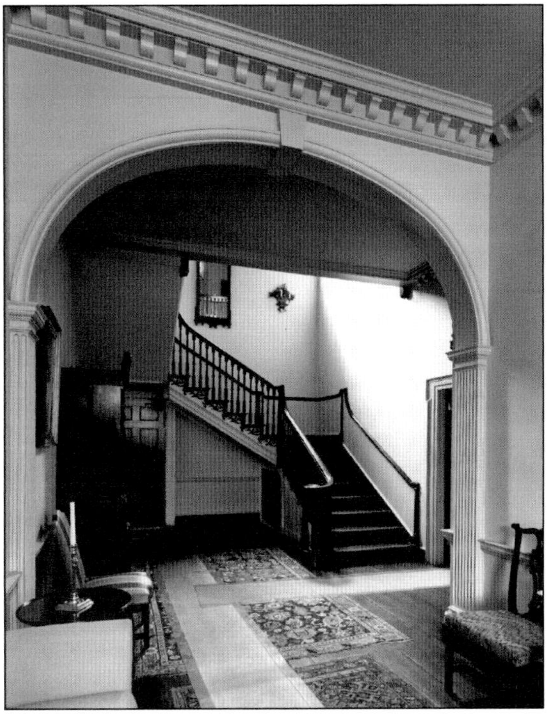

Most Georgian houses, including the John Wright Stanly House, feature a center hall design. The main staircase design—and its similarity to the stairs and several other architectural features in Tryon Palace—led to the theory that John Hawks may have designed not only Tryon Palace but also the Stanly House.

The John Wright Stanly House opened to the public in 1972 after six years of restoration work. The work restored the house to its Federal era appearance and included period-appropriate gardens. First Lady Pat Nixon was the honored guest at the dedication ceremony, and she cut the ribbon to officially open the Stanly House to visitors.

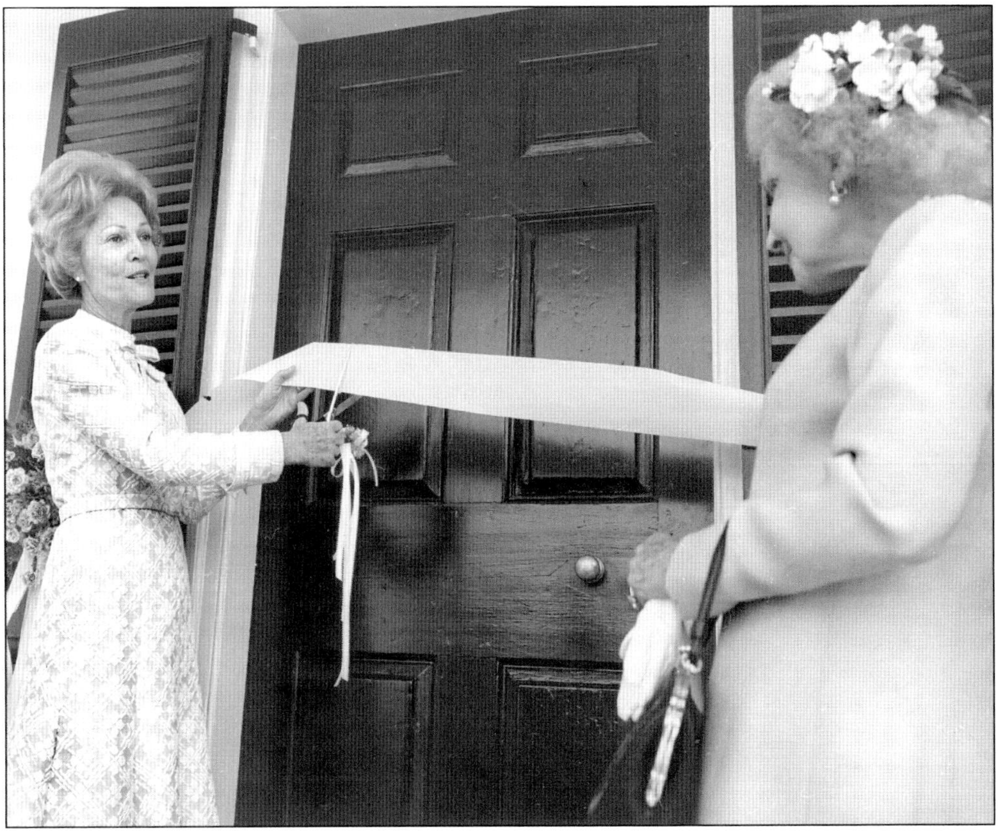

Costumed interpreters provided tours of the Stanly House beginning when it first opened in 1972. Here, interpreters pose by the fountain at the back of the Stanly Garden, a part of the original restoration plan. The fountain remains a part of the Stanly House gardens, but its appearance has changed over time.

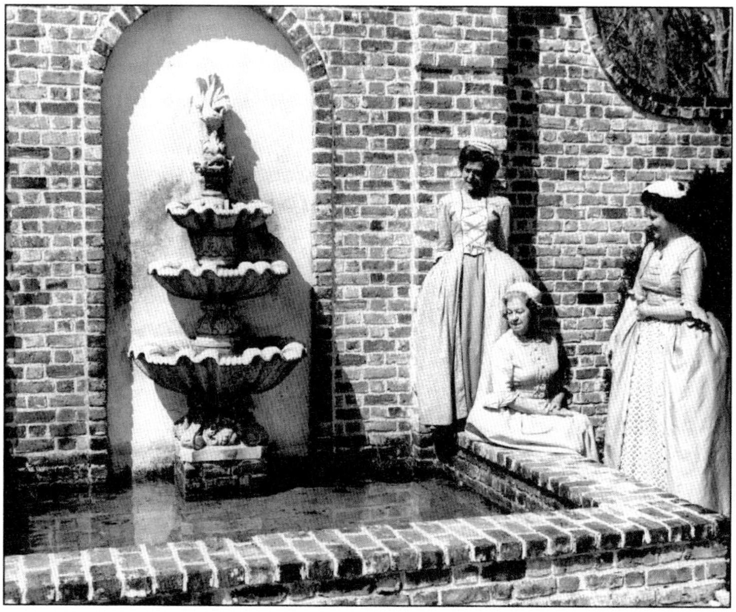

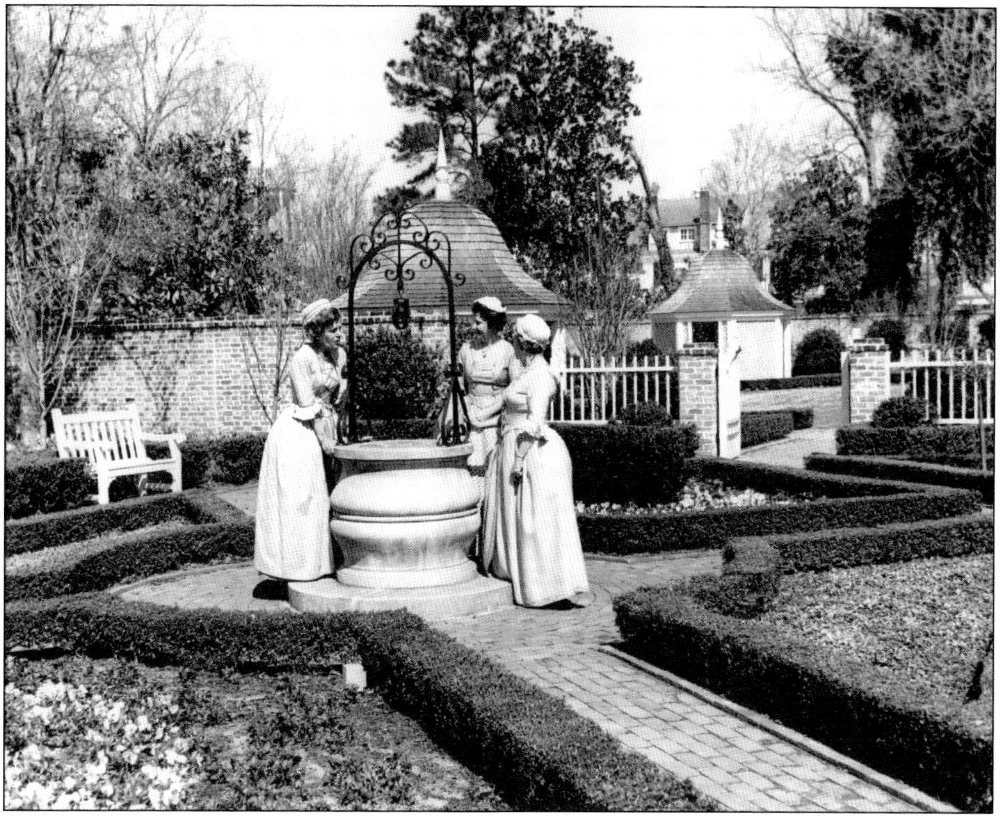

The Parterre Gardens incorporated a well in the center that became a popular spot for costumed interpreters to chat between tours. The Stanly gardens are visible through the gate, including the two large octagonal garden houses that appear similar to gazebos. The Parterre Gardens were renamed the Carraway Garden, and an extension was added on Pollock Street.

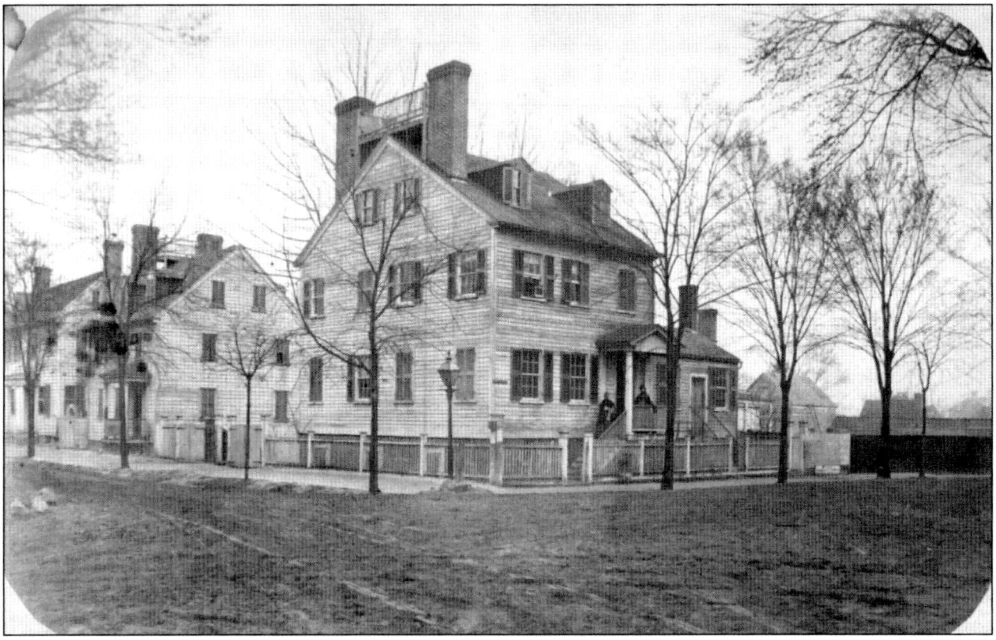

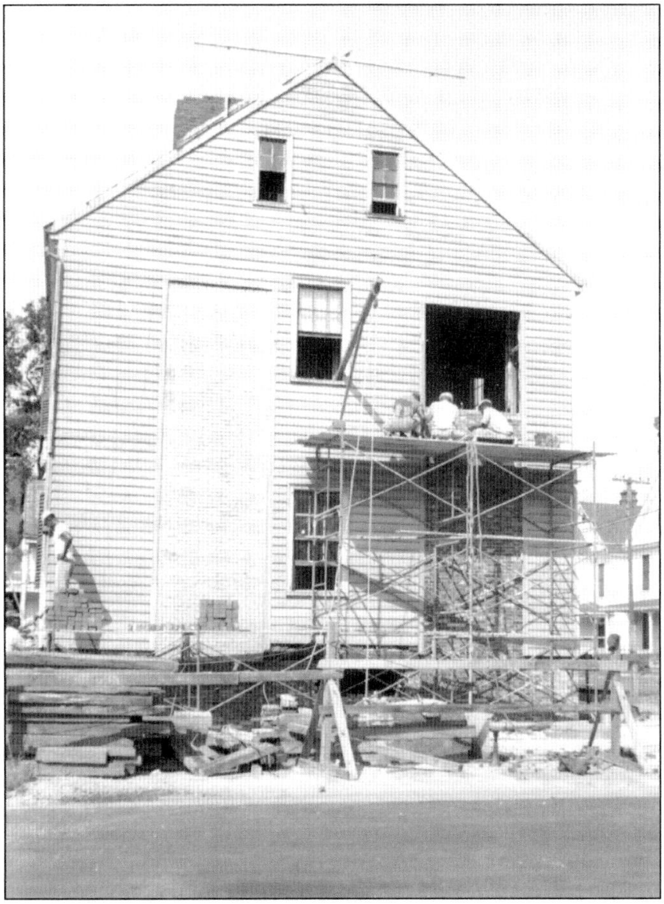

The Daves House was built by John Pough Daves (1789–1838), the oldest surviving son of Major John Daves (1748–1804) and Mary Haynes Long Daves (1751–1822), on land purchased after the Tryon Palace fire of 1798. The house was completed around 1813, the same year Daves married his first wife. She passed away within a year, and Daves married twice more before his death.

The Daves House was built in the Federal style with a side-hall plan. The layout of the house mirrors that of the Dixon House. The main gates to the palace grounds are located between the Dixon and Daves Houses. When Tryon Palace opened in 1959, the Daves House was used for staff offices.

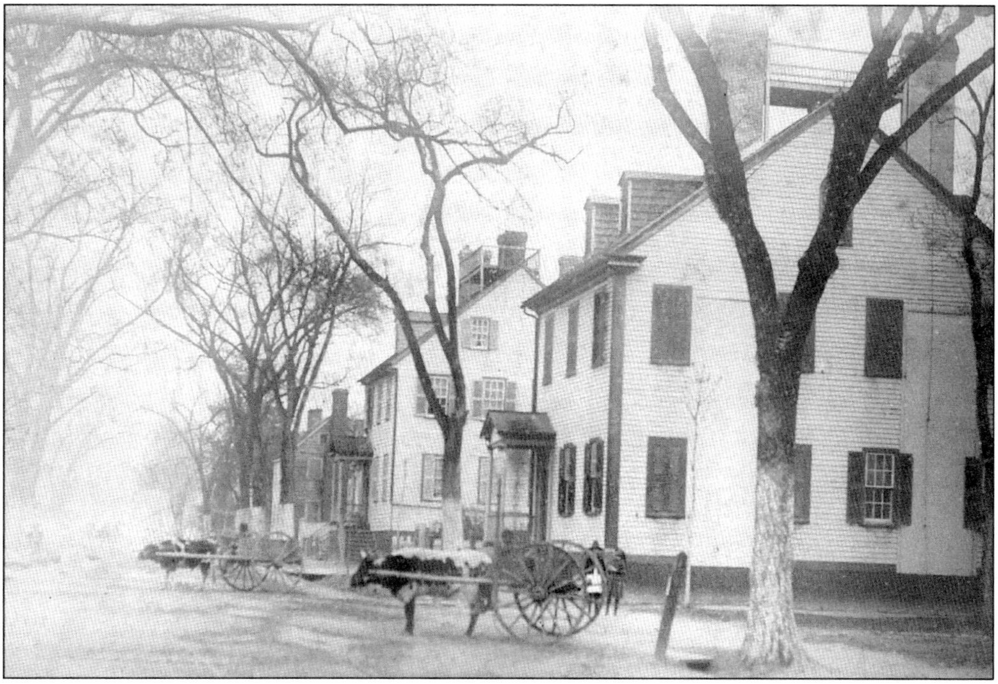

The Dixon House was built by George W. Dixon, a merchant and tailor from New Bern. He purchased the lot in 1826 for $750 and had the house constructed before 1830, when he moved in with his wife Antoinette and their family. The Dixons suffered severely from the economic depression of 1837 and were forced to declare bankruptcy in 1839. The house was sold as a foreclosure for $2,205.

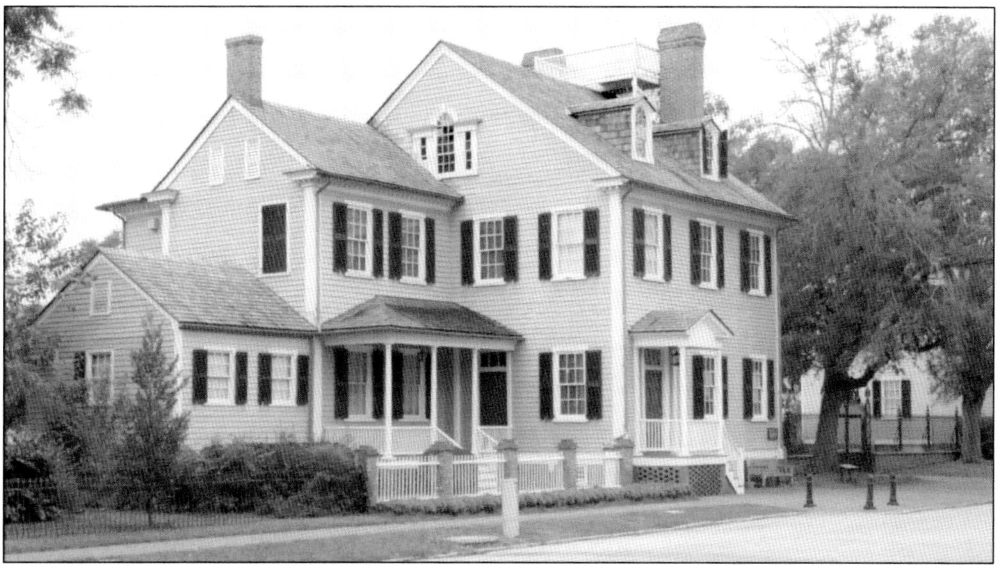

New Bern was occupied by Union solders after 1862. Different regiments were quartered in individual houses, and soldiers used private houses for regimental hospitals, where minor illnesses and injuries would have been treated. The Dixon House was used by the Ninth Vermont Regiment. The value of the home suffered as a result of the Civil War, and when it was sold in 1877, the price was only two-thirds of its prewar value.

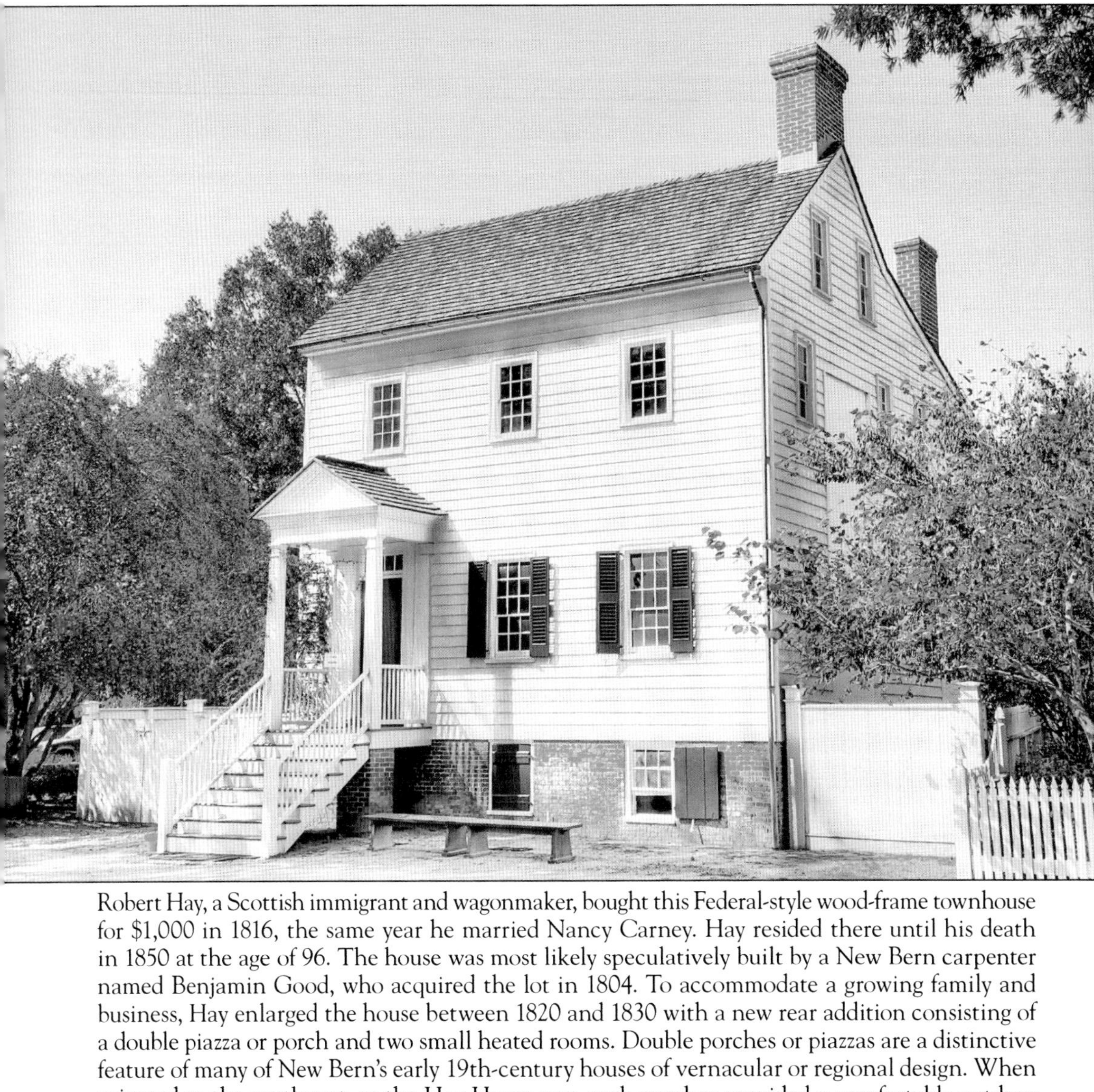

Robert Hay, a Scottish immigrant and wagonmaker, bought this Federal-style wood-frame townhouse for $1,000 in 1816, the same year he married Nancy Carney. Hay resided there until his death in 1850 at the age of 96. The house was most likely speculatively built by a New Bern carpenter named Benjamin Good, who acquired the lot in 1804. To accommodate a growing family and business, Hay enlarged the house between 1820 and 1830 with a new rear addition consisting of a double piazza or porch and two small heated rooms. Double porches or piazzas are a distinctive feature of many of New Bern's early 19th-century houses of vernacular or regional design. When oriented to the southwest, as the Hay House was, such porches provided a comfortable outdoor sitting area during the hot summer months and on sunny afternoons in winter. In the summer, the house's residents could open doors and windows to capture prevailing breezes from the nearby Trent River, and the original louvered shutters could be closed to block the hot rays of the sun.

John Jones, owner of a local turpentine distillery, built the Jones House around 1809. In 1820, he added an additional wing. During the Union occupation of New Bern during the Civil War, this house became a jail for Confederate sympathizers. Legend has it that the notorious Confederate spy Emeline Pigott was confined in this house.

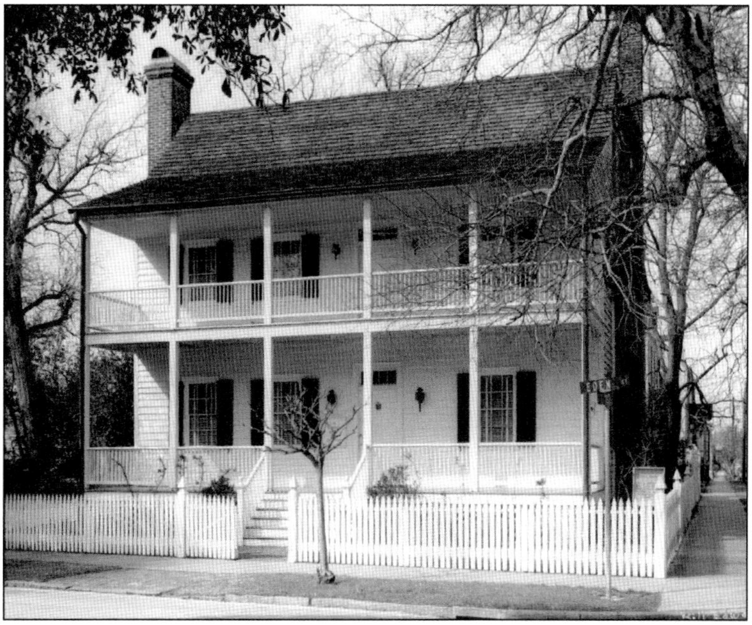

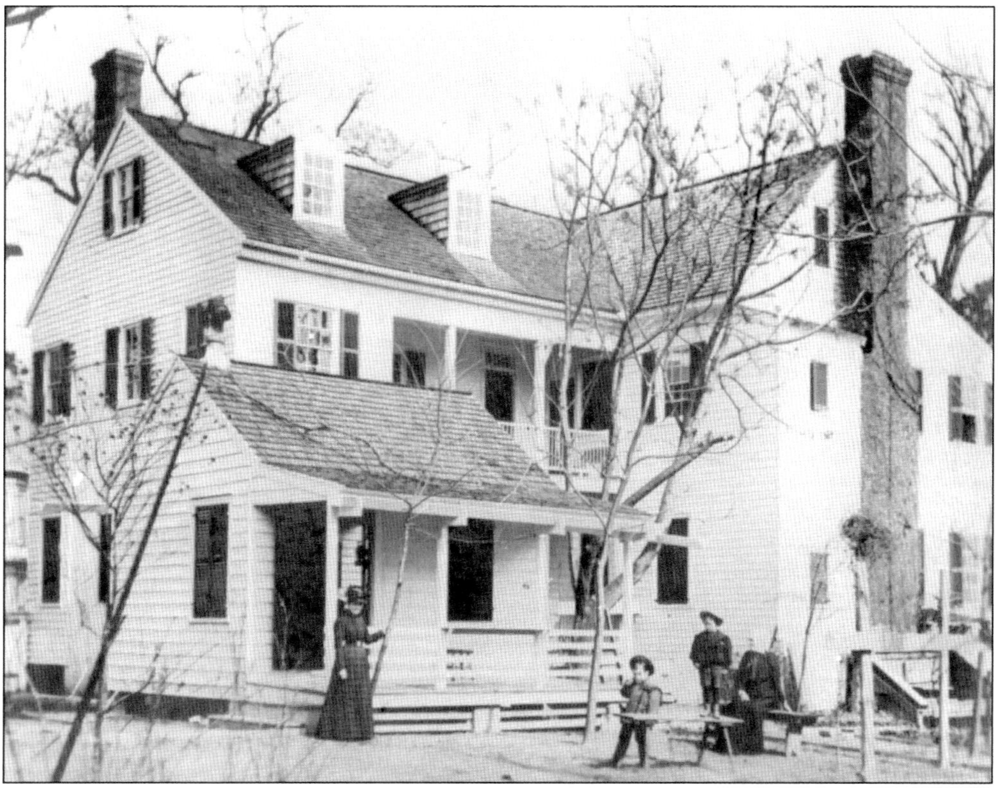

This photograph shows the rear of the Jones House around 1900. The building underwent significant restorations in order to return it to the appearance of the 1809 house. The separate kitchen wing, visible in the center front of this image, was removed, as was the "closet" wing, visible on the right side of the image. The open porch areas were also enclosed.

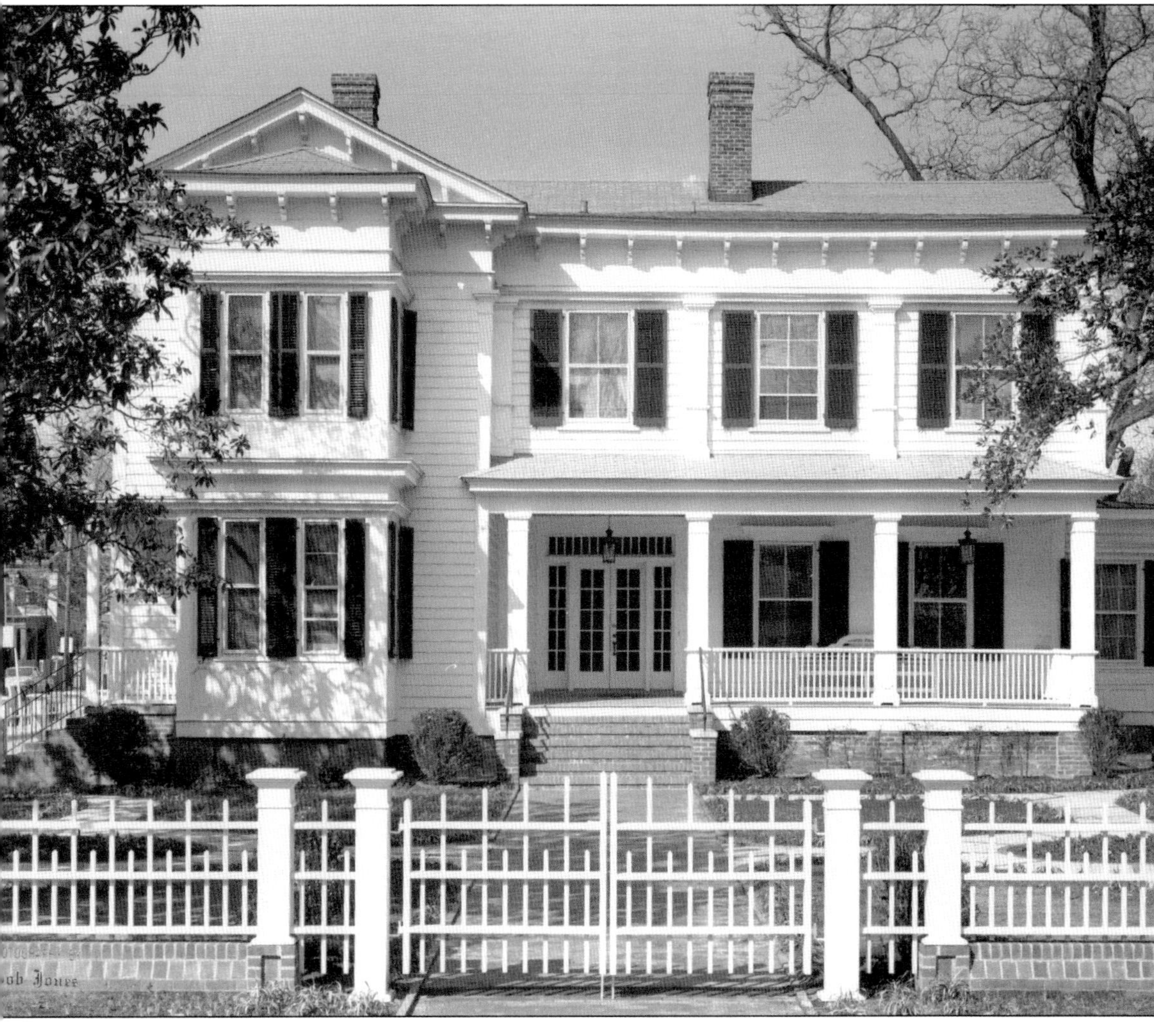

The Commission House, also known as the Lehman-Duffy House, was constructed between 1886 and 1888. The house has a central hall plan typical of the 1880s, with extensive remodeling from the c. 1920 Colonial Revival period. The land was originally owned by the Daves family, but by 1886, it had come into the possession of local lawyer Robert B. Lehman. Lehman lived in the house for two years, outfitting it with the latest conveniences, including hot and cold running water and a heated range in the kitchen. In 1888, he sold it to Sophia Bryan Duffy, wife of Dr. Charles Duffy. The Duffys resided in the house until 1920. By 1923, the Mohn family purchased the home and owned it until 1973, when the Tryon Palace Commission purchased it. After limited restoration work, the house came into use as an office space and area used for hosting special events.

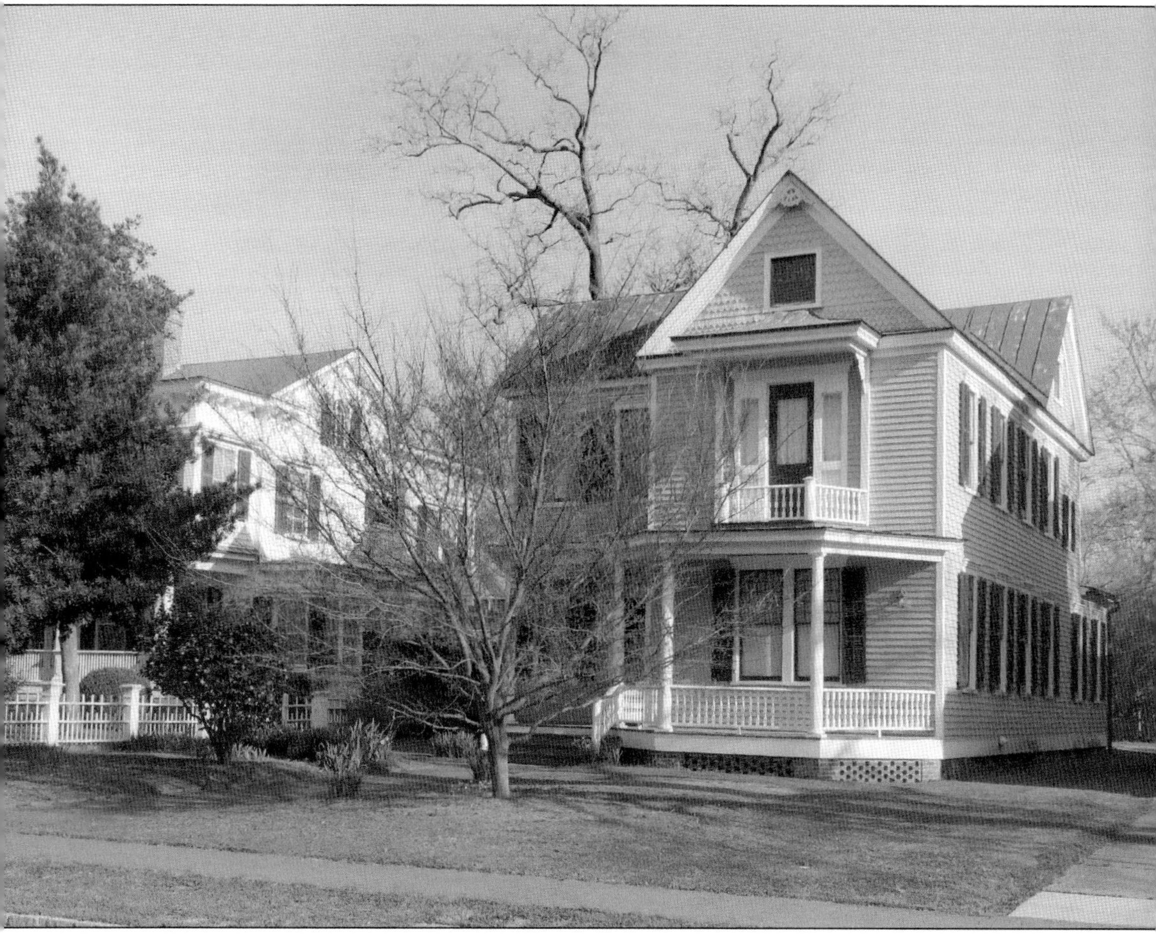

The Disosway House is a late-Victorian house originally built by John and Lyda Disosway, of New Bern, sometime between 1880 and 1890. In 1896, the Disoways sold the house to Capt. Wentworth Smith, who sold it to Charles Laban Abernethy in 1914. The house remained in the Abernethy family until 1983; under their care, several alternations were made during the 1920s, including the addition of a front-porch sunroom. Located next to the Commission House, the Disosway House provided the palace the perfect opportunity to create a permanent home for the Carraway Research Library. After extensive restoration work to return the house to its original Victorian-era design, the library moved to the Disosway House and opened in the summer of 2004. The Carraway Research Library is named in honor of Gertrude Sprague Carraway, who served as the first director of Tryon Palace.

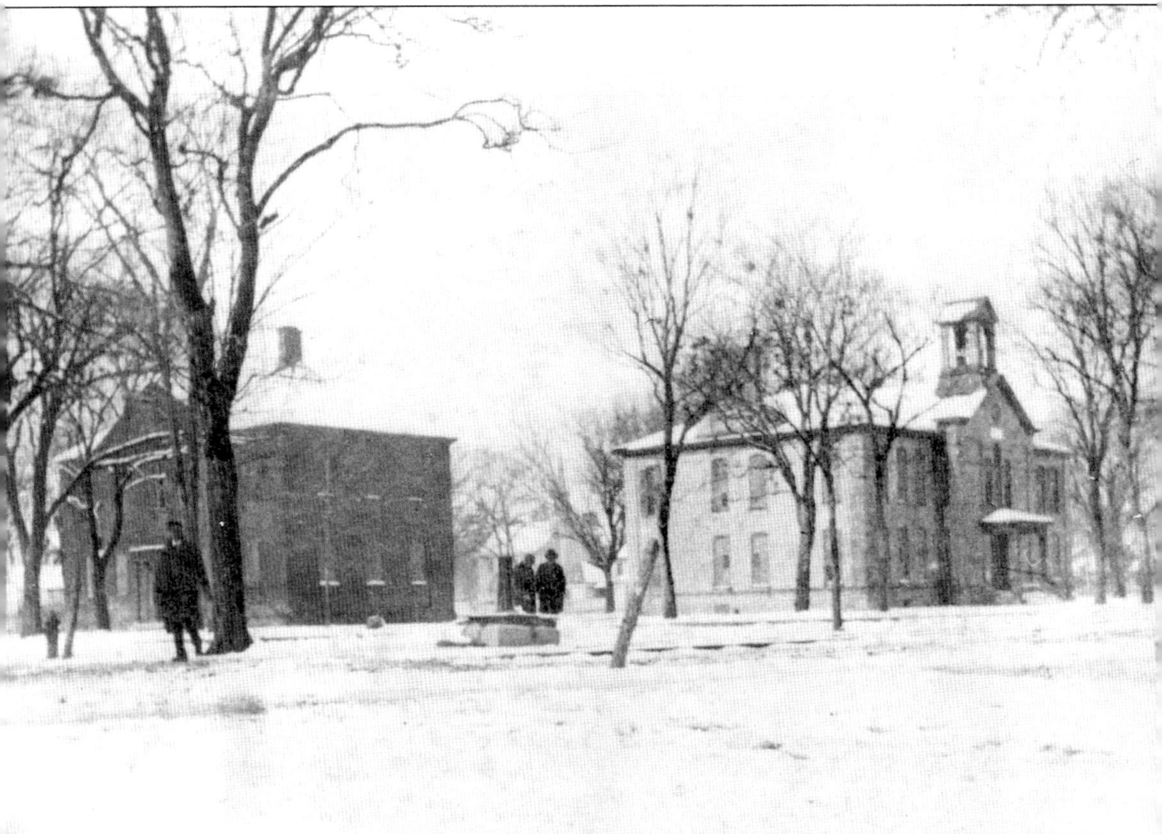

The New Bern Academy, the first school chartered by the State of North Carolina, opened in 1764. Two years later, the general assembly levied taxes to pay for the maintenance of the school, but the original building was destroyed by a fire in 1795. A new brick building was constructed and opened in 1810. During the Civil War, the New Bern Academy was temporarily closed to students and used as a military hospital. The hospital primarily treated victims of spinal meningitis, smallpox, and yellow fever, as well as wartime casualties. The success of the New Bern Academy led to a second school being opened on the property. The New Bern Graded School, more commonly referred to as the Bell Building, was completed in 1884, and in 1899, both schools joined the New Bern school system. They remained in use until 1971.

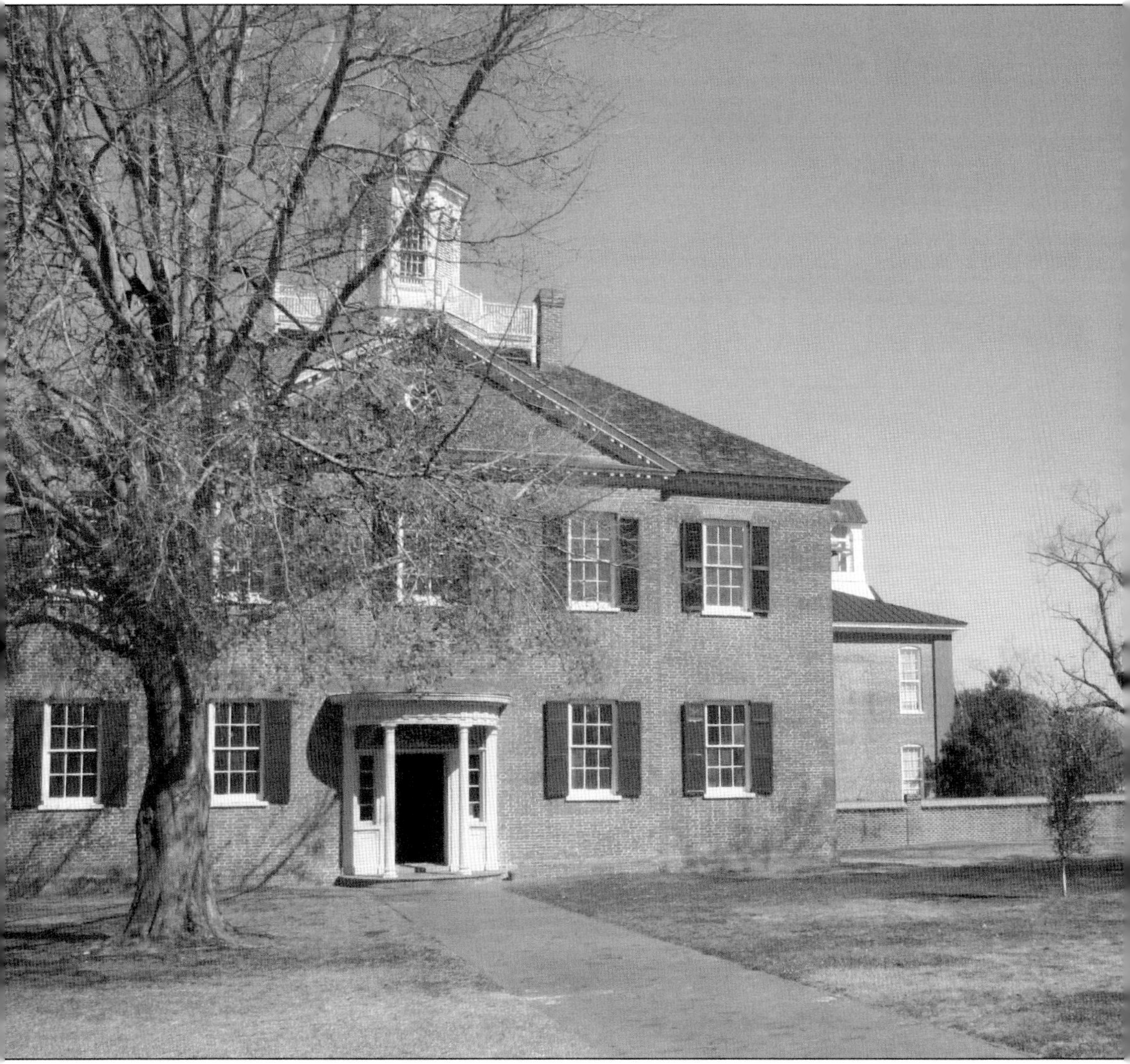

The New Bern Academy Historical Commission, established in 1975, worked diligently with local partners to restore the academy and preserve its history. In 1990, the academy opened as part of the Tryon Palace complex. In honor of its proud wartime history, Tryon Palace established the New Bern Academy as its Civil War museum. The museum contains exhibits about the city's occupation, the role of the academy during the war, and personal stories from residents who lived in the area from 1861 to 1865. During special Civil War weekends, visitors are invited to watch artillery demonstrations and engage with interpreters to learn more about New Bern during the Civil War.

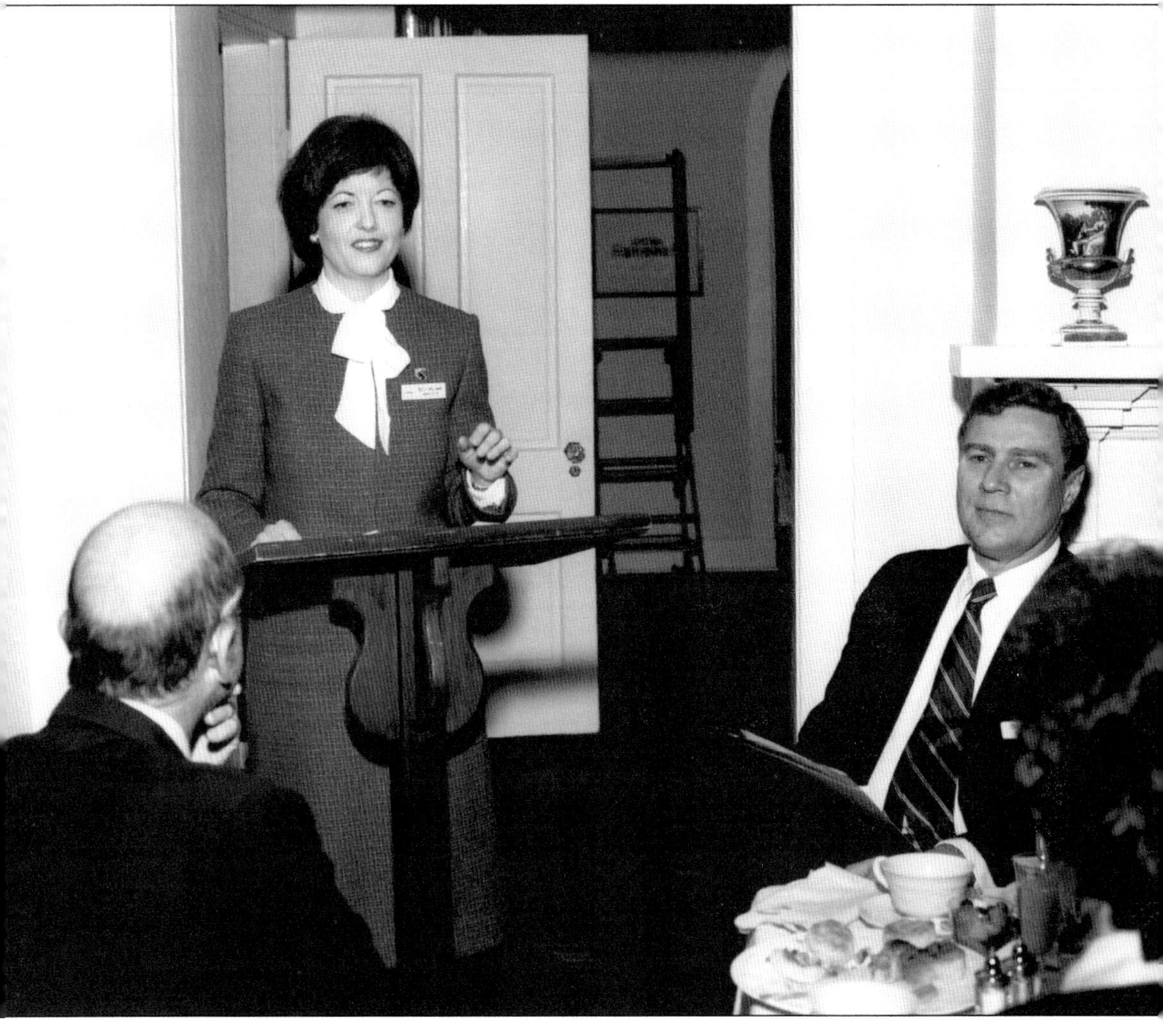

Kay Williams was named director of Tryon Palace in 1983 and served in that position for three decades. During her tenure, she saw the expansion of the African American history program and creation of the North Carolina History Center. A strong advocate for excellence in history and museum service, Williams oversaw Tryon Palace's first accreditation by the American Association of Museums (AAM) and supported the use of new technology and tools to engage a more diverse audience. She advocated for the North Carolina History Center to be a space that used the latest technologies to engage young audience members with history, which strongly influenced the exhibit design in the Pepsi Family Center and digital tours. Under her leadership, the history center was designed, built, and eventually opened on October 2010. In this c. 1988 photograph, Kay Williams speaks with a group at Tryon Palace.

Barbour Boat Works is visible in the background looking from the south lawn toward the Trent River. Founded by Herbert William Barbour in 1932, Barbour Boat Works started by producing small wooden ships, but during World War II, the company received several US Navy contracts and began creating large vessels. Barbour Boat Works continued to produce both personal and commercial vessels until the company closed in the 1990s. The Tryon Palace Commission purchased the property in 1998.

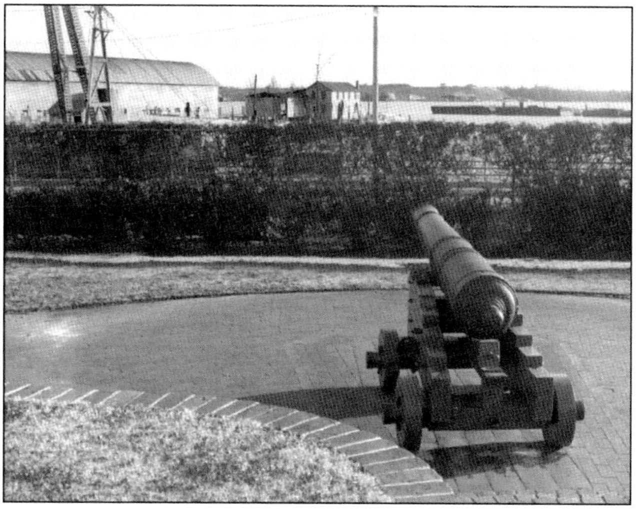

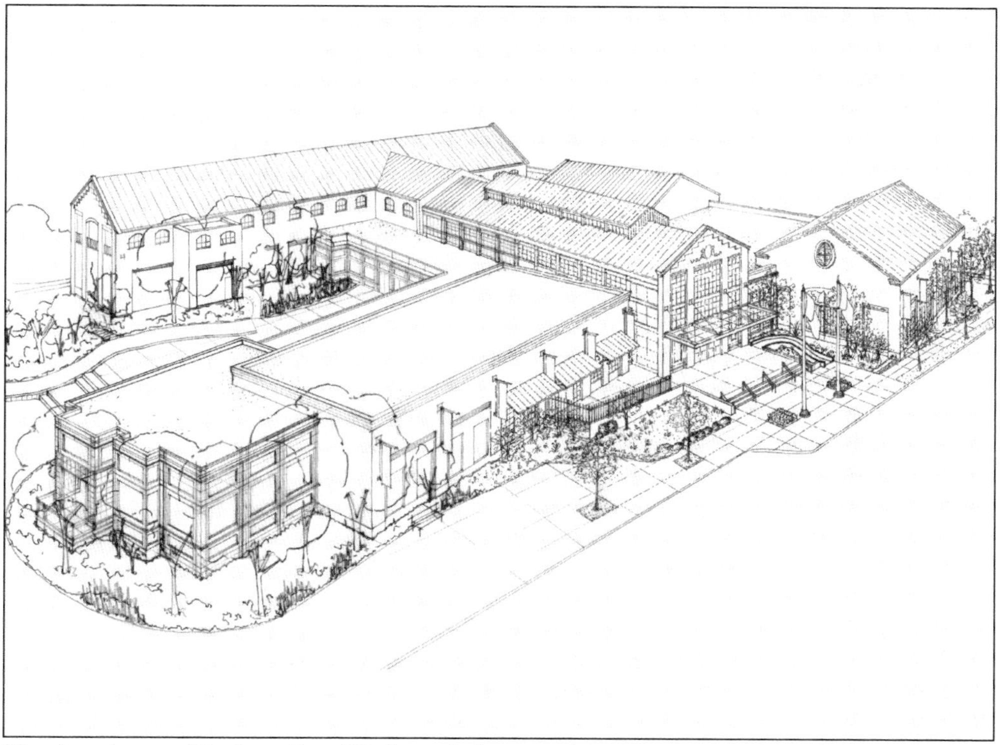

The demolition of Barbour Boat Works and cleanup of the site had been completed by 1999. At the same time, a design team was being established for the new North Carolina History Center. BJAC, from Raleigh, North Carolina, was named the project coordinator; Quinn Evans Architect, from Washington, DC, was named design architect; EDAW/AECOM from Alexandria, Virginia, was named landscape architect; and ESI Design from New York City was named exhibit planner. The conceptual design was completed in 2001, remediation of the Superfund site was completed in 2005, and the wetlands restoration was finished by the end of 2006. Design development was completed by the beginning of summer 2006, and construction of the North Carolina History Education Center began in September 2008. This schematic drawing of the North Carolina History Center shows the intended design.

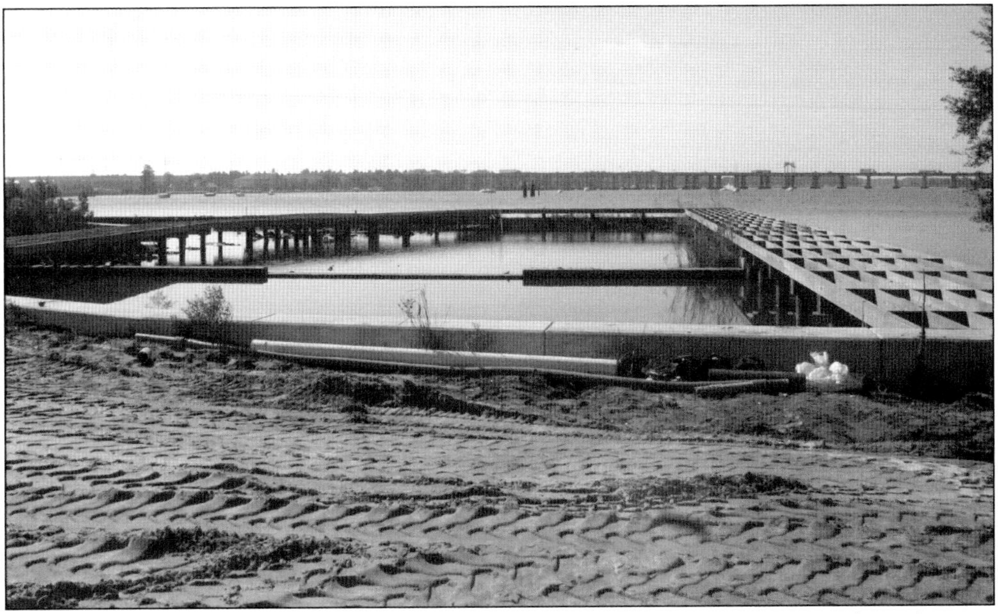

As a part of the development of the North Carolina History Center, Tryon Palace chose to include wetlands and a native-species garden along the Trent River waterfront. The Etteinne Mitchell Garden and Bate Commons create a positive environmental impact at the site while simultaneously providing visitors with a beautiful view of the Trent River. This photograph shows the initial stages of the construction of the walkway through the gardens.

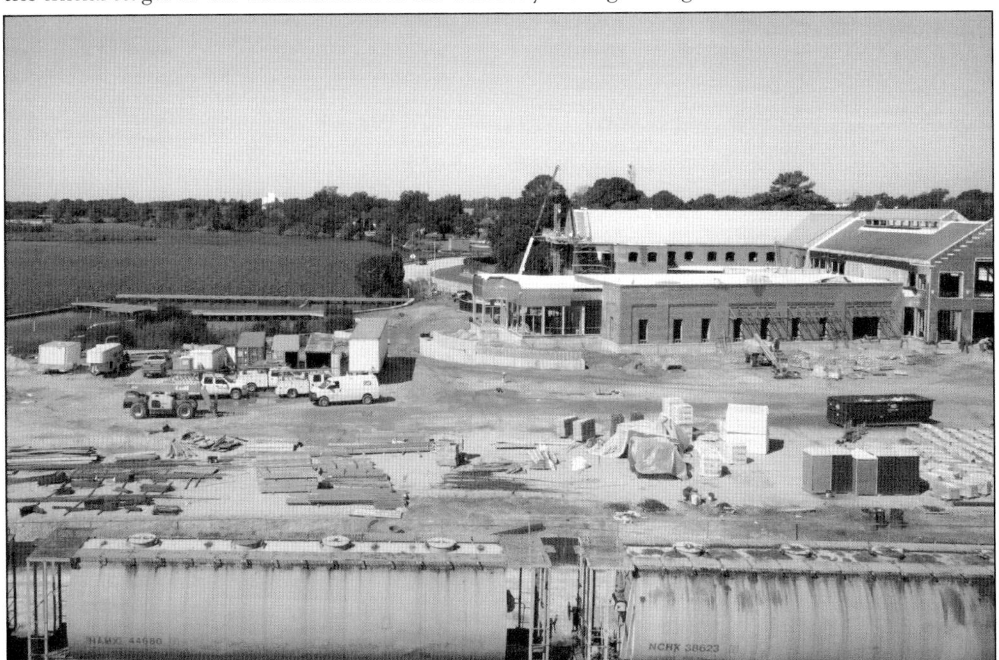

This photograph shows the North Carolina History Center construction site on September 28, 2009—approximately 13 months before the site opened. Although the construction team had encountered a few issues earlier in the year, they were back on schedule and adding the brick facing to the center by September.

The North Carolina History Center entrance at Mattocks Hall (pictured here under construction in 2009) drew inspiration from the 18th- and 19th-century brick riverfront wharves once common to North Carolina's coastal cities. Examples of surviving brick wharves still exist in nearby Washington, North Carolina.

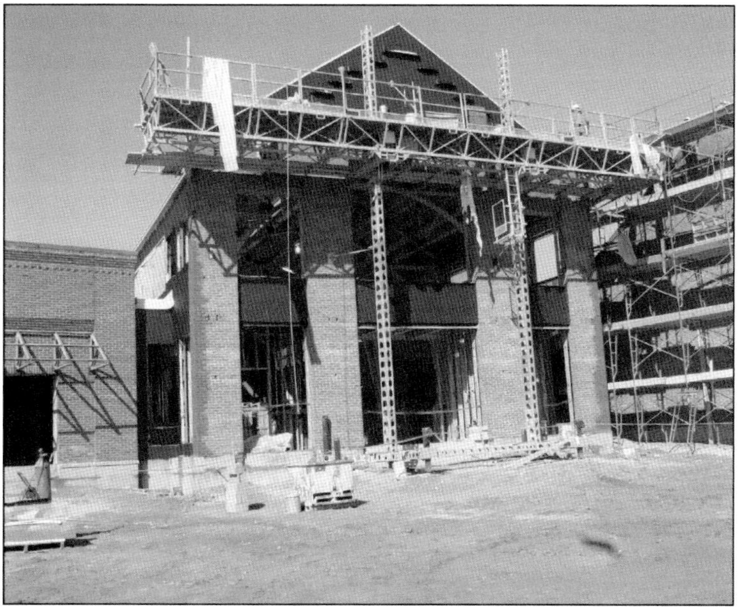

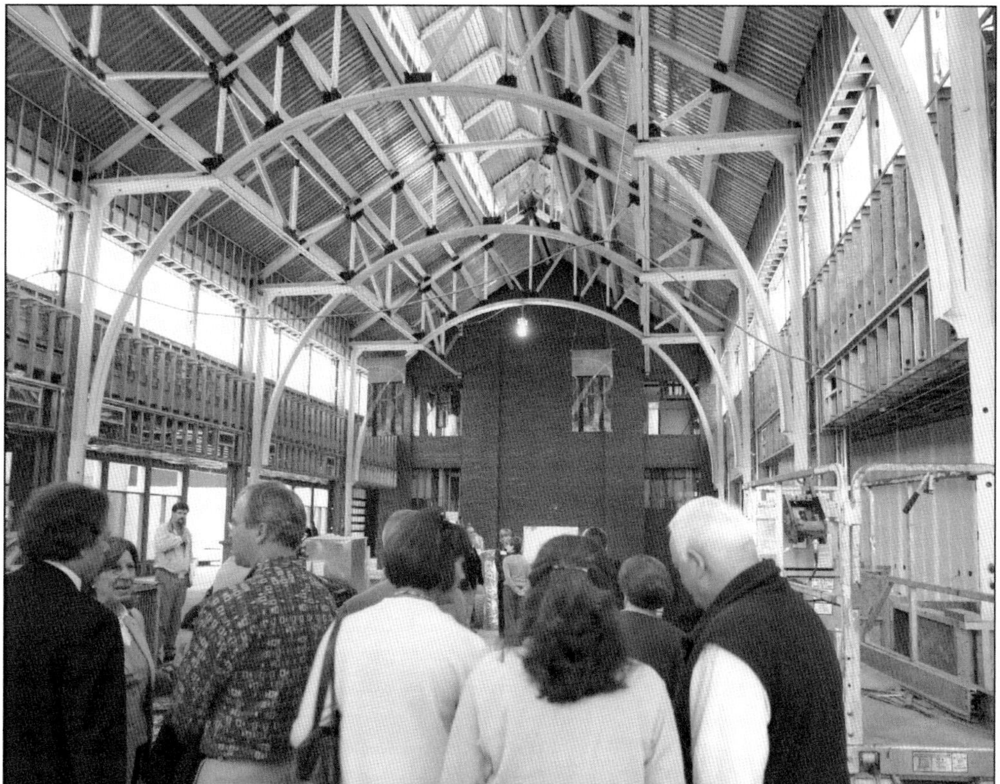

During a biannual meeting of the Tryon Palace Commission in October 2009, commission members were invited to tour the North Carolina History Center construction site and personally view the progress of the project. Commission members were excited to see the progress that had been made on Mattocks Hall.

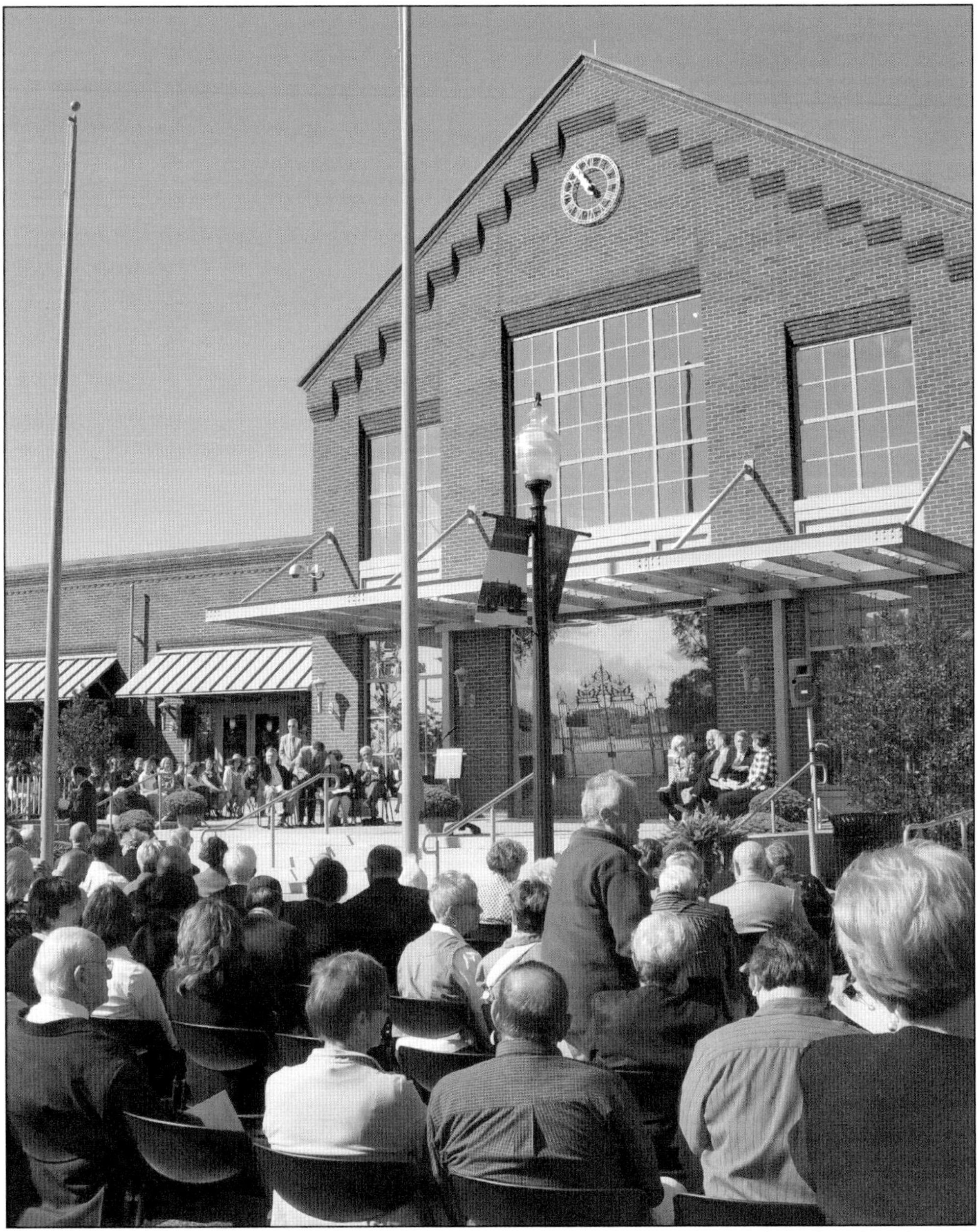

Opening celebrations for the North Carolina History Center began on Thursday, October 21, 2010, with an evening gala for Tryon Palace Commission members and supporters of the center's construction. The following day, the building opened to the general public. The weekend included a series of special events that highlighted the center's two museums (the Pepsi Family Center and the Regional History Museum), its different galleries, and its theaters. A special program held outside of Mattocks Hall featured a wide range of speakers, including Gov. Beverly Perdue. That same year, the North Carolina History Center played a key role in hosting many of New Bern's 300th anniversary events, including educational activities and a performing-arts series in the new Cullman Performance Hall and Duffy Exhibition Gallery. The history center continues to host a wide range of exhibits and events.

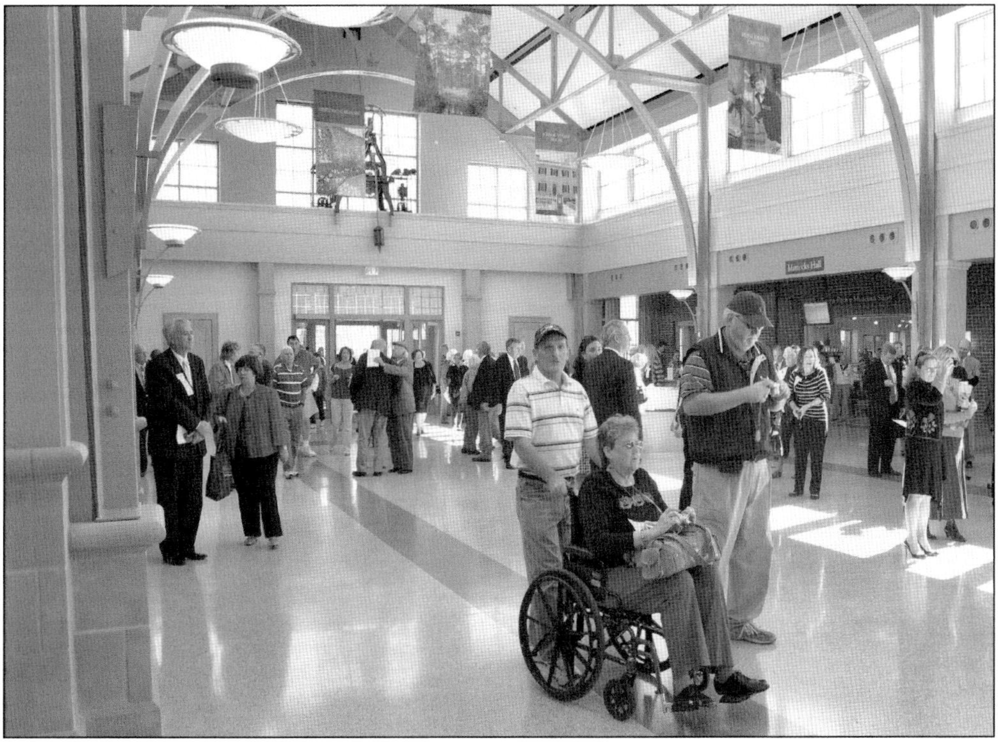

On Friday, October 22, 2010, the general public had their first opportunity to see inside the North Carolina History Center. A wide range of visitors eagerly explored the center's two museums, multiple galleries, and theaters. In honor of the special event, a Jonkonnu performance was held in Mattocks Hall in front of the Tryon Palace interactive screen. The history center is designed to engage a diverse audience with North Carolina's regional history using new technology. Today, many visitors—including school groups, families and adults—begin a trip to Tryon Palace with a visit to the North Carolina History Center to see the exhibits and orientation film.

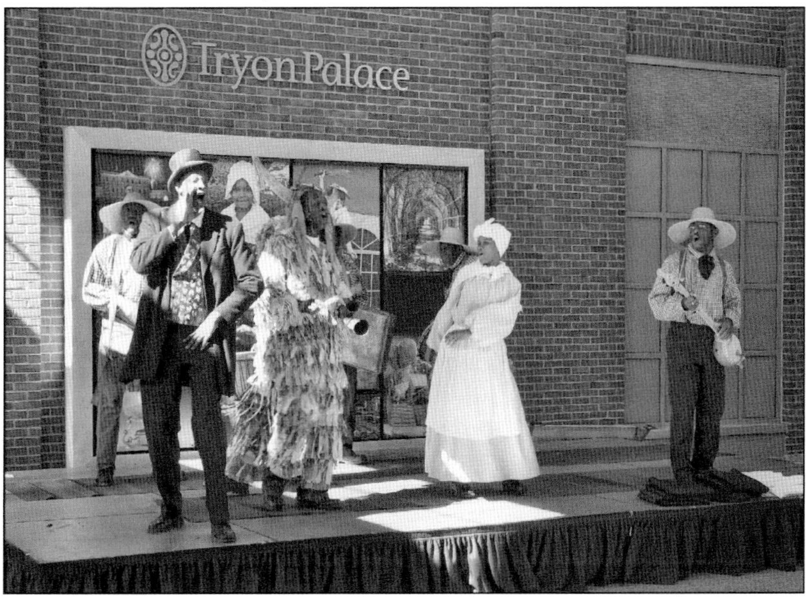

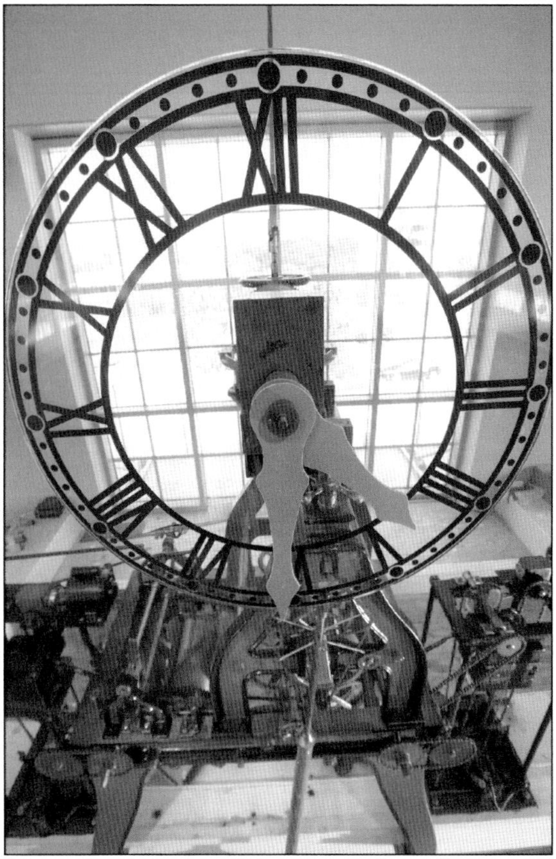

The 1910 Seth Thomas Model 17 gravity tower clock was originally located in New Bern's municipal building. The clock underwent repairs in 1974 and was removed in 2000. Fortunately, the Eastern North Carolina Chapter 191 of the National Association of Watch and Clock Collectors, Inc., began an extensive restoration project in 2007 that brought the clock back to its former glory. The finished, functioning clock moved to its current location—at the North Carolina History Center—in 2010.

The completed Etteinne Mitchell Garden overlooks the Trent River and contains plants native to North Carolina. This sustainable garden was designed with a wide variety of plants that thrive in the varying coastal climate and can survive both flooding and dry spells.

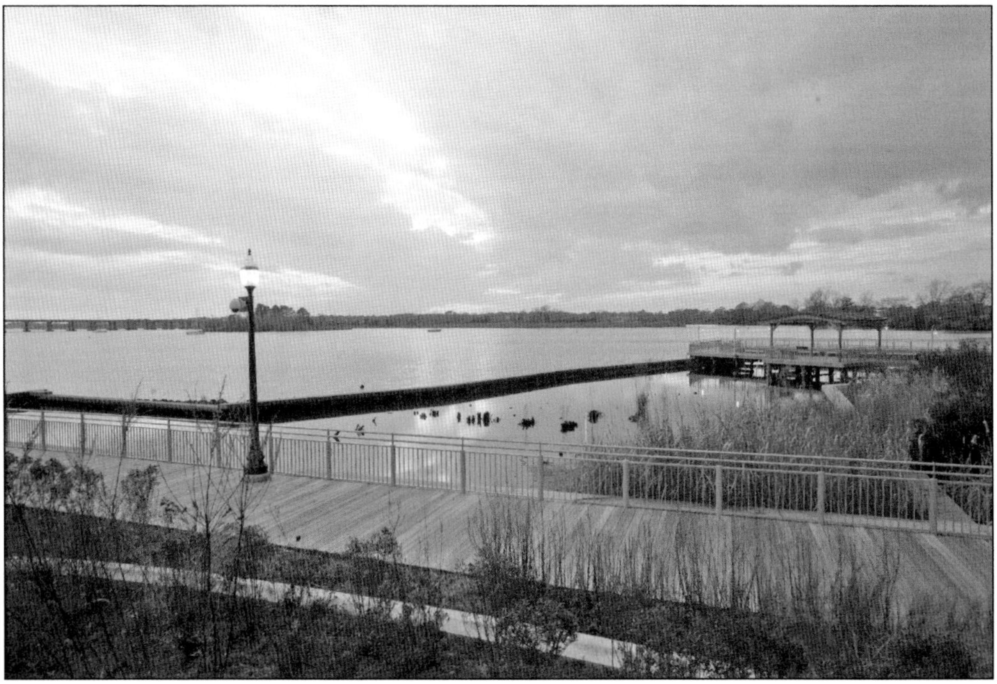

Six

Celebrations and Traditions

When the reconstructed Tryon Palace opened in 1959, it marked the beginning of a long series of new traditions and celebrations that would be introduced at the site. The people behind the palace are dedicated to preserving the past and teaching North Carolina's schoolchildren about history, and they welcome students from all over the region for programs that explore the site and its colonial past. Children have the opportunity to experience history firsthand via quilting demonstrations, militia drills, and much more. Tryon Palace is also dedicated to making the arts accessible to the general public with events such as concerts, which began in the 1960s. By 1980, the palace wanted a way to celebrate the holiday season and began hosting annual Candlelight tours. During the winter holiday seasons, the grounds are decorated using period styles and materials, and guides present special tours that highlight the holiday season. In 2000, Tryon Palace celebrated its African American heritage with the inaugural performance of Jonkonnu, which soon became part of the annual Candlelight tradition. As Tryon Palace moves forward, its directors and commission continue to develop new traditions by participating in an ever-growing number of projects intended to help educate the public about North Carolina's history.

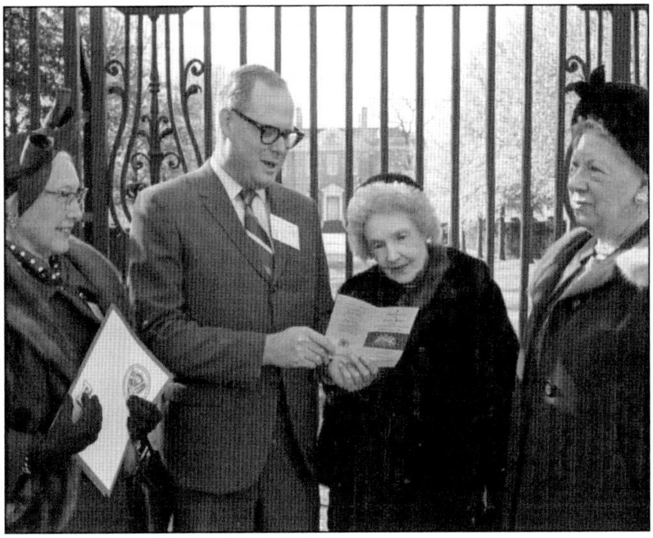

Between 1969 and 1999, Tryon Palace held an annual Decorative Arts Symposium that had support from institutions of learning (such as East Carolina University and the University of North Carolina at Greensboro) and featured contributions from furniture, ceramics, and silver experts. Pictured here at the first symposium are, from left to right, Virginia Horne, Dr. David J. Middleton (of Eastern Carolina University), May Gordon Latham Kellenberger, and Gertrude Carraway.

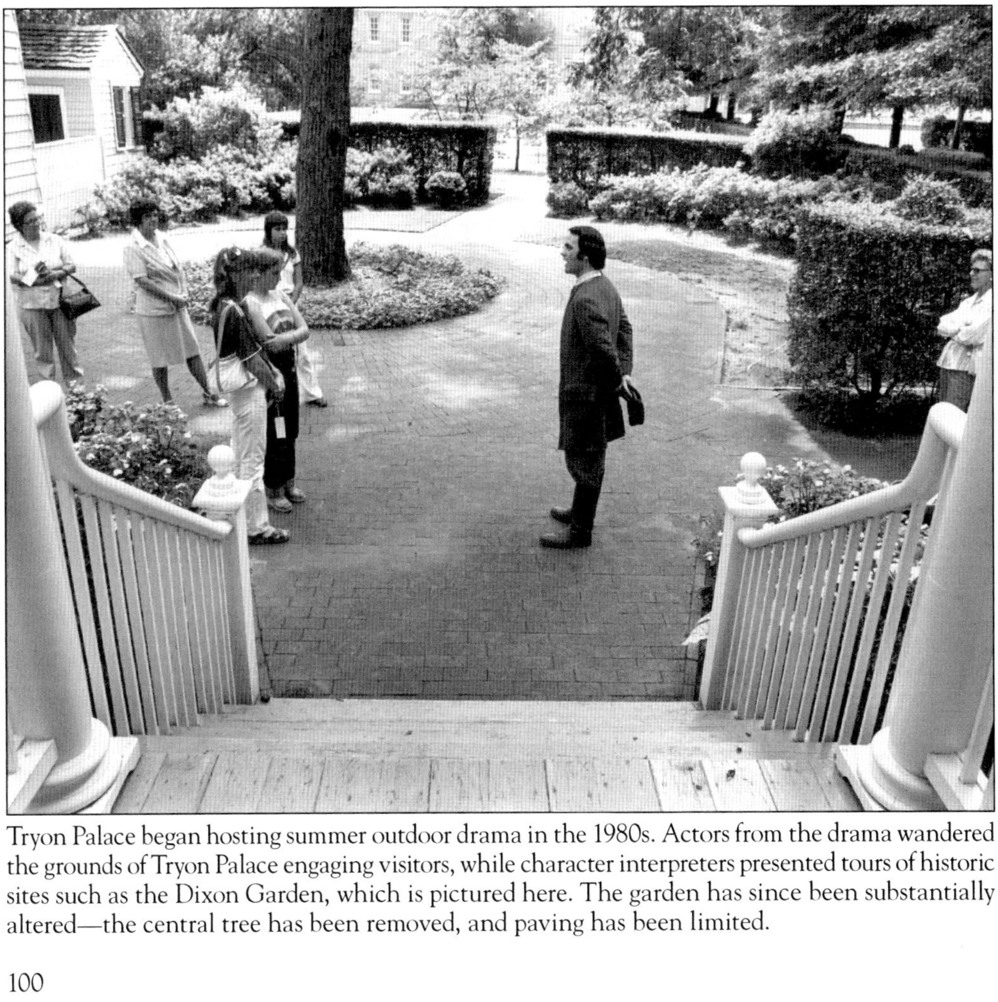

Tryon Palace began hosting summer outdoor drama in the 1980s. Actors from the drama wandered the grounds of Tryon Palace engaging visitors, while character interpreters presented tours of historic sites such as the Dixon Garden, which is pictured here. The garden has since been substantially altered—the central tree has been removed, and paving has been limited.

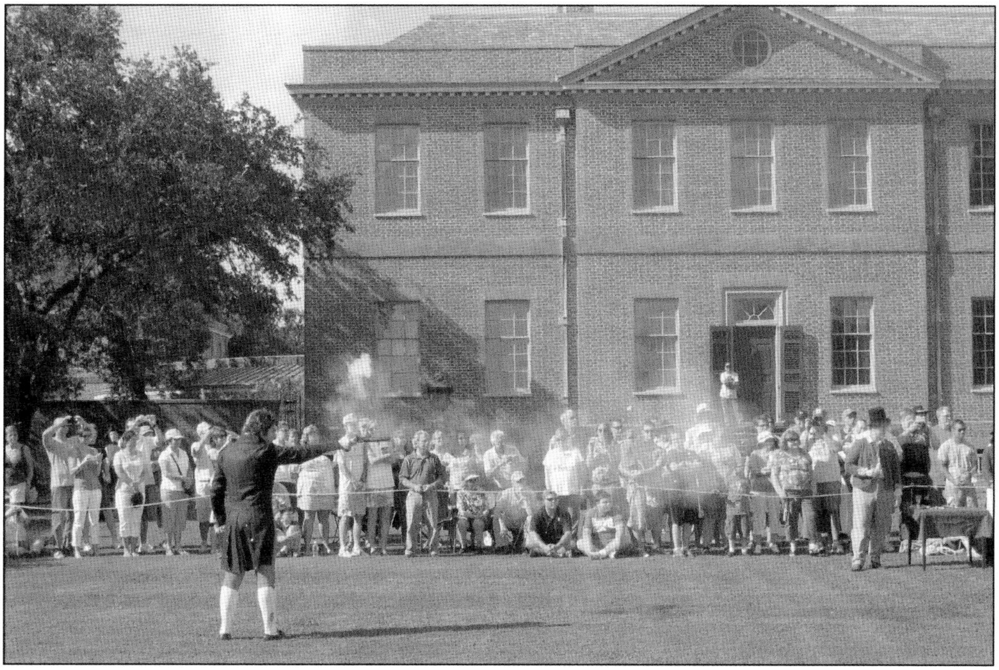

The popularity of the outdoor dramas led to the annual Stanly-Spaight Duel. This dramatic reenactment is usually held during Labor Day weekend and tells the true story of the duel between John Stanly Jr. and Richard Dobbs Spaight, which occurred on September 5, 1802. Stanly and Spaight were bitter political rivals from prominent New Bern families. Stanly (a lawyer) and Spaight (who served as governor of North Carolina) fired four rounds between them. Spaight was mortally wounded, and Stanly fled the city; he did not return until after he received a pardon in 1803, arranged by longtime friend Judge William Gaston.

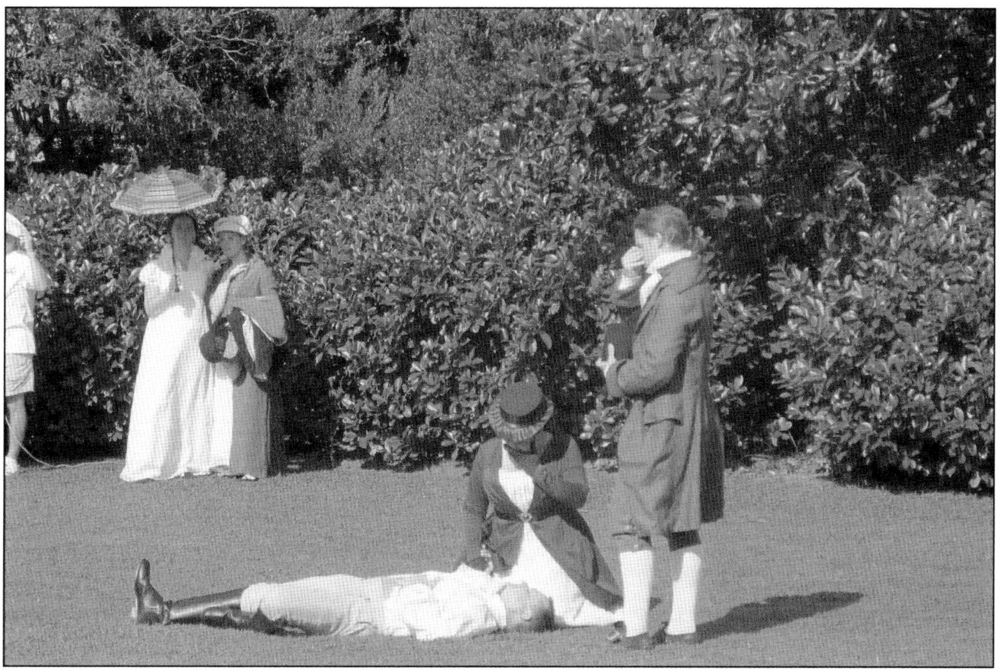

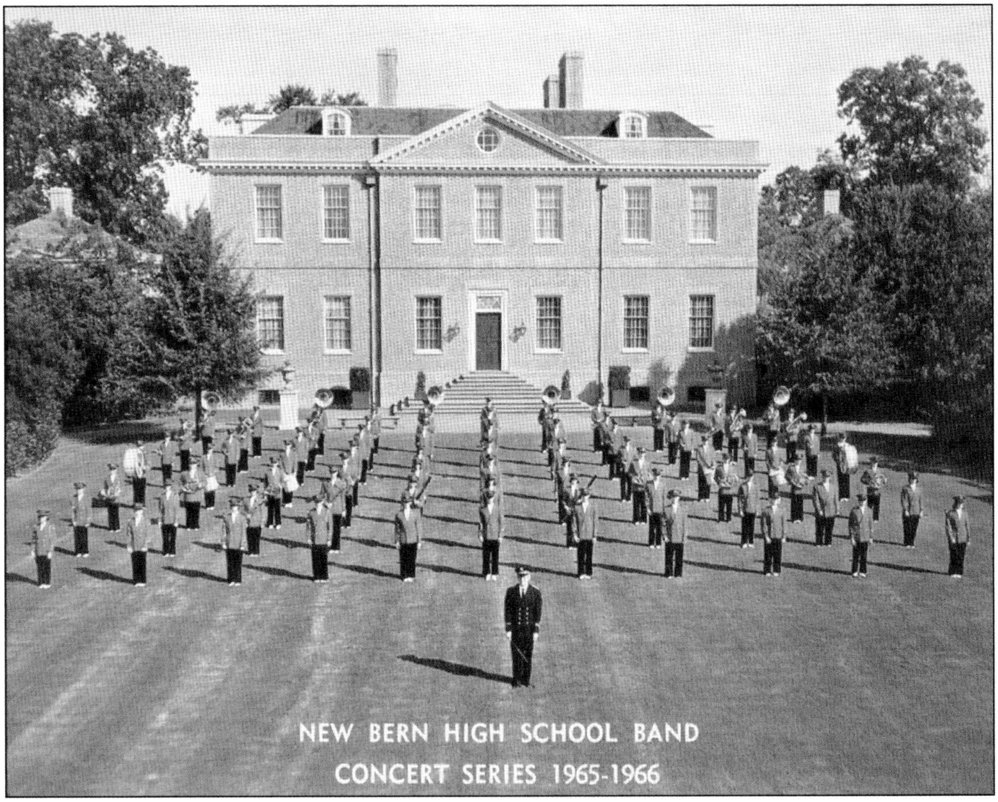

From the conception of the restored Tryon Palace, its administrators have encouraged an appreciation of the arts engrained by Maude Moore Latham, a strong supporter of the humanities and a champion of the concert series and performances held on-site for many years. This postcard shows the New Bern High School Band, which performed a series of concerts on the south lawn at Tryon Palace in 1965 and 1966.

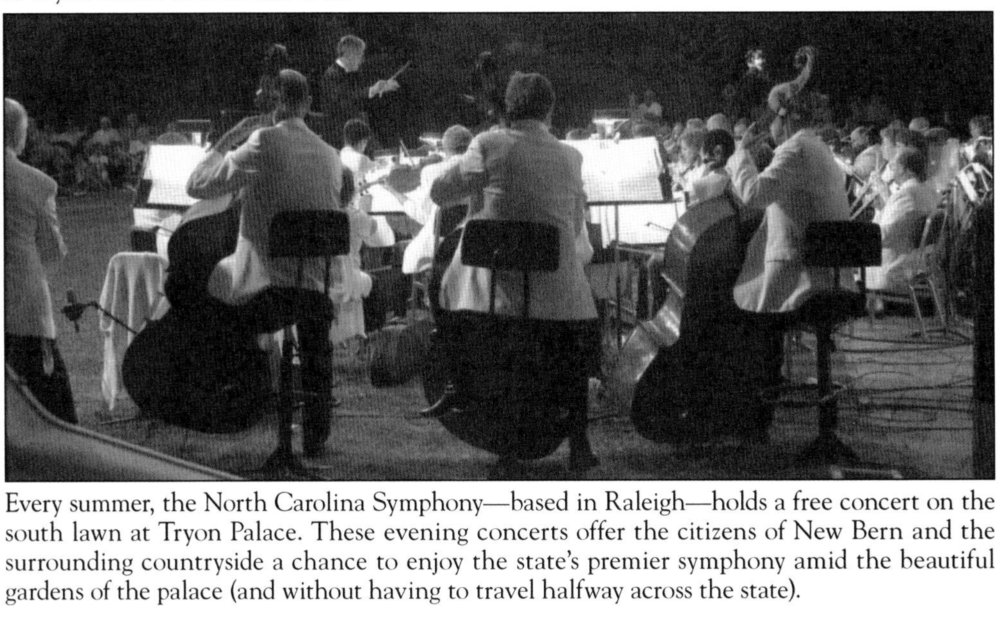

Every summer, the North Carolina Symphony—based in Raleigh—holds a free concert on the south lawn at Tryon Palace. These evening concerts offer the citizens of New Bern and the surrounding countryside a chance to enjoy the state's premier symphony amid the beautiful gardens of the palace (and without having to travel halfway across the state).

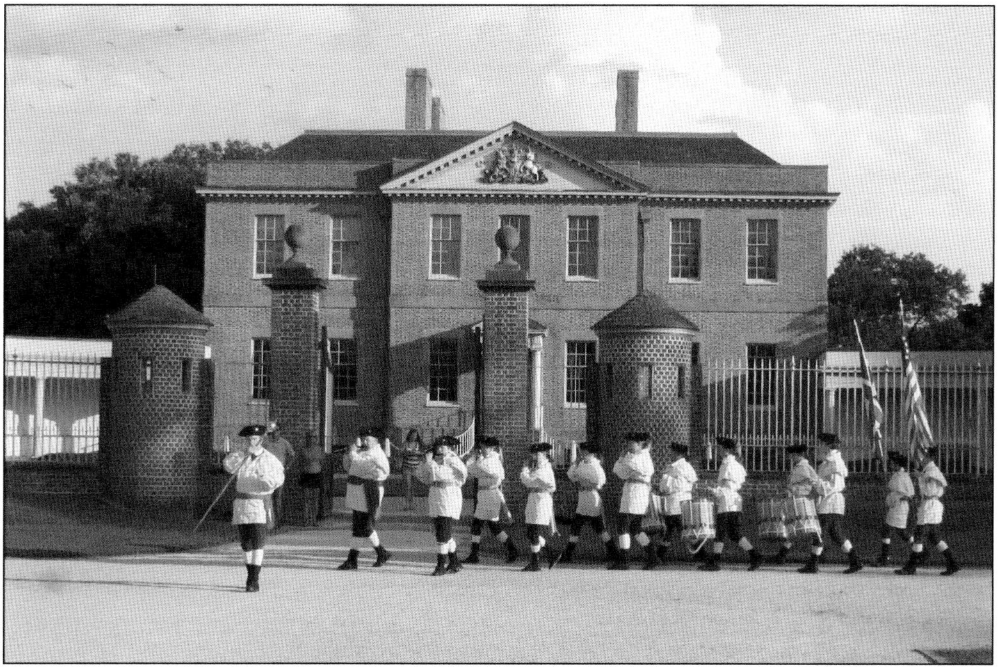

Musicians were an important part of the military in the 18th century. Fifes and drums played from sunrise to sunset and served as a primary mode of communication from commanders to troops during battles. The high-pitched sound of the fife made it the perfect instrument to be paired with the drum, as it could be heard over the noise of combat. Music also served more mundane functions in daily life at camp by signaling meals, drills, and inspections. Tryon Palace established a Fife and Drum Corps early in its history; this organization is primarily composed of volunteers who play at many of Tryon Palace's special events, including Fourth of July celebrations.

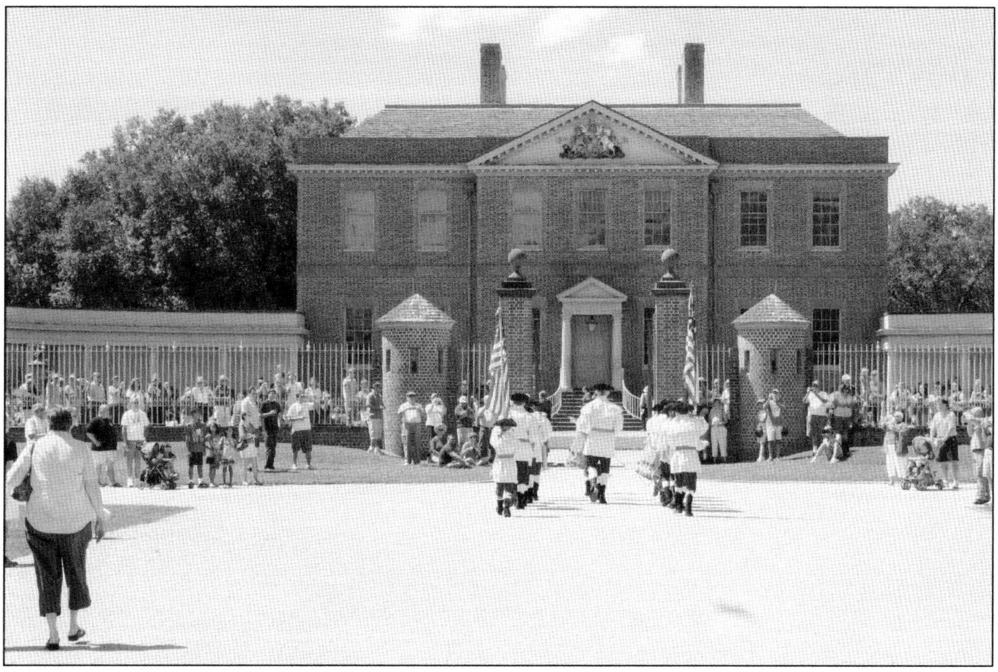

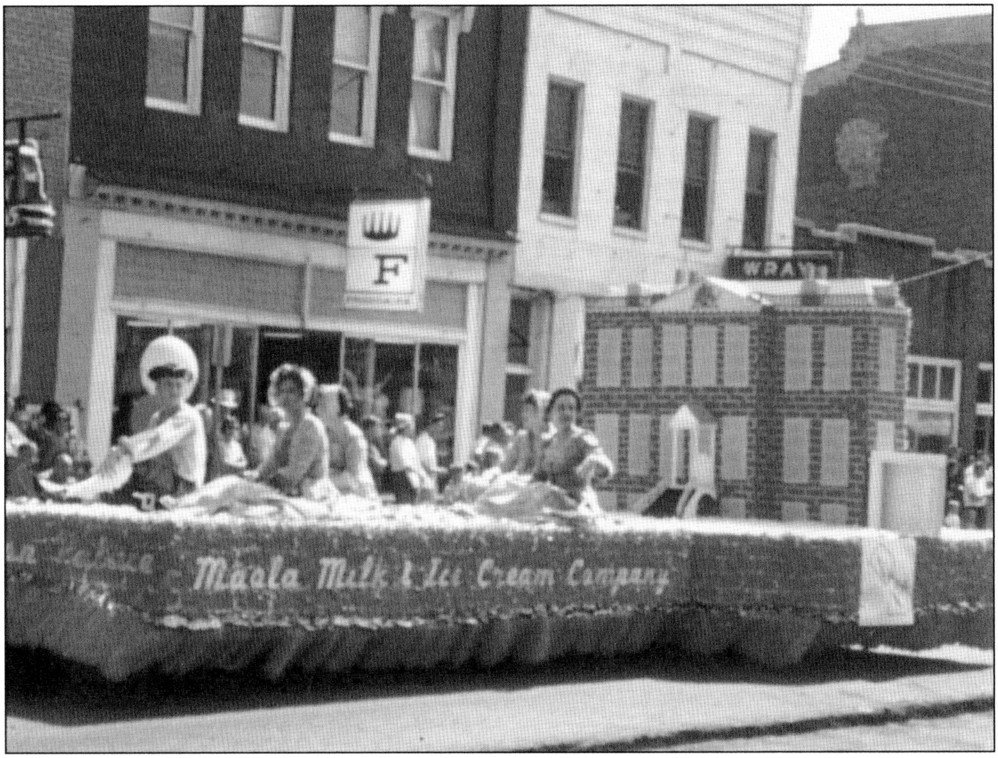

In 1960, New Bern celebrated the 250th anniversary of the town's founding. As part of the special historic events, the town held a parade that June. The parade, which traveled along Broad and Craven Streets, included two floats related to Tryon Palace—the Tryon Palace float, which was sponsored by local dairy Maola Milk and Ice Cream Company, and the Governor Tryon float. The Tryon Palace float featured the facade of the main building and several costumed guides, while the Governor Tryon float featured costumed interpreters and showcased traditional 18th-century occupations.

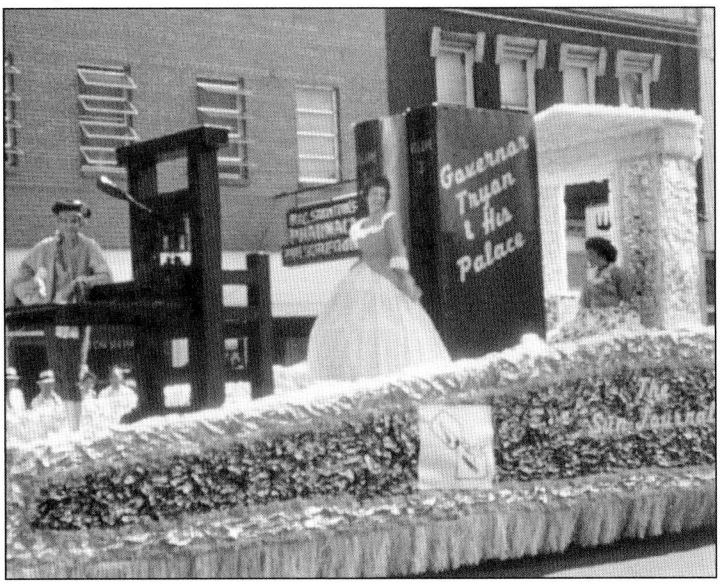

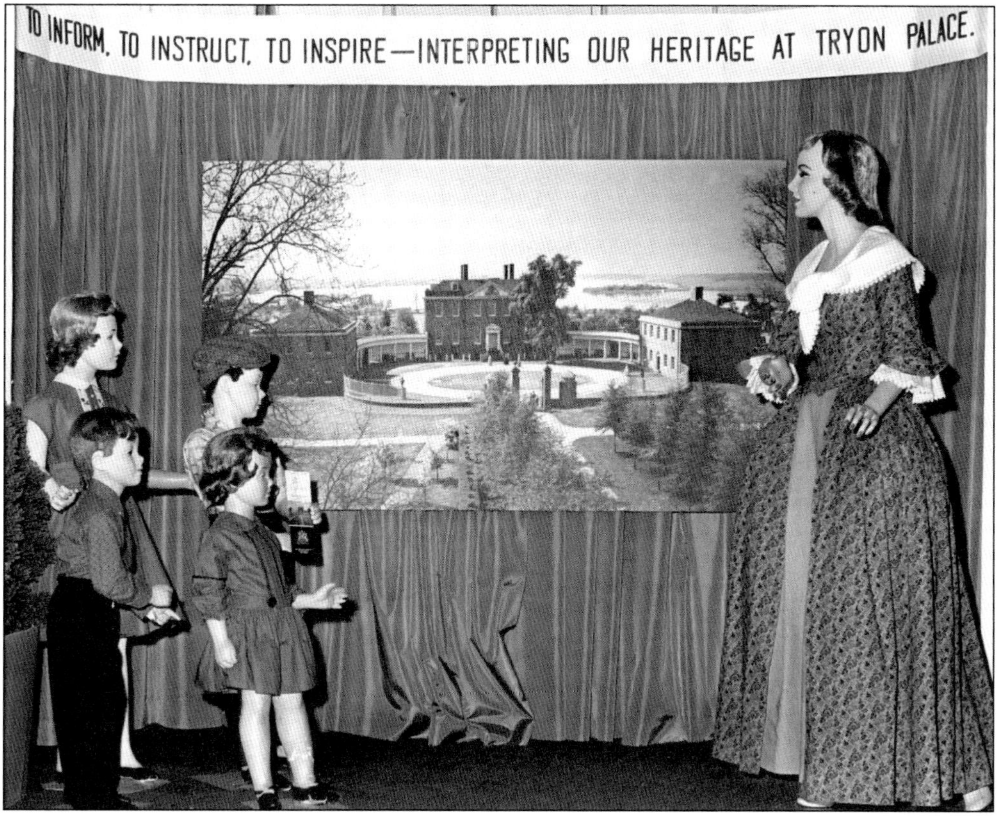

In 1963, Tryon Palace set up an exhibit at the North Carolina State Fair to promote the site and its available tours. The exhibit (pictured above) features an adult mannequin dressed in period costume (just as a guide would be) and four child-sized mannequins dressed in contemporary clothing and "listening" to a tour of the palace, which is pictured in the background. Across the top of the exhibit is Tryon Palace's slogan: "To inform, to instruct, to inspire—interpreting our heritage at Tryon Palace." The palace eventually developed an iconic quality for many North Carolina schoolchildren. Joey Bryant completed the diorama pictured below for Mrs. Burnas' eighth-grade class at Creedmoor School in Granville County.

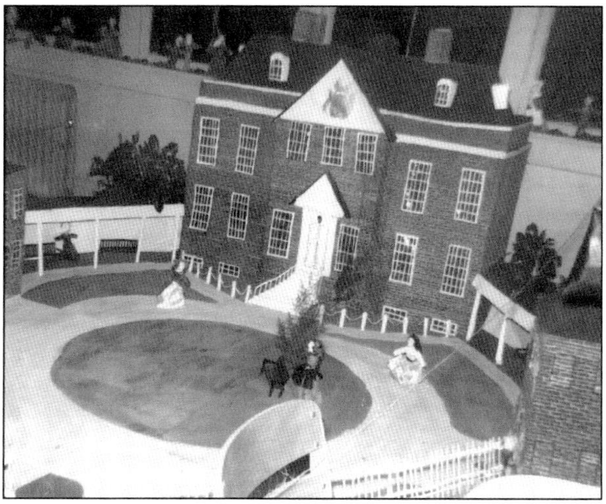

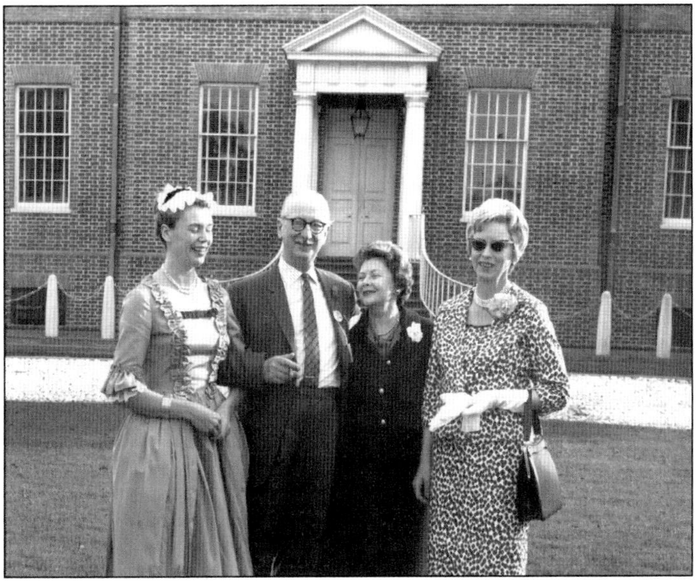

Sir George and Lady Bellew visited Tryon Palace in the early 1960s, which gave them—members of the British aristocracy—an opportunity to tour a historic building that served as home to state and royal governors alike. Their hostess and guide during their visit was Mrs. Ray Ipock. Pictured here are, from left to right, Ipock, Sir George Bellew, Mrs. James M. Tyler, and Lady Bellew.

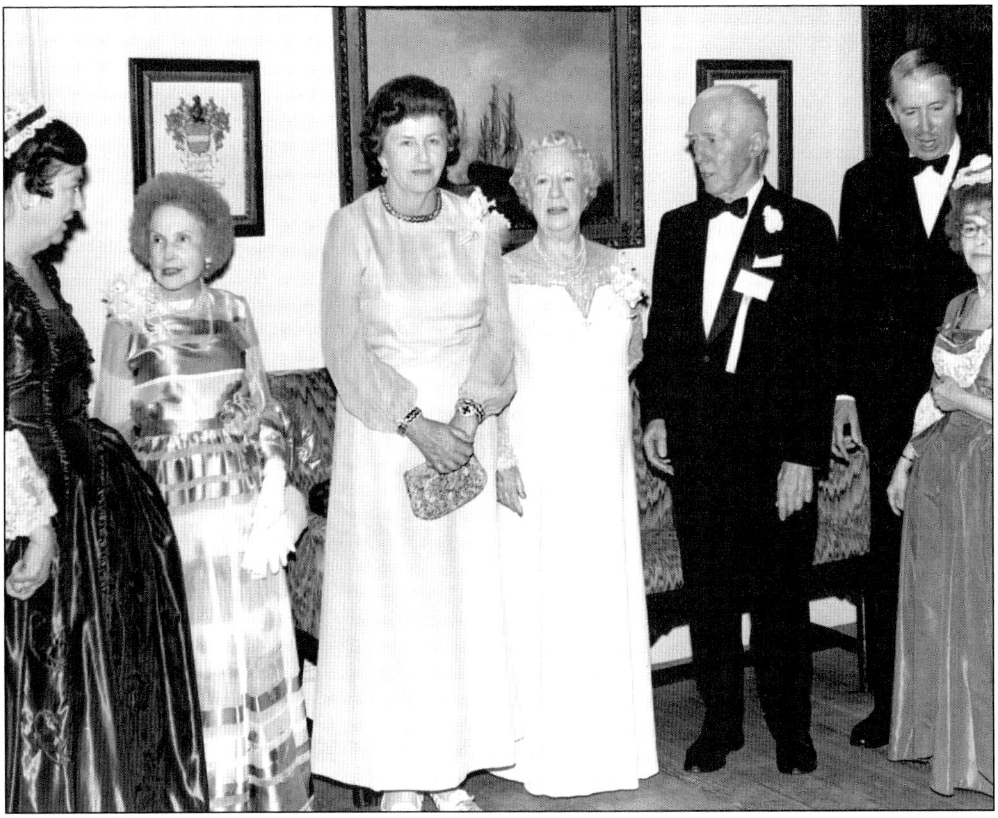

Lord and Lady Tryon—George and Etheldreda Josephine Burrell—visited Tryon Palace on April 4 and 5 in 1970. The Tryon Palace Commission hosted them and gave them a private tour of the palace. Lord and Lady Tryon supported the reconstruction and provided family portraits of William Tryon's father for the palace. They had previously met the Kellenbergers and Horne sisters while the four were in England looking for period pieces to furnish the palace.

Edward Vason Jones, the lead architect for the restoration of the John Wright Stanly House, became close to First Lady Patricia "Pat" Nixon during his work at the White House. He was instrumental in having her appear at the reopening of the Stanly House on April 19, 1972. Pictured are, from left to right, unidentified, May Gordon Latham Kellenberger, First Lady Patricia Nixon, and John A. Kellenberger.

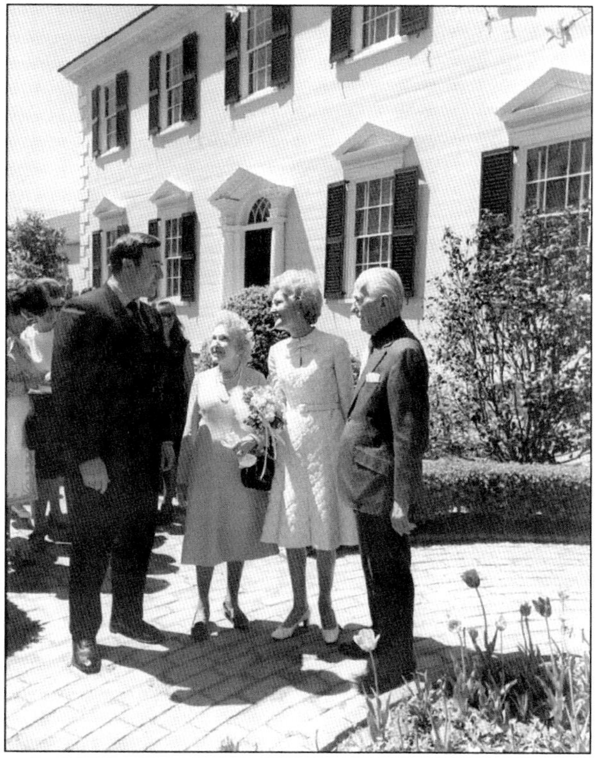

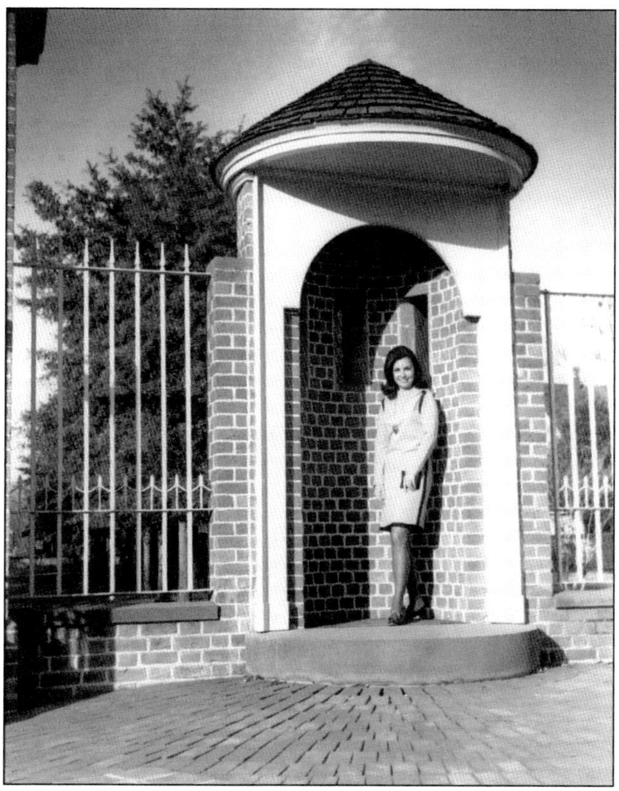

Several television news personalities have visited Tryon Palace. Among them is Kay Currie, who was the morning and midday weathercaster for WITN-NBC from 1975 to 1984. In this photograph, she is standing in one of the guard posts at the gate in front of the palace.

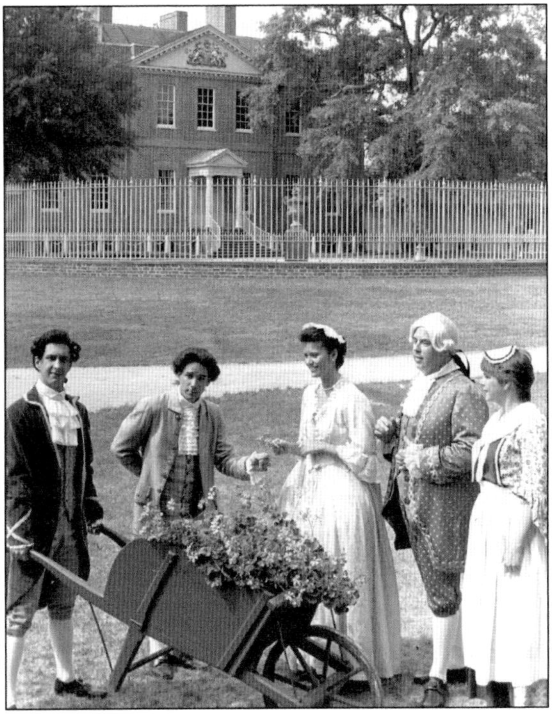

Tryon Palace used a wide range of costumed interpreters to tell the many stories of the palace. The earliest interpreters portrayed New Bern's elites, who were members of the North Carolina General Assembly or who would have been invited to the palace on special occasions. By focusing on these historic figures, the palace was able to tell the story of two royal governors and the state governors who worked and lived in Tryon Palace. A changing audience and a new attempt to make history more inclusive have led to other members of the household being interpreted, including the household staff and local merchants and farmers who supplied the palace. This ever-widening cast of characters has allowed Tryon Palace to tell a more complete story of colonial North Carolina.

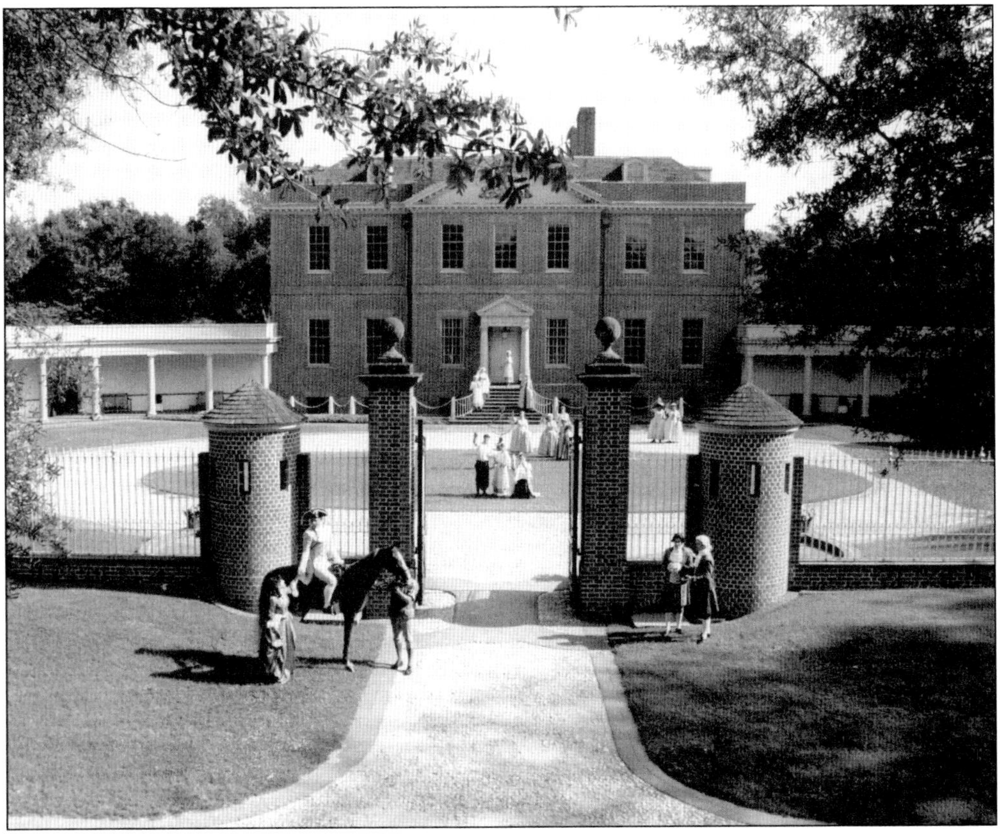

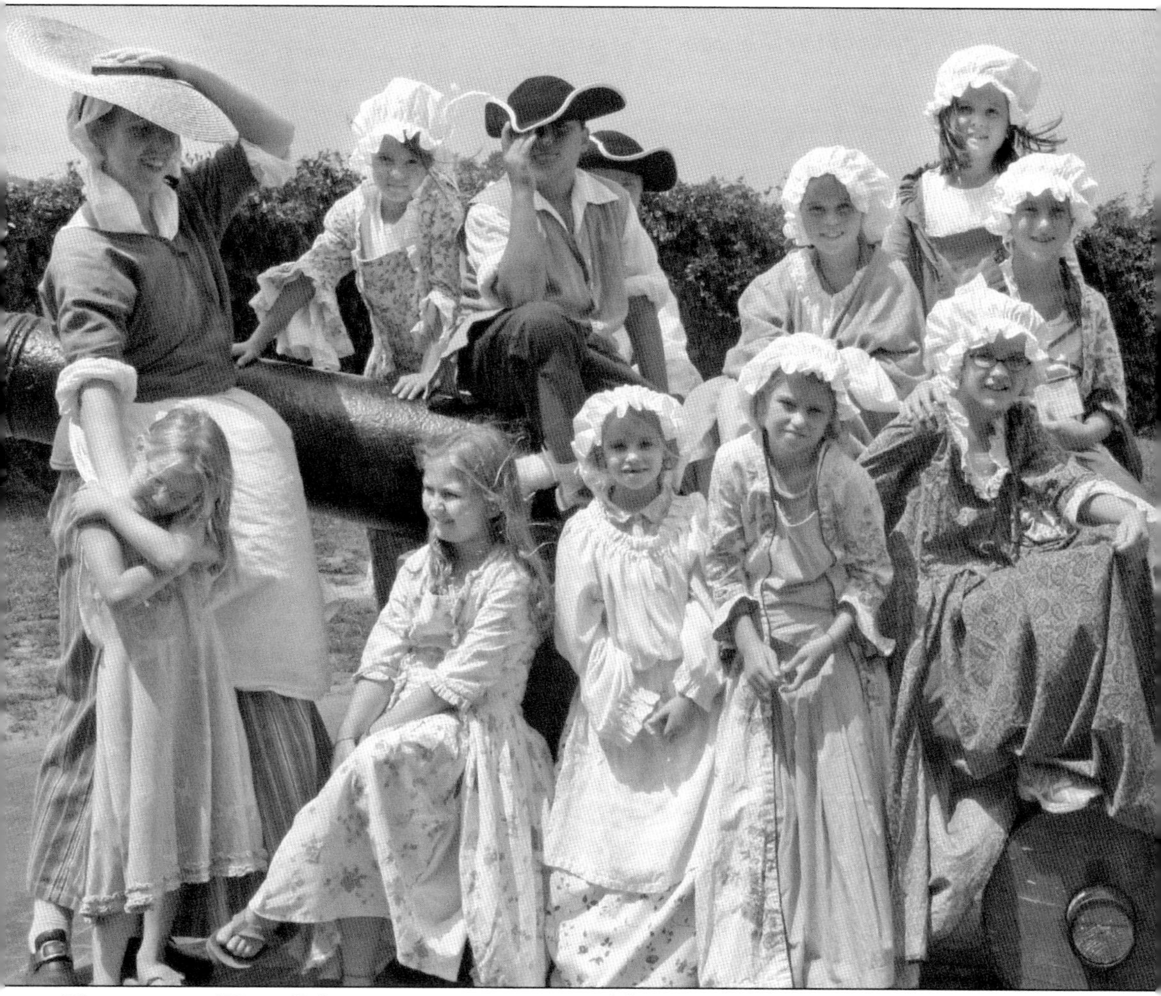

The mission of Tryon Palace is to engage current and future generations in the history of North Carolina—from early settlement and development of statehood through the mid-20th century—by collecting, interpreting, and preserving objects, buildings, landscapes, and events that enrich understanding of the creation of the state and the nation. In order to achieve this mission, Tryon Palace actively engages children of all ages in a wide range of programs. The palace's summer camps are among the most popular programs. The camp programs allow children to learn about and develop a deep appreciation for history through the use of costumes, games, and hands-on activities. Campers are fully immersed in the experience, and one might imagine a few of them becoming interpreters in the future.

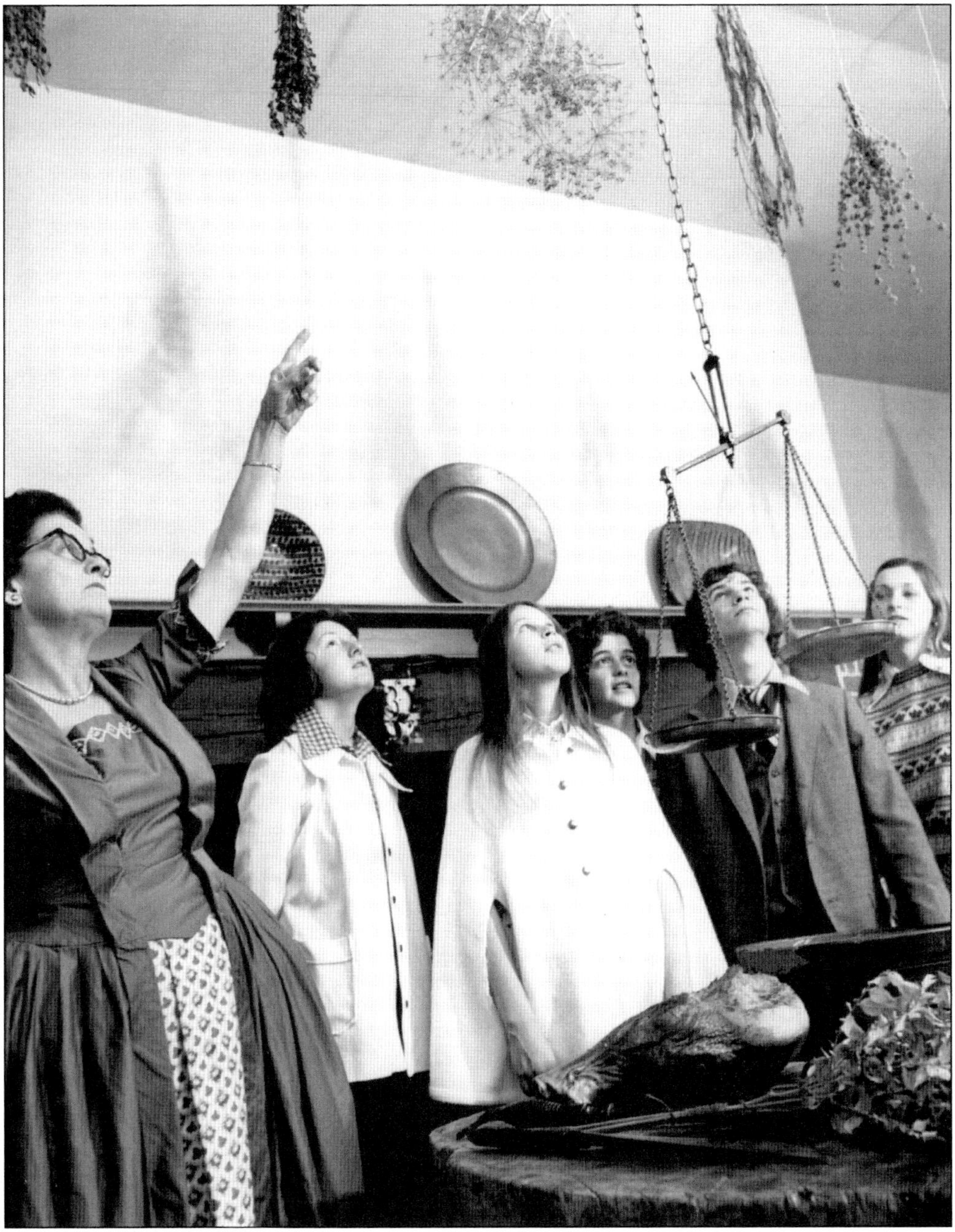

School tours in the 1970s included a visit to the kitchen office, where students learned about the lives of the staff who kept the palace functioning. Students touring the kitchen area were given the opportunity to learn about the different tools used for cooking on an open hearth and the wide range of herbs grown in the kitchen garden that were essential to the preparation of meals. In this photograph, a palace hostess points out drying herbs to a school group. While the kitchen garden provided valuable produce nearly year-round, some produce had to be preserved to have stores for the winter months. The best way to preserve herbs during the 18th century was by drying them. The beams in the kitchen office provide and ideal location to dry summer herbs for the winter.

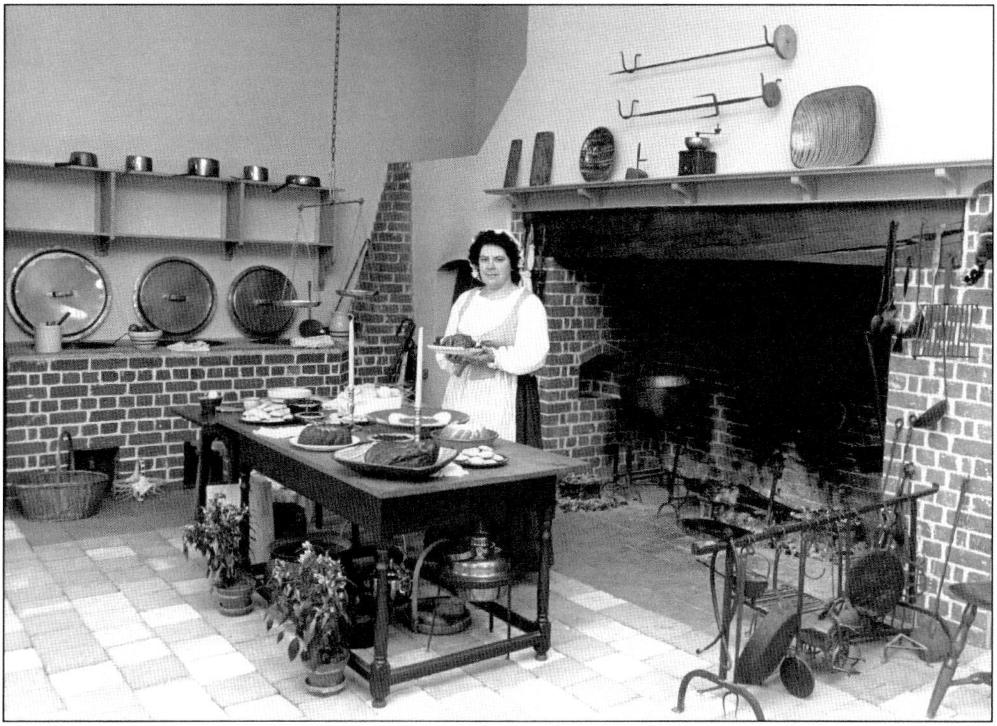

Cooking demonstrations are held daily in the kitchen office, presenting visitors with a taste of life in the 18th century. This 1970s photograph shows the wide range of foods prepared by the cooks. This food was not all cooked on the same day; instead, interpreters in the kitchen office focused on limited selections allowing them to interact with visitors while preparing meals.

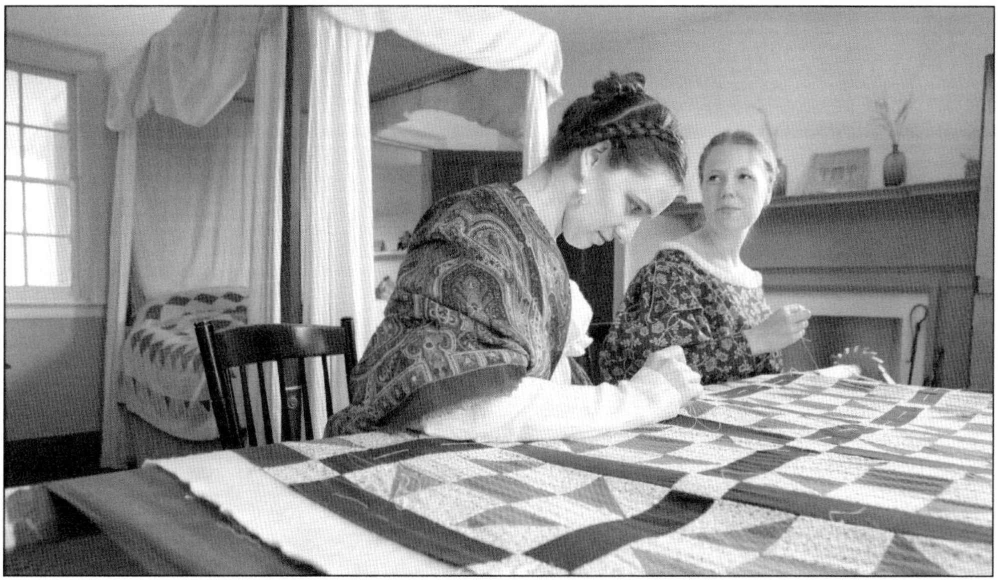

The dedicated staff and volunteers at Tryon Palace provide visitors with an opportunity to try a wide range of activities that would have been common in the 18th and 19th centuries. Quilting is a very popular activity, and volunteers demonstrate basic quilting skills and provide visitors with the tools to try quilting for themselves.

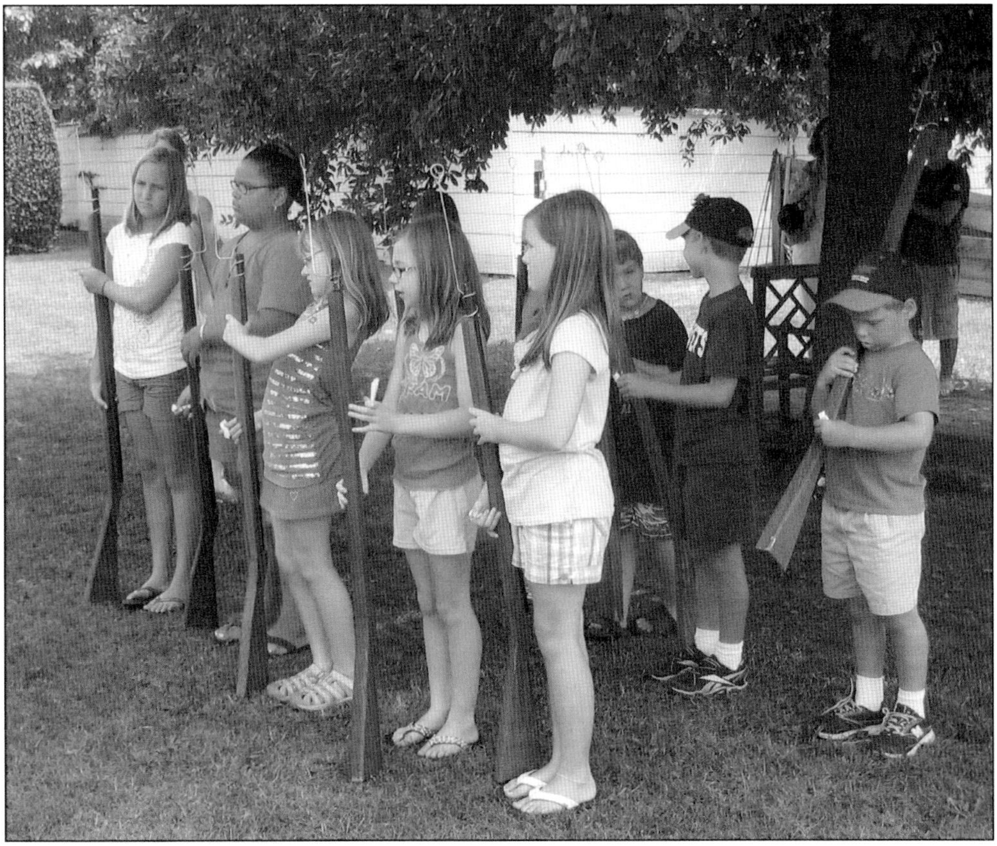

Tryon Palace hosts more than just summer camps and school groups. With a focus on education, the palace has expanded its educational services by offering tours and programs to outside groups who wish to tour the site and providing special daylong events for home-schooled and family groups. These events allow these visitors to enjoy Tryon Palace and participate in activities that the site has to offer. Militia drills, which teach children about military life during the colonial and revolutionary eras, are popular and informative. The drills provide a small peek at what life was like for New Bernians in the 1700s.

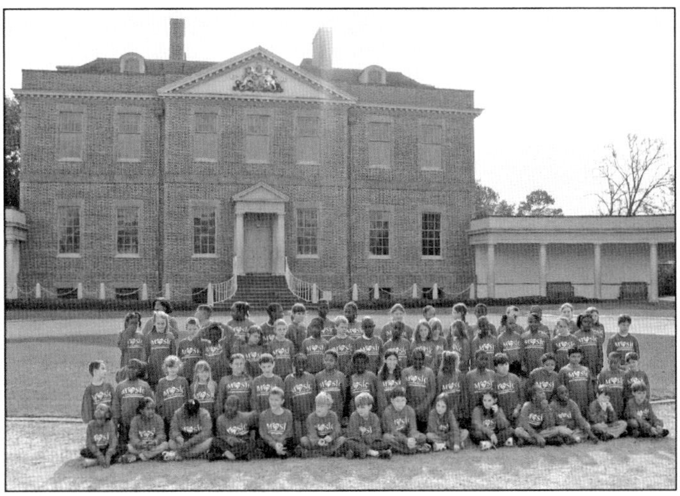

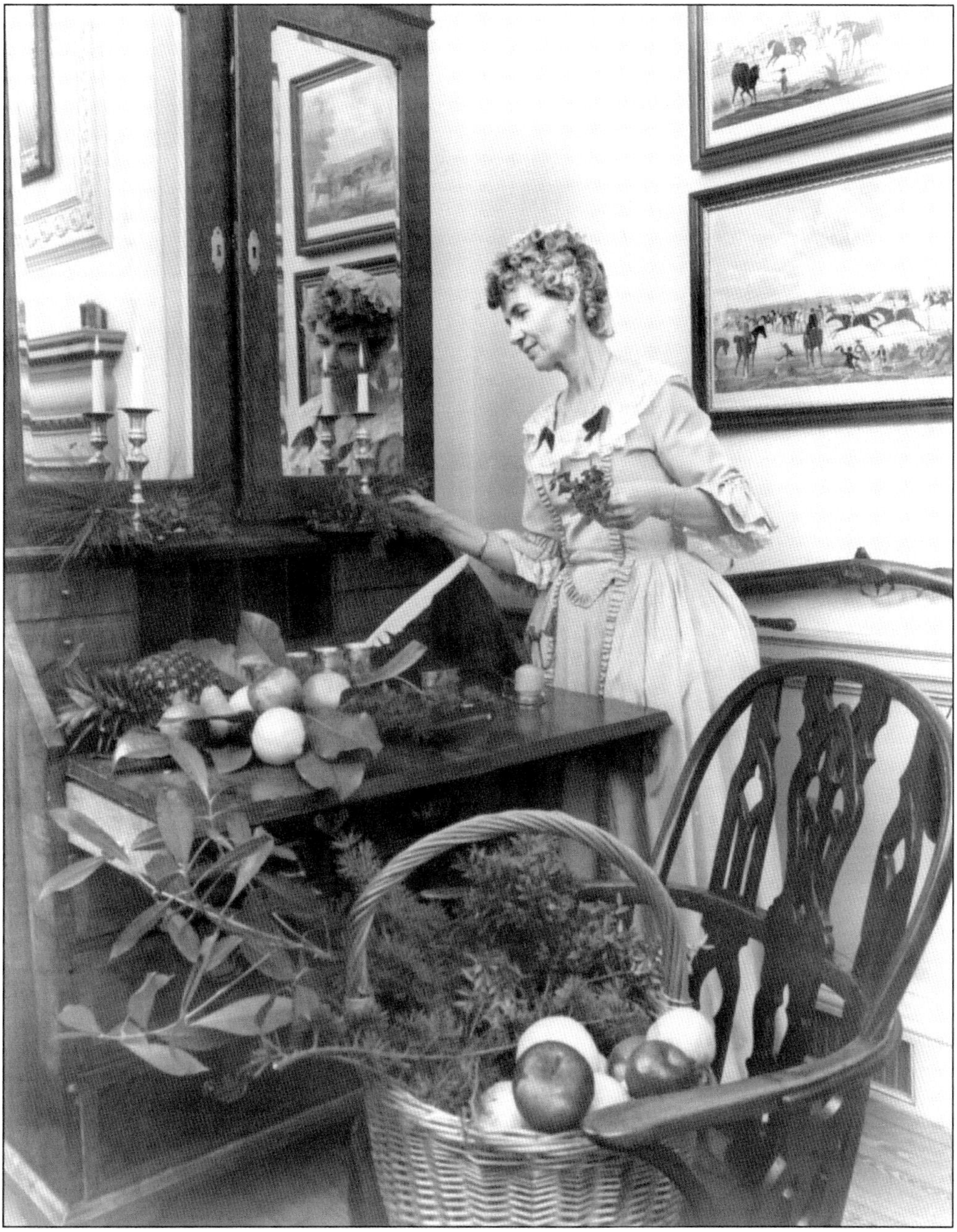

During the first holiday seasons after the restoration, Tryon Palace included a few small decorations, but it was not until 1979 that the palace presented a series of decorations or festivities. Though their historical accuracy may be questionable, the styles espoused by Colonial Williamsburg had a profound impact on the holiday decor of colonial American sites. In 1979, volunteers and staff worked to incorporate period decorations (in the Colonial Williamsburg style) into the palace and grounds. Palace hostesses learn about Christmas traditions and the history of decorating and incorporate that information into their tours of the palace. This photograph shows Tryon Palace hostess Bettye Paramore arranging decorative fruit and greenery for the opening of the holiday season on December 9, 1979.

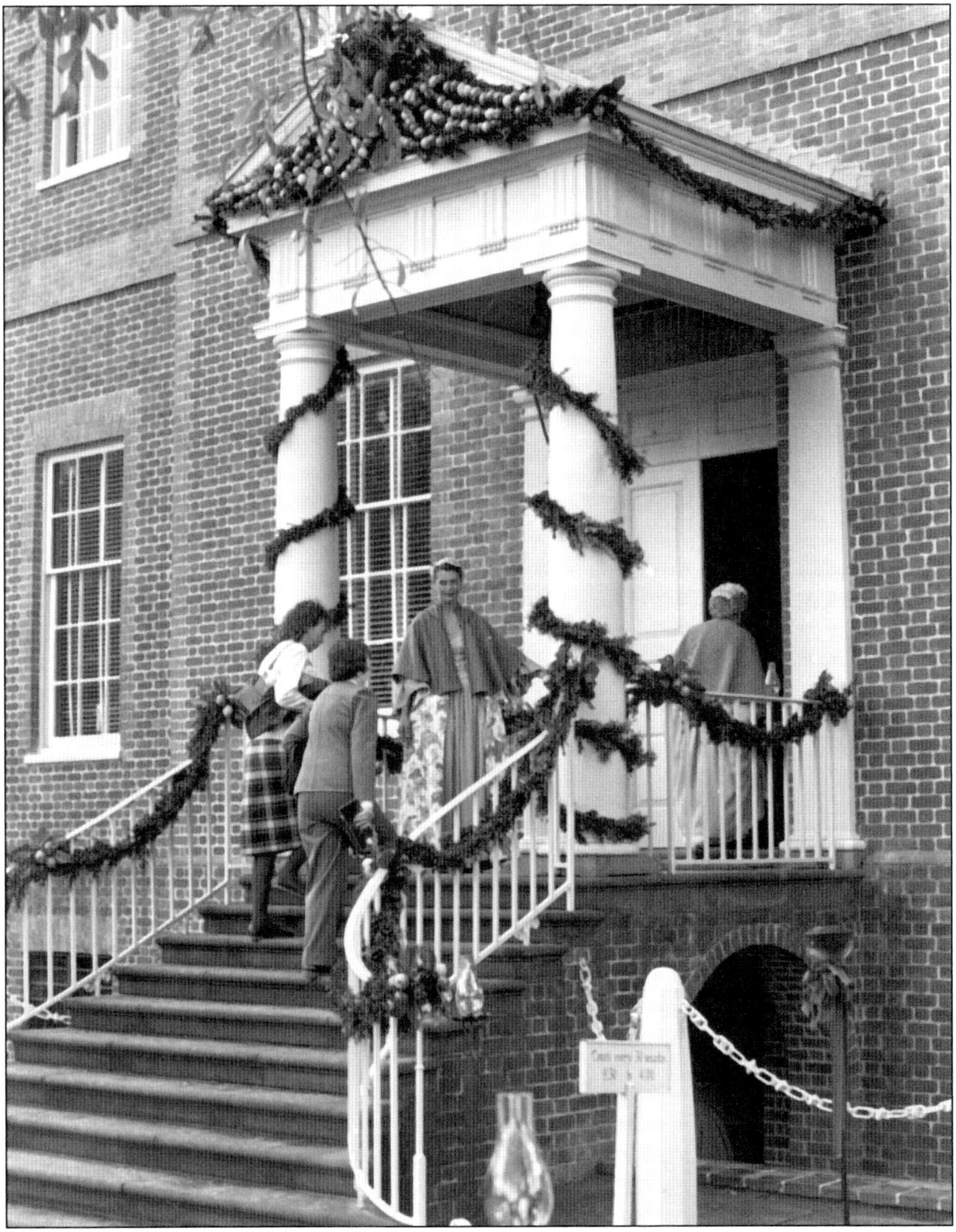

Tryon Palace decorated for the Christmas holidays for the first time in 1979. The earliest decorations relied heavily on evergreens and fruit by incorporating them into garlands, wreaths, and other floral displays. This photograph shows the holiday decorations on the front entrance to the palace. The banisters and support pillars are wrapped in evergreen boughs, while the pediment is decorated with apples and pineapples. The use of fruit became very popular for holiday ornamentation; however, 18th-century New Bernians would have preferred to eat the fruit rather than use it for decorations. Holiday tours at the palace focused on 18th-century holiday traditions, the prevalence of family parties during the holiday season, and Twelfth Night. In 1980, these events eventually became part of the palace's annual holiday celebration known as Candlelight.

By the 1980s, the holiday season at the palace had become extremely popular thanks to the extensive decorations and entertainment for the visitors. The main stairs had minimal decoration but featured a costumed musician on the first floor. For the holiday season, the palace revived the harpsichord, which was a popular instrument in the 18th century.

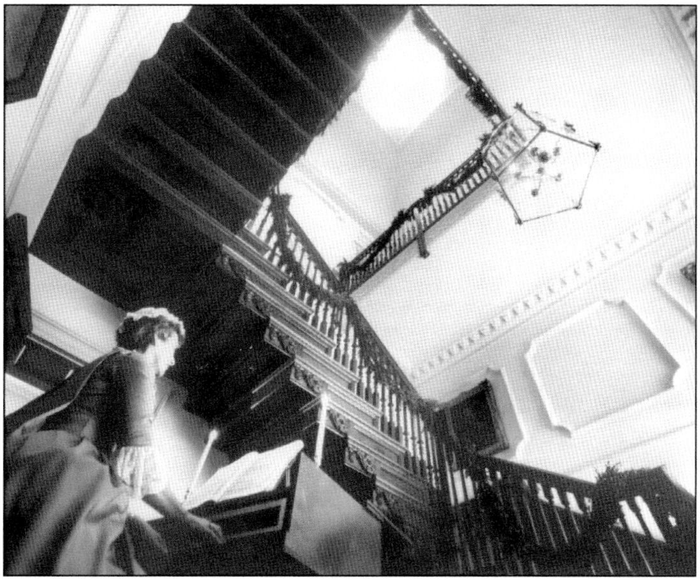

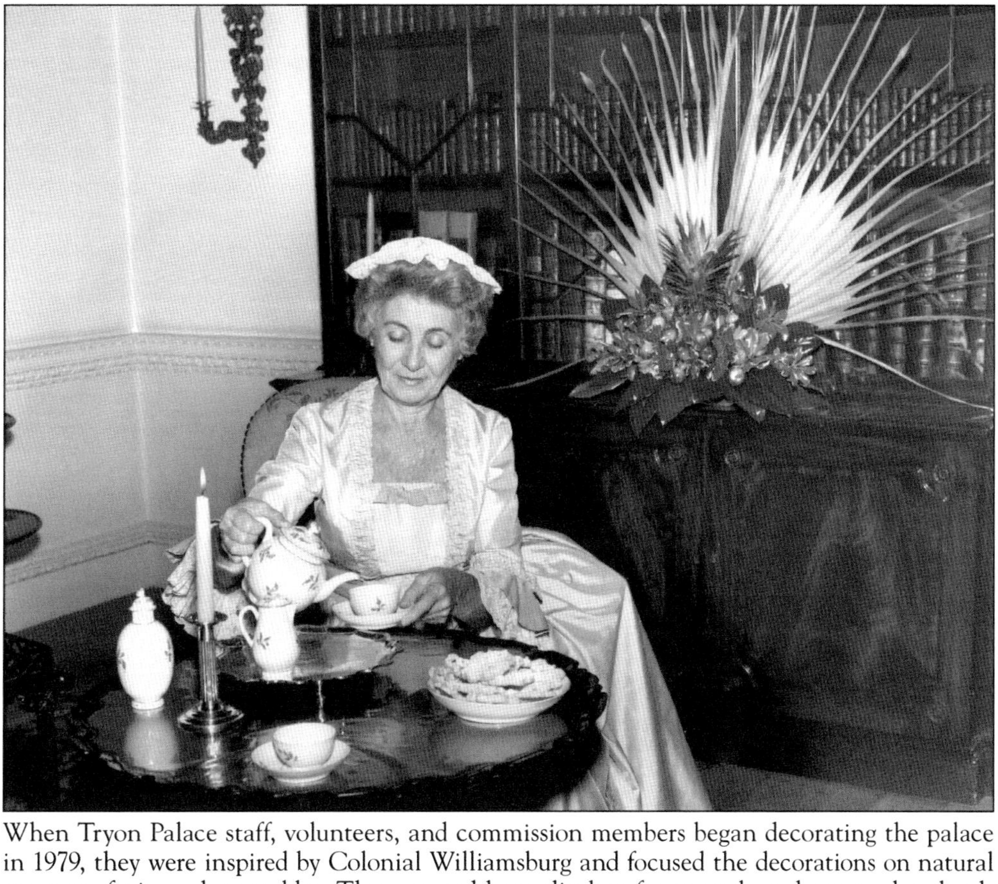

When Tryon Palace staff, volunteers, and commission members began decorating the palace in 1979, they were inspired by Colonial Williamsburg and focused the decorations on natural greenery, fruit, and vegetables. They created large displays for mantels and wrapped garlands around banisters. In this 1979 photograph, costumed hostess Jane Constantine sits with a tea set to greet visitors during the first 18th-century Christmas at Tryon Palace.

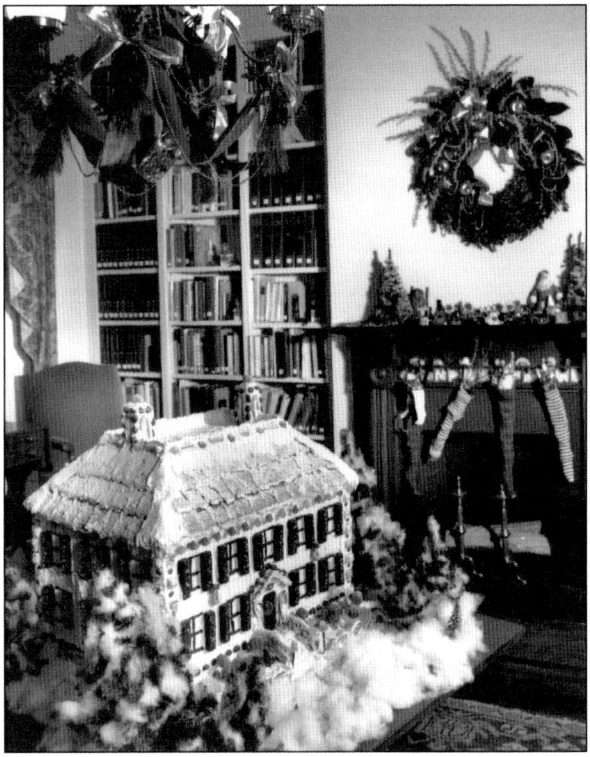

The Commission House, which is normally used for meetings and office space, is opened during the holiday season for Tryon Palace's annual Candlelight tours. The theme for the house changes annually with each holiday celebration, with topics that have ranged from the Victorian period through World War II. In this c. 1982 photograph, the decorators decided to have a little fun by using a gingerbread version of the John Wright Stanly House as a decoration in the Commission House.

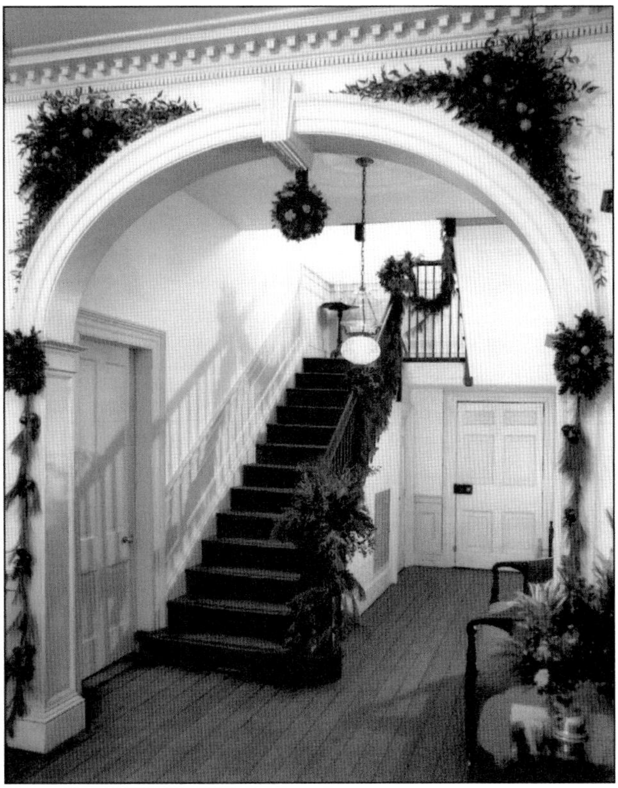

The Dixon House, which dates to the Federal period, is traditionally decorated with simple evergreen boughs—no trees or ornaments—for the holiday season in keeping with 18th-century practices. This photograph shows the transverse arch and staircase in the Dixon House decorated for Candlelight in the early 1980s.

In the weeks leading up to the holiday season, the gardening and maintenance staff works closely with volunteers to ensure that all the decorations are prepared and installed on the palace grounds. This 1985 photograph shows Tryon Palace horticulturalist W. Herb Rea arranging Candlelight greenery above the entryway to the stable office.

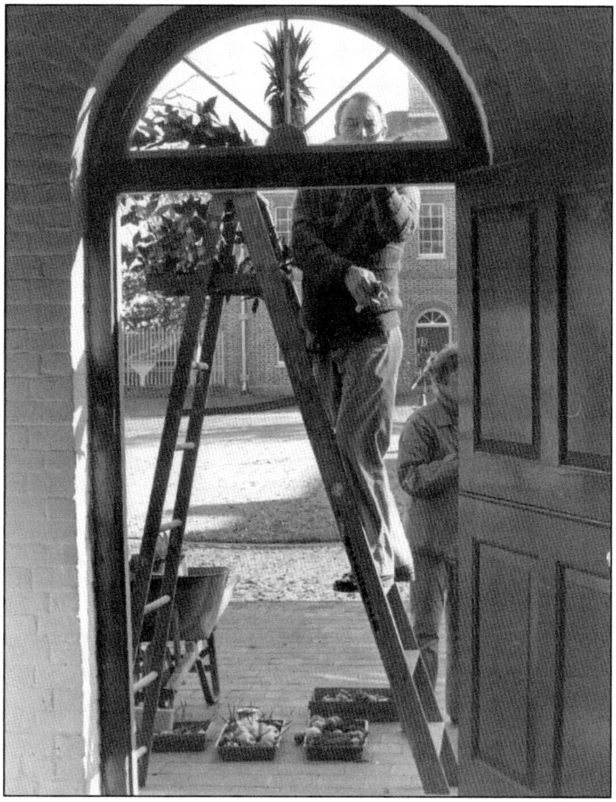

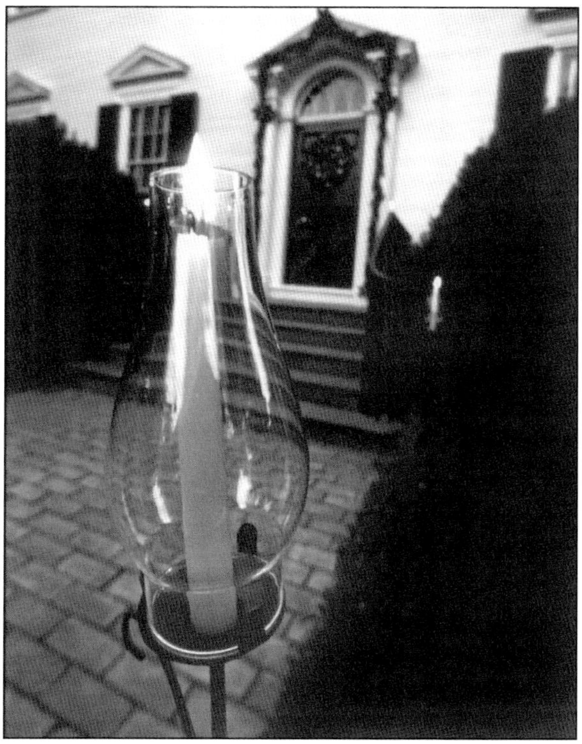

The holiday Candlelight tour is so named because of the candles that light the palace walkways throughout the event. Over 100 candle stands are placed throughout the grounds by the gardening and maintenance staff. The photograph shows just one of the many candles that light the evening tours.

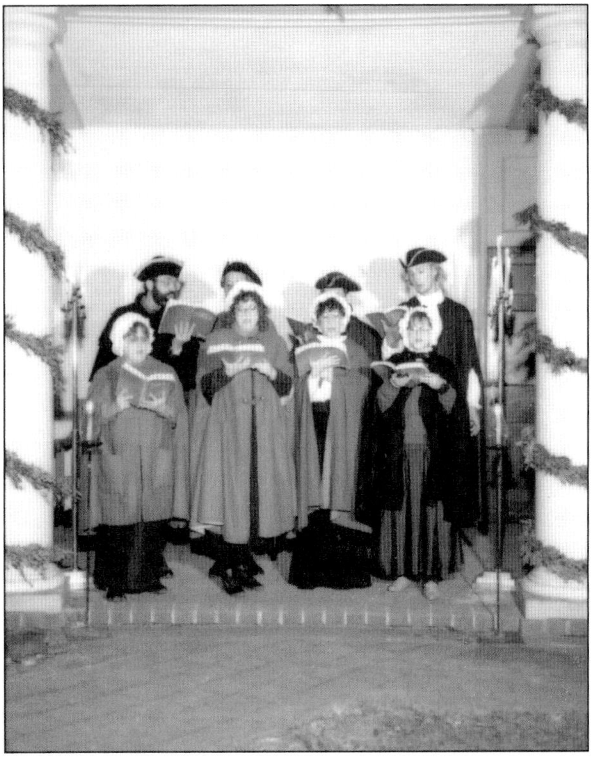

Music is an important part of Candlelight. Since the tours began, Tryon Palace has tried to incorporate period musical performances and holiday songs into the celebrations for visitors' enjoyment. This photograph shows a small choral group dressed in costume and performing under the colonnade at the palace during Candlelight in 1988.

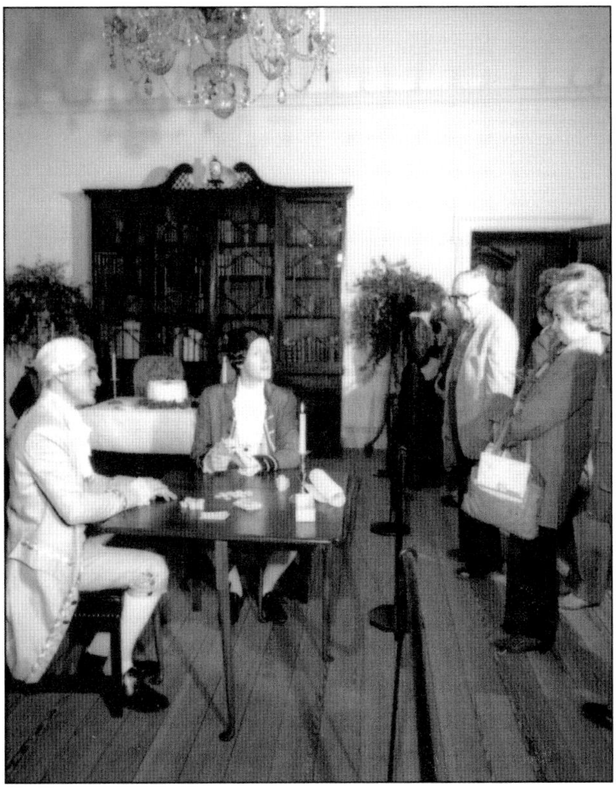

During Candlelight, visitors inside the palace are greeted by decorations and character interpreters. This 1988 image shows interpreters greeting visitors in the palace's south parlor, which is decorated for a small intimate gathering of family and close friends. The two interpreters are playing a card game, and the dessert table is visible in the background.

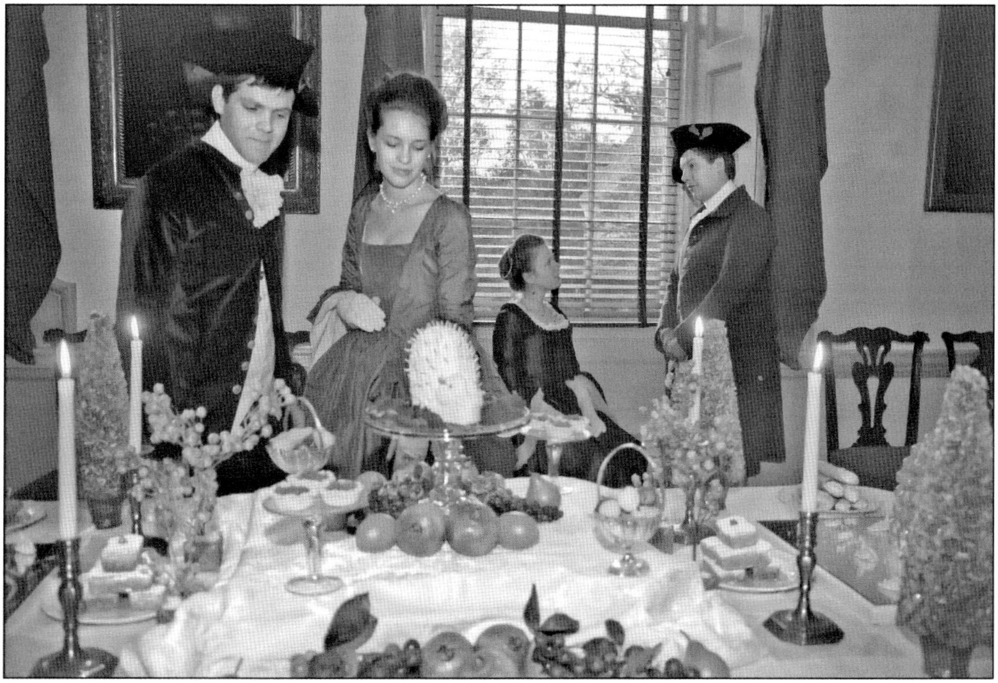

In the early 2000s, Tryon Palace returned to a more historical approach to the holiday season. First-person interpreters began telling the stories of past holiday seasons on the properties, and decorations were simplified to bring them more in line with actual 18th-century holiday traditions by focusing on the food and greenery.

The seasonal decorations used outside the buildings are mostly made of all-natural materials, including fruits and vegetables that would have been available in the 18th century. These wreaths and garlands have been a hallmark of Candlelight since 1980 and are greatly admired by hungry critters in winter.

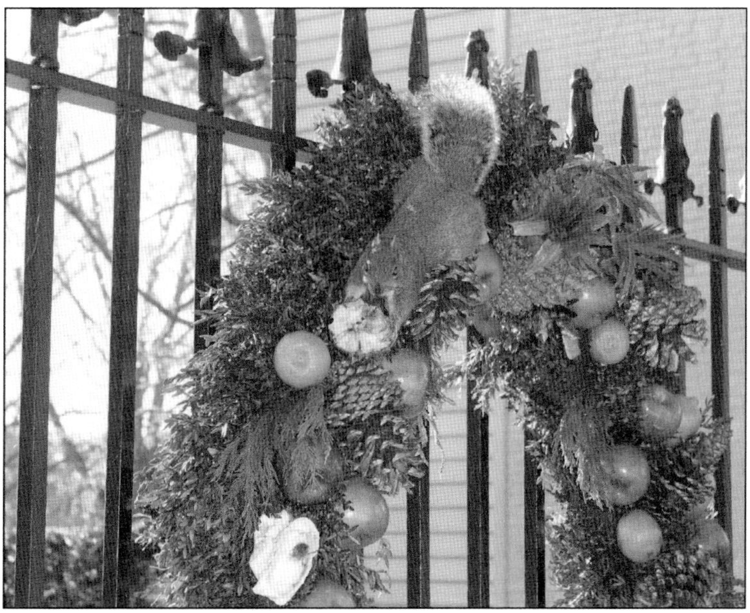

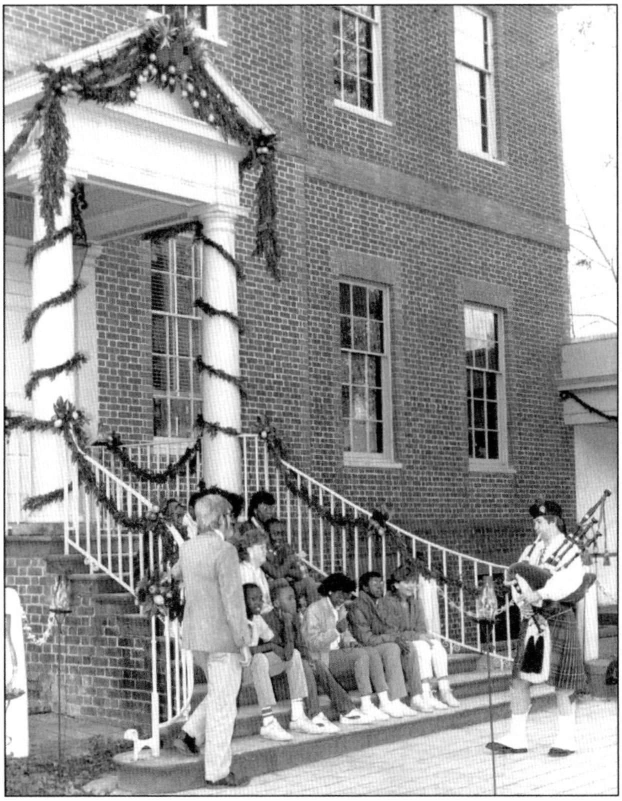

Each year, Tryon Palace slightly changes the decorations and theme for the Candlelight tour. The front entrance to the palace is still decorated with fruit and greenery, but by the late 1980s, the amount of fruit used on the pediment had been reduced. Musical interludes included a highland bagpipe performance by Loyal Osterlund to usher visitors into the palace on Candlelight tours.

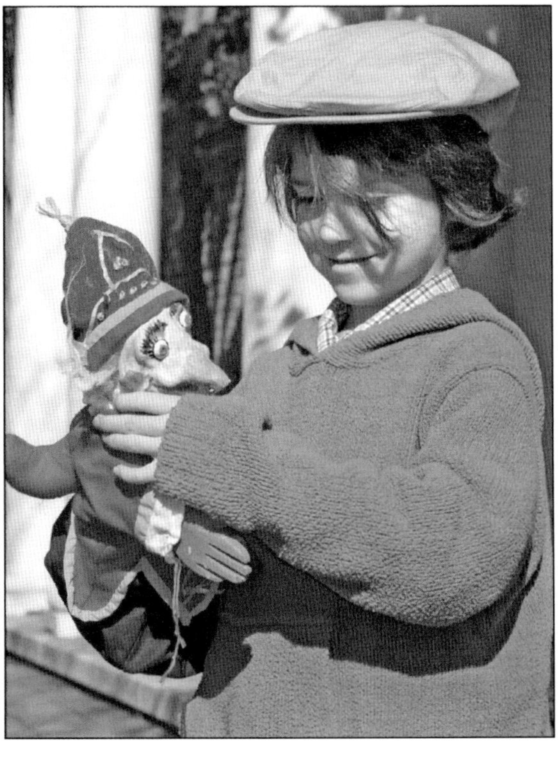

Candlelight also features entertainment. Children enjoy the "Punch and Judy" puppet shows, a European tradition that dates from the Middle Ages. This early form of theater was first associated with festival events, and by the late 18th and early 19th centuries, theater productions had become a regular part of Christmas celebrations in England.

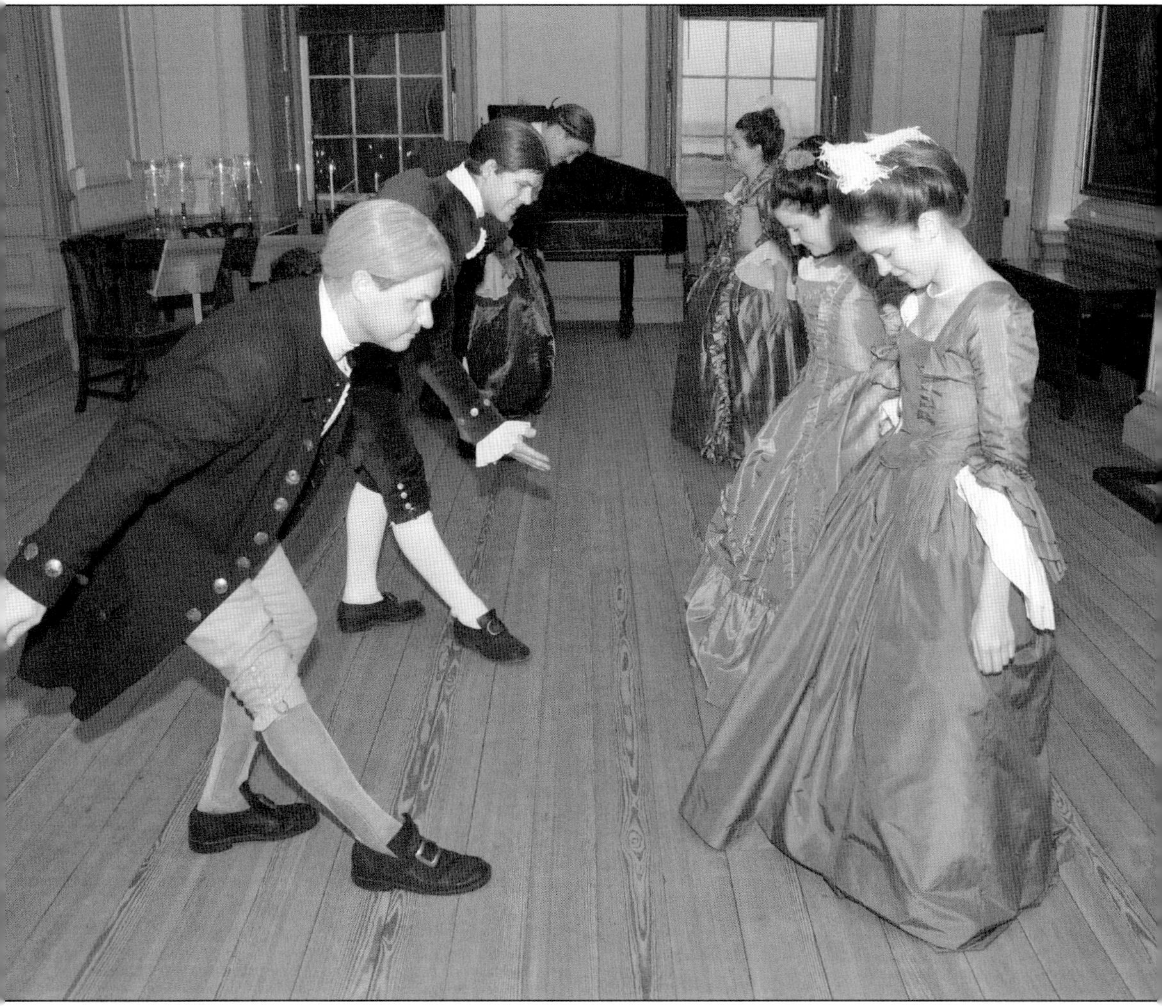

Tryon Palace's Candlelight tradition has included performances of dances popular in the colonial period. The palace contains several rooms suited for hosting 18th-century dances. The dancers include staff, volunteers, and guest performers. All participants are thoroughly trained prior to the holiday season during a series of rehearsals. These dances were referred to as "*contredanse*" in France and "cotillion" in England and the United States. The *contredanse allemande*, a Viennese figure dance for four couples, was popular in the colonial period; this dance required a couple to maneuver through a series of 12 alternating figures before returning to the main figure. In the 18th century, dance instruction manuals assisted members of society with learning the latest dances. Today, interpreters use the surviving manuals to re-create the dances for visitors. This photograph illustrates dancers in the courtesy pose, which is the most common way these dances begin.

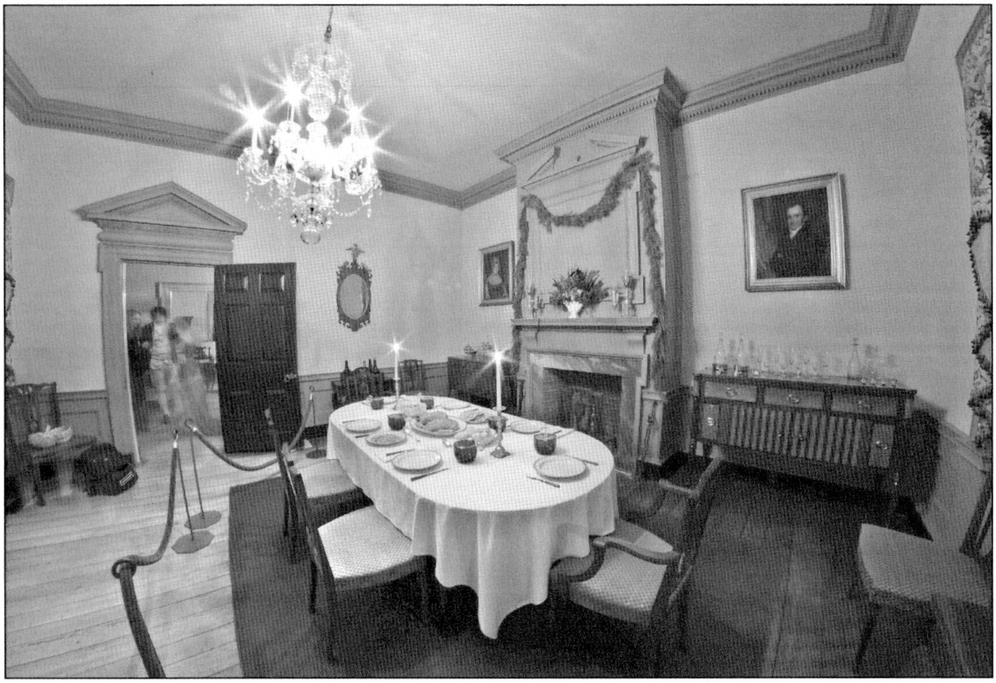

The John Wright Stanly House is traditionally interpreted for Twelfth Night, which was the last day most families celebrated during the Christmas holidays during the 18th century and through the Federal period. The dining room (above), which is located to the right of the main hall at the front of the house, is set for a holiday meal featuring special dishes that take on elaborate forms. In the front parlor (below), located to the left of the main hall, dinner guests play card games as part of the evening's entertainments. The interpreters pictured below are, clockwise from far left, Alma Gibbons, Andrew Duppstadt, Jeff Bockert, and Laura Rogers.

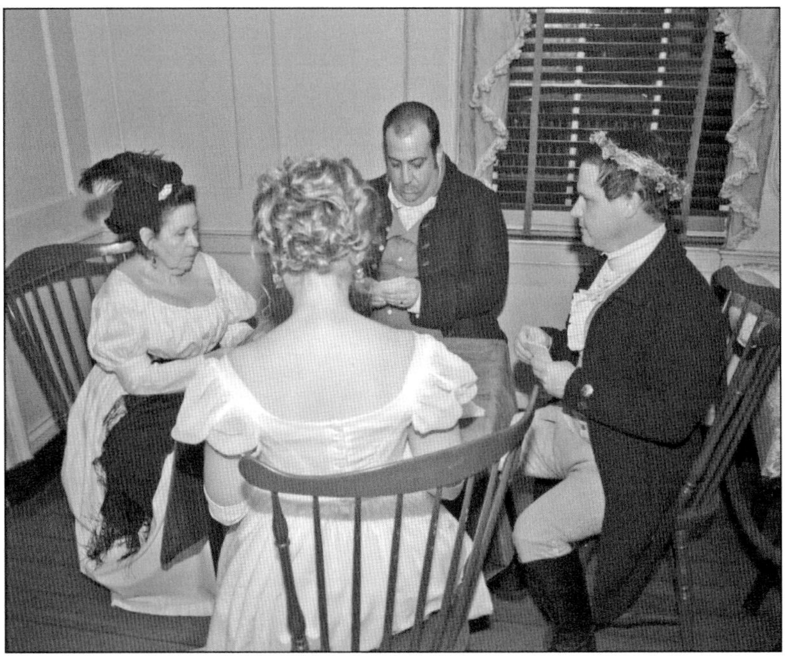

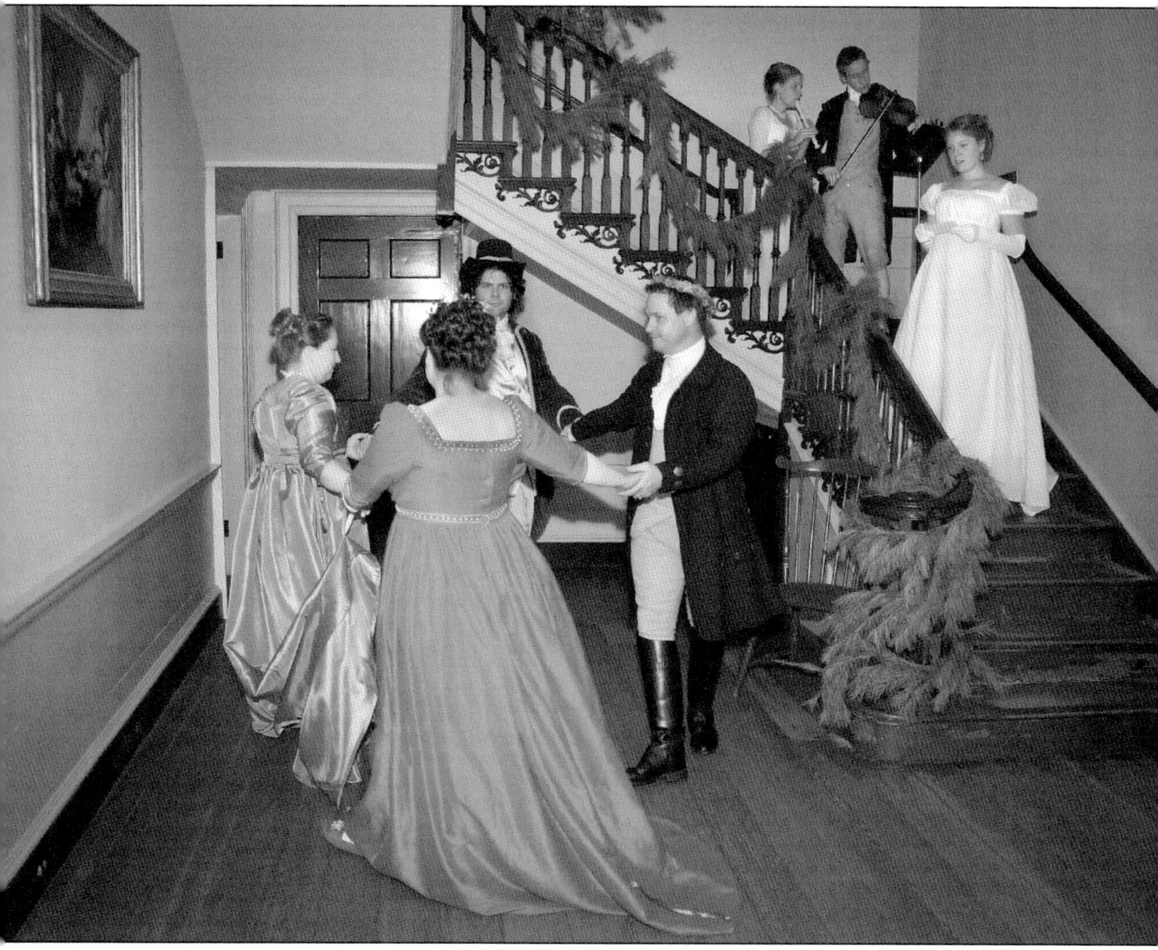

The central hall of the John Wright Stanly House is shown decorated for Twelfth Night. This holiday—which, by the late 18th century, fell on January 5—marked the end of the Christmas season. Traditional foods served on these evenings included the tortell and king's cake. The king's cake had a bean baked into it, and whoever got the slice of cake with the bean in it became king of the festivities. Longstanding superstition required that all decorations be taken down the day after Twelfth Night lest one risk bringing bad luck on the household. Visitors who take the Candlelight tours enjoy a festive family party at the Stanly House with dancing in the Center Hall. In this image, Rebecca Arthur, Karen Ipock, Matt Arthur, and Jeff Bockert are dancing as Seth and Jenna Poppe play from the landing on the stairs and Laura Rogers watches.

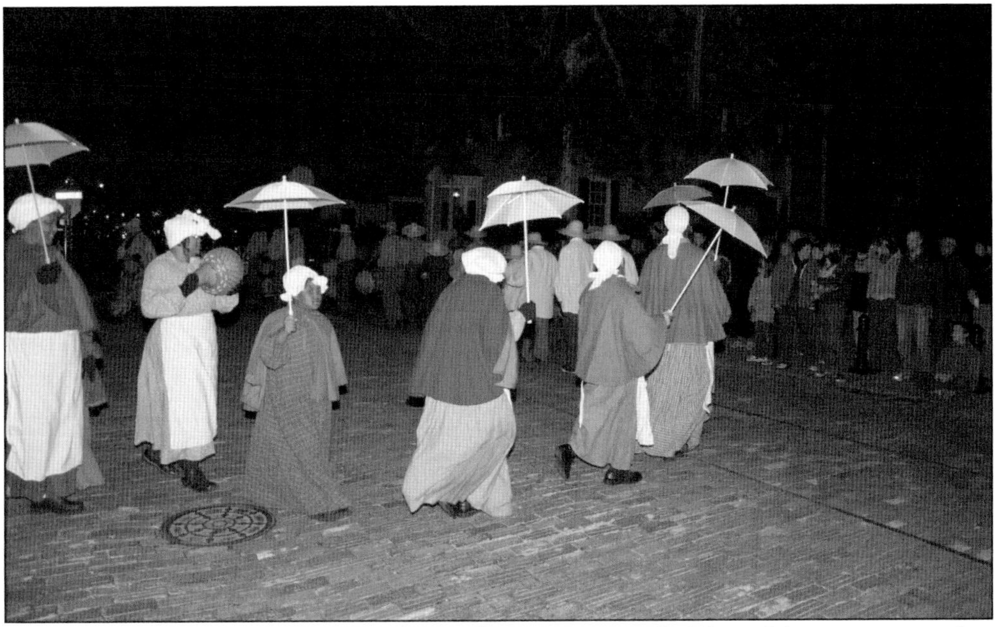

Jonkonnu (pronounced "John Canoe"), an African American holiday celebration practiced in North Carolina and the Caribbean Islands during the 19th century, became a regular part of Tryon Palace's Candlelight celebrations in 2000. Jonkonnu tells an important part of the story of enslaved African Americans that had previously been neglected during the palace's holiday celebrations. While Jonkonnu is traditionally associated with Christmas, its popularity has resulted in performances at special events throughout the year. The performers include staff, volunteers, and paid performers.

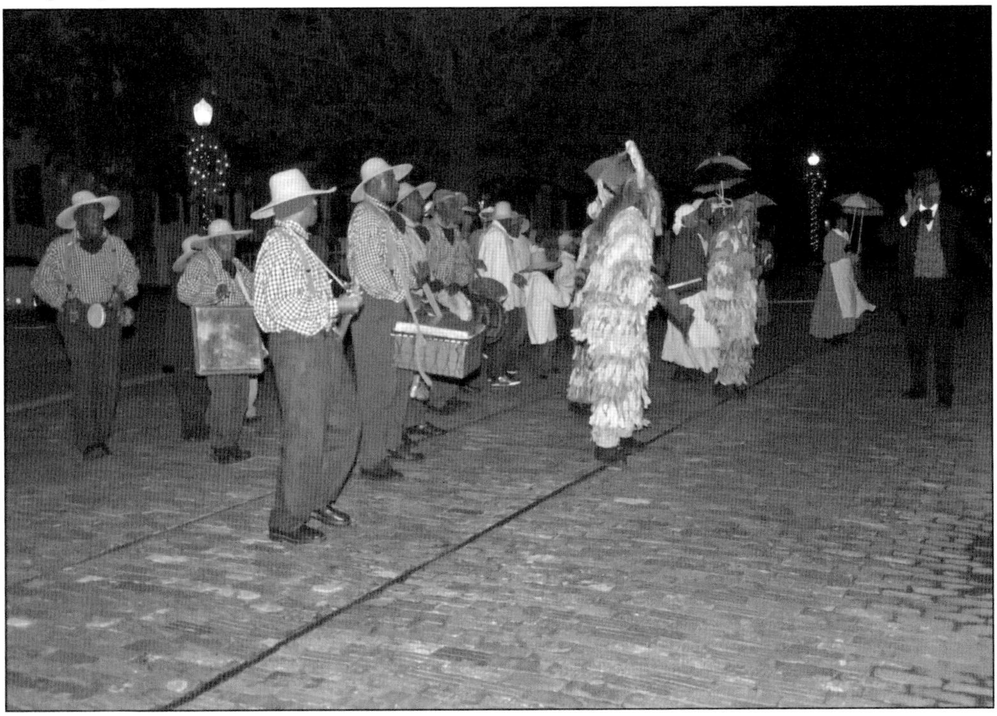

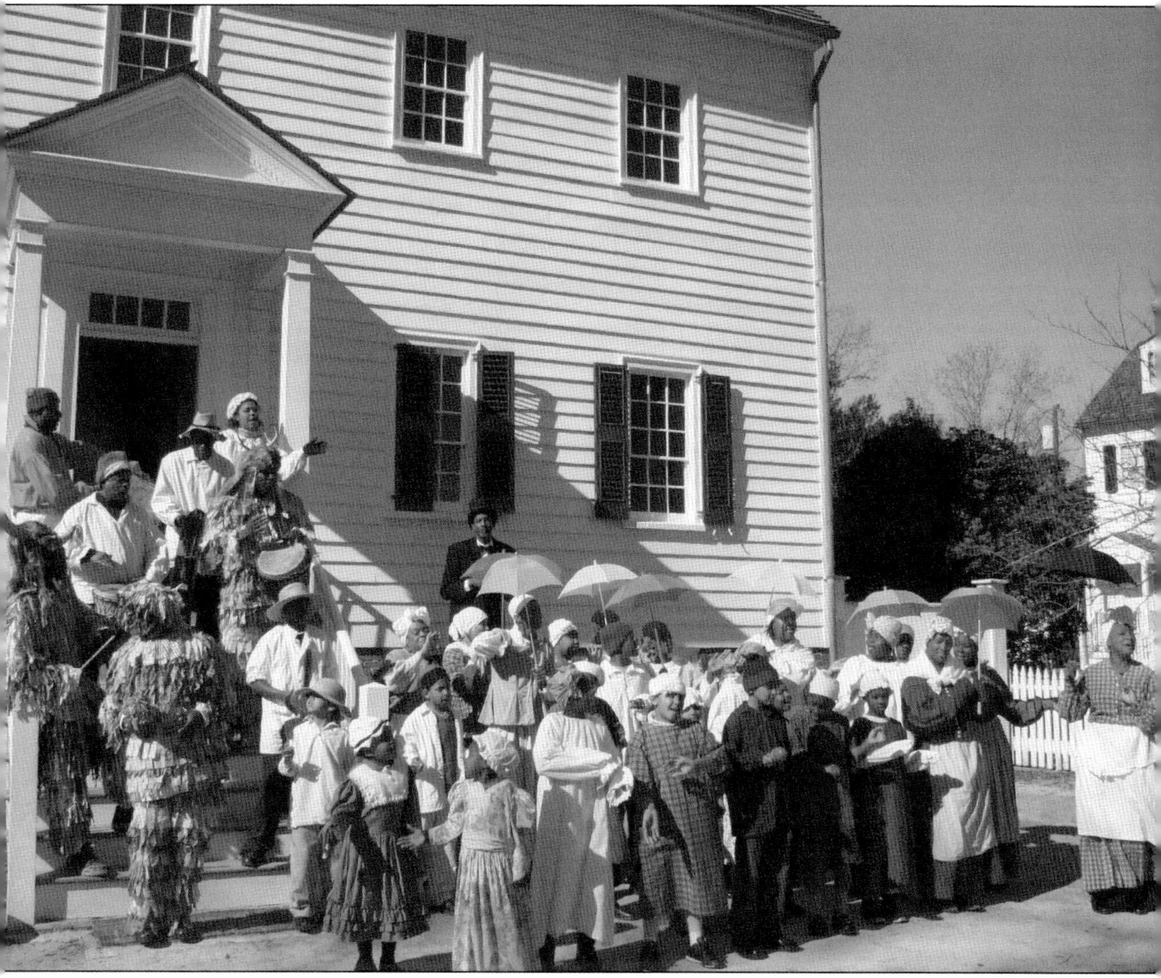

Jonkonnu was practiced in nearby Edenton, North Carolina, as early as 1824, but the practice did not spread beyond Eastern North Carolina in the United States. The origins of the celebration are linked to slave ships from West Africa and Jamaica. Jonkonnu is still a cherished part of holiday celebrations on several Caribbean islands. The celebration includes music and dance, with performers using a call-and-response format in the songs and featuring two iconic figures—the "ragman," whose costume is composed of colorful rags (with each representing a different spirit), and the "fancy man," who is attired in formal wear and leads the singing.

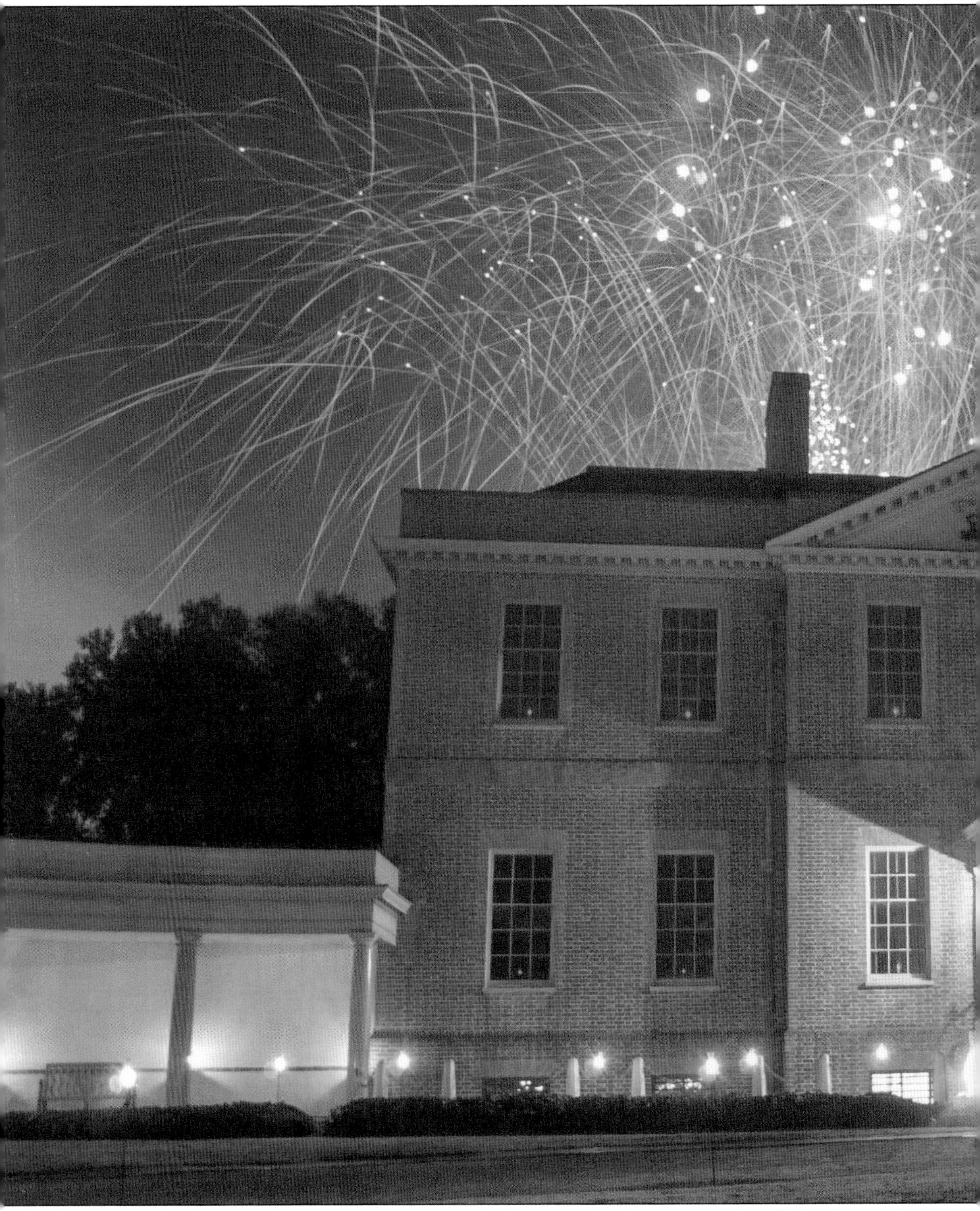

Royal Governor William Tryon commissioned a fireworks display in December 1770 to honor the opening of the new government house known as Tryon Palace. Since the early 2000s, the palace has continued this tradition, holding a black-powder fireworks display each December as part of the palace's holiday celebration. During the colonial period, fireworks displays would not have

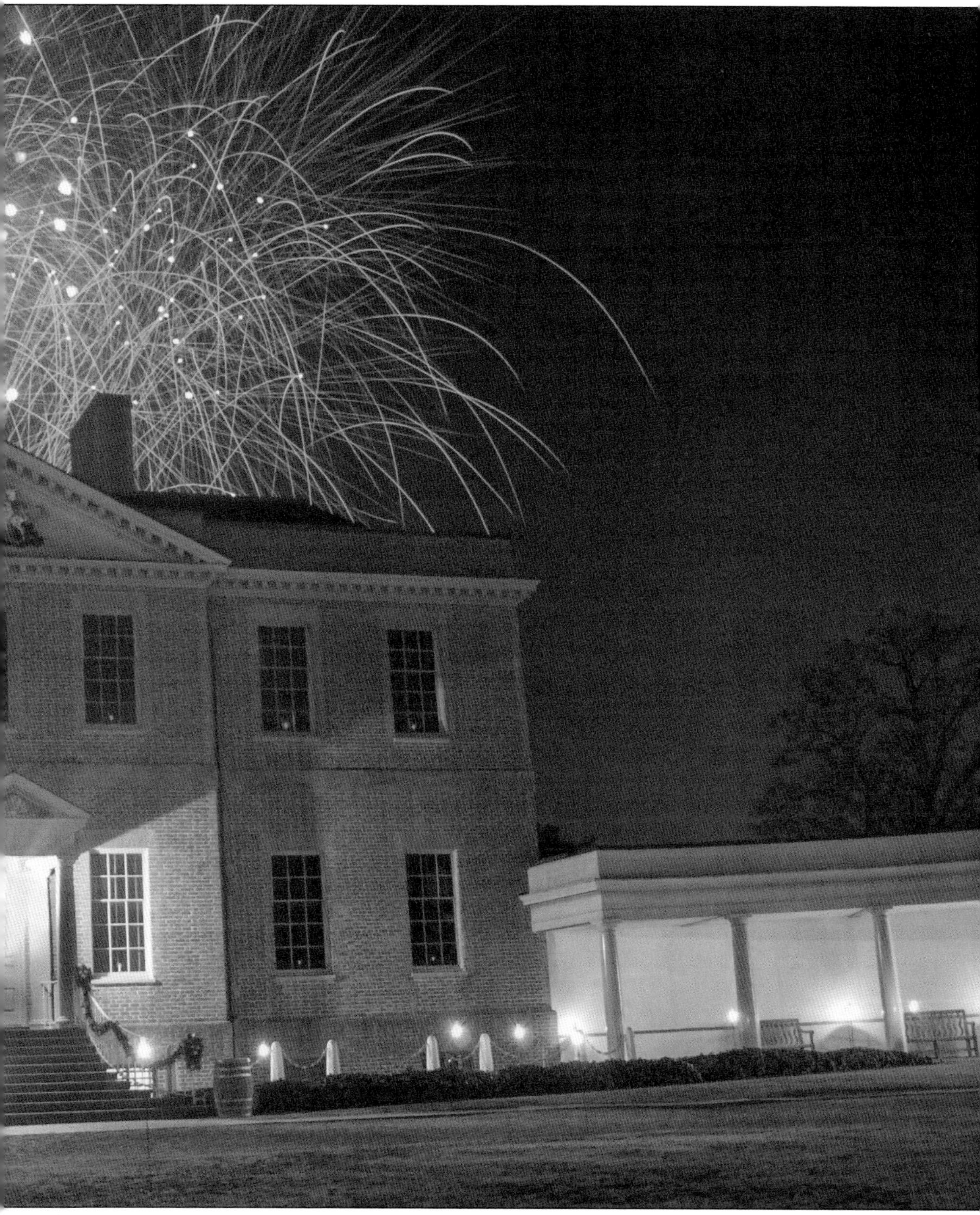

been a part of Christmas celebrations, which were marked in North Carolina by parties among kinsmen and expansive meals. While Governor Tryon used the display solely to commemorate the opening of the palace, the modern tradition, influenced by contemporary holiday celebrations, incorporates the spectacle into the palace's Candlelight festivities.

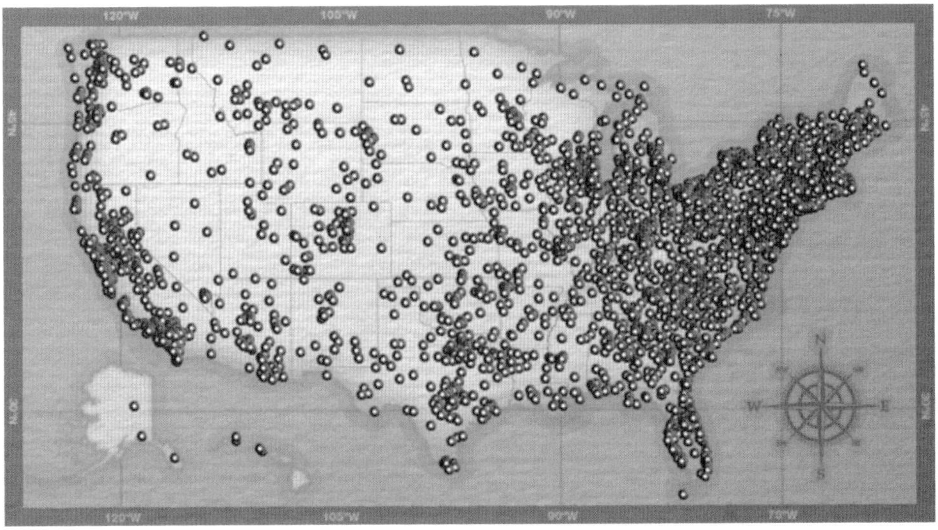

Consistent with our mission to preserve history on a local level, this book was printed in South Carolina on American-made paper and manufactured entirely in the United States. Products carrying the accredited Forest Stewardship Council (FSC) label are printed on 100 percent FSC-certified paper.

MADE IN THE USA